The Cultural World in *Beowulf*

Beowulf is one of the most important poems in Old English and the first major poem in a European vernacular language. It dramatizes behaviour in a complex social world – a martial, aristocratic world that we often distort by imposing on it our own biases and values. In this cross-disciplinary study, John Hill looks at *Beowulf* from a comparative ethnological point of view. He provides a thorough examination of the socio-cultural dimensions of the text and compares the social milieu of *Beowulf* to that of similarly organized cultures. Through examination of historical analogs in northern Europe and France, as well as past and present societies on the Pacific rim in Southeast Asia, a complex and extended society is uncovered and an astonishingly different *Beowulf* is illuminated.

The study is divided into five major essays: on ethnology and social drama, the temporal world, the legal world, the economy of honour, and the psychological world. Hill presents a realm where genealogies incorporate social and political statements: in this world gift giving has subtle and manipulative dimensions, both violent and peaceful exchange form a political economy, acts of revenge can be baleful or have jural force, and kinship is as much a constructable fact as a natural one. Family and kinship relations, revenge themes, heroic poetry, myth, legality, and political discussions all bring the importance of the social institutions in *Beowulf* to the foreground, allowing for a fuller understanding of the poem and its implications for Anglo-Saxon society.

(Anthropological Horizons)

JOHN HILL is with the Department of English at the United States Naval Academy.

Anthropological Horizons
Editor: Michael Lambek, University of Toronto

This series, begun in 1991, focuses on theoretically informed ethnographic works addressing issues of mind and body, knowledge and power, equality and inequality, the individual and the collective. Interdisciplinary in its perspective, the series makes a unique contribution in several other academic disciplines: women's studies, history, philosophy, psychology, political science, and sociology.

1 **The Varieties of Sensory Experience**
A Sourcebook in the Anthropology of the Senses
Edited by David Howes

2 **Arctic Homeland**
Kinship, Community, and Development in Northwest Greenland
Mark Nuttall

3 **Knowledge and Practice in Mayotte**
Local Discourses of Islam, Sorcery, and Spirit Possession
Michael Lambek

4 **Deathly Waters and Hungry Mountains**
Agrarian Ritual and Class Formation in an Andean Town
Peter Gose

5 **Paradise**
Class, Commuters, and Ethnicity in Rural Ontario
Stanley R. Barrett

6 **The Cultural World in *Beowulf***
John M. Hill

John M. Hill

THE CULTURAL WORLD IN *BEOWULF*

UNIVERSITY OF TORONTO PRESS
Toronto Buffalo London

Published by University of Toronto Press Incorporated
Toronto Buffalo London
Printed in Canada

ISBN 0-8020-2981-7 (cloth)
ISBN 0-8020-7438-3 (paper)

Printed on acid-free paper

Canadian Cataloguing in Publication Data

Hill, John M.
The cultural world in Beowulf

(Anthropological horizons)
Includes index.
ISBN 0-8020-2981-7 (bound) ISBN 0-8020-7438-3 (pbk.)

1. Beowulf. 2. Epic poetry, English (Old) – History and criticism. I. Title. II. Series.

PR1585.H55 1995 829'.3 C94-932033-1

University of Toronto Press acknowledges the financial assistance to its publishing program of the Canada Council and the Ontario Arts Council.

For Barbara and Katherine
My Kitchen Cabinet

Contents

Acknowledgments

Acknowledgments reveal the debts we know and thus our self-conscious, authorial identity. Appropriately enough for a book on *Beowulf* and such topics as gift giving and constructed kinship, the close and extended kindred of influential predecessors, colleagues, and collaborators is large. The scholarship of some predecessors is so fundamental that without them this book could not have been conceived. I think here mainly of the great editor, Frederick Klaeber, the historians Frederic Seebohm and D.H. Green, the germanicist Vilhelm Grønbech, the literary historian H. Munro Chadwick, and such anthropologists as Marcel Mauss, Bronislaw Malinowski, Marshall Sahlins, and Marilyn Strathern. I also owe much to a host of literary scholars, whose contributions appear in both the text and notes.

Robert D. Stevick and Robert O. Payne first guided me through Beowulf and the daunting commentary surrounding it. My debt to them is inestimable. Several generations of students, first at Smith College, and then at the U.S. Naval Academy shared my enthusiasm and sparked scholarly essays underlying sections of this book. But my anthropological interests found a comprehensive voice only after Ross Samson and Pam Graves invited me to a 1988 conference at Glasgow University on New Perspectives in Viking Studies. The exposure there to anthropologists, archaeologists, and historians suggested startlingly different ways of addressing old problems. While a scholar in residence at Denison University, I received helpful advice about British anthropology from Keith Maynard and Susan Didick. Readers for the University of Toronto Press suggested additional anthropological readings appropriate for the kind of society *Beowulf* dramatizes. To William McKellin, whose advice helped shape this study's interdisciplinary argument, I owe what one owes a generous collaborator. To Michael Lambek I owe useful suggestions for directing the book to anthropologists as well as to Anglo-Saxon scholars and Beowulf specialists.

Along the way a number of literary scholars encouraged papers on topics in this book for various Old English sessions: I especially thank George Clark, Ward Parks, and John P. Hermann in this connection, and John D. Niles and Robert E. Bjork for inviting me to a 1993 conference on *Beowulf* at the University of California, Berkeley. John Niles's review of an early draft was invaluable. His suggestions, cautionary advice, and encouragement were astute and energizing.

Finally, I thank the editors at University of Toronto Press, especially Prudence Tracy, who first saw promise in this study, and Suzanne Rancourt who took it on after Prudence's untimely death. To Miriam Skey, the copy editor, I owe innumerable improvements in style and continuity. She also spotted many lapses and corrected mistakes. In these editors I feel especially blest; my only regret is that Prudence Tracy did not live to see this project reach its present form.

Publication of this book has been aided by a grant from the U.S. Naval Academy's Research and Professional Development Committee. Special thanks go to Dean Carl S. Schneider for his resourceful support.

The Cultural World in *Beowulf*

Introduction

Early in this century specialists in medieval English literature and history wrote in the current anthropological and legalistic terms about the nature of early Germanic society. Their focus was the time before and during the early periods of written law codes, charters, wills, histories, and, of course, literary texts. When scholars such as Schücking, Grønbech (who more than any other scholar of his generation explored Germanic gift giving), Seebohm, the Chadwicks, Lawrence, and Phillpotts turned from attempts to understand such 'institutions' as early medieval coinage or social organization, they tended to focus on questions concerning implied social stratification, land-holding rights, and the Germanic kindred. They inquired into whether or not the kindred involved an ancient, matrilineal organization, what the obligations of so-called kinsmen were toward each other, if there was a folk-land held in common that differed significantly from bookland, if a king could alienate common land, and of course the kinds of social ranks and feud-related arrangements that various law codes express in their distinctions regarding compensation following upon losses, injuries, deaths, and violations of such proscriptions as the king's peace.

Rarely did these scholars think of myth or primitive religion as deeply implicated in social arrangements, especially in jural customs; nor did they focus on such central matters as feud settlement or revenge in any comparative, global way. Indeed, their anthropological reading, although expansive, mainly concerned questions of social evolution and progress (or else devolution); it was not ethnologically comparative. Such study had to await a sense of significant differences between seemingly similar 'primitive' cultures. This sense became manifest in several areas: the publication of field work by such anthropologists as Malinowski and Boas's students (notably Alfred Kroeber and Margaret Mead); the development of British structural anthropology from Rivers and Radcliffe-Brown, through Evans-Pritchard, and on to Fortes; and more recently a number of reevaluations concerning such ideas as kinship, lineage, descent, and kindred.[1]

Medieval English historians have only recently noted these developments in comparative ethnology. With a few exceptions, again usually in kinship studies in the 1950s, we have had to wait until the last twenty years for any appreciable interest in cross-cultural comparisons of gift-giving, the meaning of myth, the functions of genealogies, and the reciprocal operations of revenge and feud settlements.[2] Perhaps this is because British structural anthropologists had a comparative method that used fully structured, integrated, ethnographic models to illuminate the social worlds of less well known peoples, thus often obscuring significant, perhaps even immense social differences between, say, 'nineteenth-century Polynesia and seventh-century England.'[3] What ought to have been an analogical method often seemed an impositional one. For less pointed reasons, literary critics, and especially readers of *Beowulf*, have been even slower, although in the last decade several studies of special kinship, gift giving, drinking behaviour, and feud have focused in anthropological ways on *Beowulf* – the only Old English poem to recreate a complex and extended social world for us.

Beowulf dramatizes subtle behaviour in a complex social world – a non-centralized, notably martial, face-to-face, aristocratic world. We often distort this world by imposing on it our own, ethnocentric biases: about decorum and adventure; about the moral values of wealth, exchange, honour and a desire for fame, loyalty and revenge; about the social nuances of boasts, challenges, and ceremonious speech; and about ancestors, kinship, time, and change in the transitions between pagan and Christian societies. These biases are so pervasive in the scholarly commentary that many aspects of Germanic social life – such as ancestral identity, jural customs, gift giving and service in return, peace brides, the wearing of captured weapons, the role of queens, and the passing of cups in the meadhall – are simply tagged as 'background' or else considered unnuanced givens fed into the dramatic, and usually darkly interpreted, ironically framed action of the poem. A notable exception is T.A. Shippey's pointed reminder that swords, wealth, drinking, and boasting behaviour, along with honour and desire for fame function as social signs in

Beowulf; they function in 'systems which cannot be entirely, or even largely, the creation of the poet.' By missing this point we tend to oversymbolize aspects of the poem in literary directions.[4]

We can overcome those biases and that symbolizing tendency by reimagining *Beowulf*, that is, by reviewing its drama in contextual detail using the inspiration of an analogically flexible ethnology. While full-scale, ethnographical study is not possible – because of our ignorance of the particular Anglo-Saxon society out of which *Beowulf* comes – we can still reflect relevantly upon the poem.

I look to historical analogues in northern Europe and France, as well as to near past and present societies on the Pacific rim, in Southeast Asia (especially the so-called 'house societies'), among North American Indians, and elsewhere. What matters is similarity of social organization, not ethnic background or geography. Therefore I look for face-to-face, that is, non-centralized, small group societies as sources of insight where kinship structures are largely bilateral; where there is customary settlement of grievances through revenge and feud; where gift giving matters; where myths and legends are ancestral and incorporating; where the sense of time is genealogical and not deeply historical, mechanistic, and alienating; where there is hierarchy between chiefs and warriors and where there is a tendency toward monarchy.

My anthropological procedure in general is analogical, comparative, cross-temporal, and opportunistic. I look to ethnographies for societies organized in ways that recall details of the social and cultural world of Danes, Geats, and Swedes in *Beowulf*, matching features in depth wherever possible, and looking to hitherto obscure or apparently surface detail in *Beowulf* for further implications whenever similar features in ethnographies have a functioning depth. Might matters work in Beowulf's world as they seem to in a well-analysed society – especially in such areas as the social dynamics of gift exchange, the functions played by genealogies, the forms of feuds and customary settlements, the relation of brides to their fathers' families, and the relationships between leaders and their armed followers or clients? Often these questions take us into *Beowulf* in new directions, illuminating an astonishingly different *Beowulf* in some respects: the world in the poem almost leaps into social and cultural relief, becoming dynamic, complex, and subtle in ways we have not fully appreciated before.

On the whole, we have misconceived Beowulf's social world and therefore we have not read the poem well enough. Some good interpretations in *Beowulf* studies invite attention to Beowulfian depictions of such Anglo-Saxon customs as the uncle-nephew bond, the exchange of gifts, the legal obligations of the feud, the functions of drink and boast, the reciprocal, ethical vocabulary of the *comitatus*, and the identification of self with one's war-band leader and, through one's father, with paternal kin.[5] Indeed, the themes of revenge obligation within the kindred and the *comitatus* have figured prominently in literary discussion since the beginning of modern criticism. But it is fair to say that most *Beowulf* scholars only flirt with an anthropological understanding of these matters, quickly moving away from the social world of the poem into philological, textual, and literary-thematic issues. The social institutions of the poem suffer accordingly – being relegated to background, for the most part, or to a general structure of conflicting and vaguely understood obligations, which in turn is held to generate the drama of so much heroic age literature.[6]

By social world I mean a milieu that includes kinship ties, of course, as well as the institution of the kinsman-like war-band, juridical expectations, political marriage, the changeable dynamics of exchange, the incorporating as well as manipulable and identifying functions of genealogy and legend, and the shallow sense of time that descent-based or else ascent-based genealogies provide. Within each of these areas values grow regarding good and bad behaviours and unexceptional ones: the good of not weaving treachery; the values of reciprocal favouring and honouring, of trust and loyalty, of generosity, of subduing one's enemies and avenging harm or else seeking some form of compensation for it, of sharing everything in the hall except for the people's lands and lives, and so on. These values in relationships with kin and confederates so permeate institutional and material aspects of the world in *Beowulf*, and are everywhere so open to development and manipulation, that when we take them to heart the world characterized in *Beowulf* becomes other than what we have seen. In effect, we begin to revise our prior estimation of such matters as revenge (there is no critique of revenge as such in *Beowulf*), liberality, the powers of kings and queens, delight in gifts, boasting behaviour, the functions of story-telling and recollected legends, the special purposes that gift giving can acquire, the function of genealogies, the sense of time and history, and the functioning of kinship. We see kinship not as an ultimate category of relationship and identity, but as a pattern for constructed and newly significant relationships (whether through confederation, fosterage, vicinage, or actual consanguinity). Indeed we can even reimagine the hall as more than a place or centre; rather it becomes a fundamental mode of organization, cutting across kinship lines and creating a hall kinship – a kinship-band (*sibbegedriht*) – that includes queens as powerful, sometimes independent, sacral personages. Moreover, the hall encompasses both private and public activities, both secular and sacred ones, even as it is identified with a ruling family, reflecting the prestige of that family.

Thinking in these ways, we can reenter the social drama of *Beowulf* and come to a fuller understanding of such matters as Beowulf's careful approach to Hrothgar and Heorot – the challenges received and met, the juridical context of Beowulf's proposals, the mythological sanctions for his apparent role as the strong hand of law, and the special guardianship Hrothgar grants. We can reconsider these conundrums: Hrothgar's relationship with his nephew, Hrothulf; Wealhtheow's countermoves in Heorot regarding Hrothgar's proposed adoption of Beowulf; the purport of that portentous 'victory song' we call the Finnsburg digression; and the extent to which *Beowulf* is less about heroic action than about the problem of achieving settlements between previously contending parties. We can shift our approach to Hildeburh and to Freawaru; brides may be less failed peace-pledges when violence breaks out between in-laws than they are prospective peace-kin (not given away but rather a means of attachment and alliance). Similarly, Beowulf's ongoing, reciprocal alliance with Hrothgar and the Danes (one that he knows his lord, Hygelac, will support), becomes the poem's model of a harmonious relationship after earlier enmity.

We can deepen our understanding of the evolving complexity of aristocratic gift giving – the special meanings that special acts of giving can in fact acquire. We can even rethink the poet's relationship to the world of the poem, evaluating the way that story and myth join the poet to the past he recreates. This process of incorporation makes the poem's world a complex idealization for the poet, such that no alienation occurs between poet and poem. In effect the poet recreates an epic memory of the past, coming to see the past in terms of his values and those of his present – values writ large. Such emphasis, along with a pronounced, egalitarian sense of reciprocal relationships, would lift the poem as a reflection of reality above any particular, recoverable Anglo-Saxon world of hierarchy, exchange, markets and coinage, land organization and centralized administration.

As already mentioned, our appreciation of the degree to which kinship is both an actual tie and the model for analogous ties – between in-laws, neighbours, and confederated recruits – will change. These ties are often enough constructed within the exigencies of violence and they are open, even in the case of consanguinity, to new significations in changed or changing contexts. Finally, perhaps a better assessment emerges than has so far seemed possible of Beowulf's death day, of his last day alive and his first day dead, and of the dark tonalities that characterize the poem's last sections. A forward-looking, praiseworthy reorganization occurs as Wiglaf carries out Beowulf's dying request, bringing the Geats together (minus those who fled from the dragon fight) both in expectation of future violence and in fitting, superlative praise of their great, amity-weaving, kinship-supporting king. This complex, anxious task is not unknown in Anglo-Saxon England and in Scandinavia, even in Christian times.[7]

Before elaborating these perspectives, I will first offer a sketch of the poem's social content and movement. Within 3,182 lines, *Beowulf* dramatizes three monster fights, each occurring within a rough third of the poem. In the course of these fierce incidents, a world of social relationships between three groups – Danes, Geats, and Swedes – comes into focus. Other people, notably Heathobards, Frisians, and Franks figure in asides or in reminiscences concerning issues of either revenge or marriage settlement, or else raiding and feud. The foreground of monster fights is set within a seemingly historical matrix of feuding peoples – each group is a house society of sorts, that is, centred on a great hall – with the three main societies given genealogies going back at least two generations from the time of the monster-killing action in the poem. Although the poet does not say so, the approximate historical period for that action seems to be the late fifth and early sixth centuries, in areas of southern Sweden and northern Denmark (the isle of Zealand), whereas the poem probably comes down to us in an eleventh-century manuscript, from an Anglo-Saxon culture not much earlier than the ninth century and perhaps a century later.

Beowulf opens by establishing, through an agnatic line of powerful war-band leaders, a five-generation genealogy for the Danes, the greatest of people in this northern world. The fourth generation of Danes best expresses its pre-eminence in the person of Hrothgar, whose wide sway brings him to command the building of a great hall, which he names Heorot, where he will share all that is good, excepting only the lives of his people and the common land. Built by people from far and near, and thus testifying to the range of Hrothgar's command, the hall is an image of both Danish might and munificence.

The poem then rapidly moves forward to a time of paralysing strife as Hrothgar and his kinship band of warriors endure the nightly ravages of a cannibalistic ogre, Grendel (who in turn has an associative genealogy linked to Cain, and who, as an outland creature, attacks the hall out of pain over hearing songs of joy from within.) Grendel, unwilling to settle his feud with the Danes in any way, repeatedly raids Hrothgar's great hall, Heorot, until the Danes abandon the place at night. Hrothgar is one of four siblings and has three children in turn with his queen, Wealhtheow, who may have Celtic ancestry. His brother's son, Hrothulf, is also a prominent and, for many readers, an ambiguous member of Hrothgar's court. Hrothgar's sister is married to a Swedish king, Onela, and Hrothgar himself has settled a feud on behalf of a hero who may be partly Swedish, the Wægmunding Ecgtheow, who is Beowulf's father.

That settlement in part can justify Beowulf, who is a Wægmunding Geat, not a Dane, in coming to Hrothgar's aid twelve years after Grendel's depredations begin. Apparently Danes and Geats have had their moments of strife, but the immensely powerful Beowulf comes during a time of amity. Yet he comes unsummoned, of his own volition, into the land of guarded, watchful Danes and he must progress socially in such a way as to gain a hearing and have Hrothgar grant his petition: to wit, that Beowulf and his retainers be given nighttime possession of Heorot so that they might await the outlaw ogre, whom they would lawfully challenge. After a further challenge in the hall from Hunferth, Beowulf eventually receives Hrothgar's permission and a promise of reward should he survive the encounter with Grendel. In the event of his own death, Beowulf adds, he hopes that Hrothgar will send his armour, a legacy from his Geat grandfather, home to Hygelac, Beowulf's Geat uncle (mother's brother) and lord. Beowulf thus emphasizes his dual identity as his grandfather's foster son and his uncle's loyal retainer.

Night comes and the Geats wait. In the event, Beowulf triumphs by holding onto Grendel's hand so fiercely that the struggle is violent; the hall receives the brunt of the damage until the desperate Grendel wrenches free and flees, leaving behind his entire arm. The Danes celebrate, likening Beowulf's feat to that of Sigemund, the legendary dragon-slayer. Scenes of refurbishing the hall follow, along with an exchange of speeches and detailed gift giving; Hrothgar tries to adopt Beowulf in some sense and gives extraordinary treasures (dynastic objects as it turns out). Wealhtheow, Hrothgar's queen, strongly counters that attempted adoption. She would prefer that Hrothgar leave the hall and kingdom to his young sons, well protected as she says they are by their cousin, Hrothulf. Hrothgar should magnificently reward Beowulf but do no more than that. The poet has a court poet then recite a victory episode from the Danes' past. This story is told between Hrothgar's gift giving and Wealhtheow's countergifts.

The episode from the Danes' past concerns a bitter fight that has somehow broken out between long-accommodated in-laws. In the end a Danish princess, Finn's queen, Hildeburh (who apparently has not been completely given away), is brought back to her own people after her husband and his people have been slain in retaliation for deadly attacks upon Hildeburh's brother and his party of visiting Danes (during which Hildeburh's son by Finn also dies). Allusive episodes such as this one, interspersed with the plot of monster fights, suggest an associative relationship: seemingly, in the monster fights the poet would project, much enlarged, something of the dynamic and the mixed values that inform raids and feuds, their social beginnings, their settlements, and sometimes their recurrences.

In the first, great scene of gift giving Beowulf, while accepting all gifts, does not verbally respond either to Hrothgar's adoption attempt or to Wealhtheow's countergifts. But he accepts a cup of mead from Wealhtheow and drinks along with everyone else after her final words. Festivities end and the Danes bed down in the newly purged hall, while Beowulf sleeps elsewhere. In the night another ogre, Grendel's mother, comes seeking 'gallows-minded' revenge for her son's death. She seizes a veteran warrior and counsellor, the Dane, Æschere, and carries him off when threatened by other warriors, leaving his head beside the fennish lake into which she goes. She seeks her home at the bottom. In the morning, a suffering Hrothgar prevails upon Beowulf for help once more. Only he seems to have the counsel and the gifts of god-given strength and luck to help the Danes meet and slay such monsters. He agrees, dives fully armed and protectively armoured into the lake, seeks out the dam in her underwater lair, and slays her there with the help of God and a gigantic sword. He then looks around for Grendel's body; he finds and beheads it, only to have the sword's blade melt in Grendel's still hot blood. Upon returning to Heorot with the sword's hilt and Grendel's head, he recites his adventure, listens to a contemplative speech on Hrothgar's part, and is once again rewarded magnificently, although this time the great gifts are not detailed as they were before.

The next morning Beowulf and his retainers depart for their homeland, with Hrothgar's loving, tearful blessing. Before departing Beowulf enunciates a continuing, reciprocal tie between Danes and Geats should the future hold any further threats for the Danes from any foe. After arriving home, Beowulf recounts his adventures to Hygelac, in Hygelac's hall, noting in passing that he thinks Hrothgar's efforts at a future peace-kinship with the Heathobards will fail. He then hands on to Hygelac, his uncle and lord, the greatest of Hrothgar's gifts, adding that for Beowulf all still depends upon Hygelac, to whom he is absolutely loyal (thus putting to rest possibly unsettling implications concerning his repeated service for the Danes).

Hygelac in turn rewards Beowulf with a subkingship, vast landholdings, a hall, and a throne. Time passes; strife occurs between Geats and Swedes and Geats, Franks, and Frisians. Hygelac dies in Friesland in a raid against the Franks and his son, Heardred, dies in a later Swedish attack on the Geat stronghold – an attack driven by generational strife among the Swedes. Two Swedish princes, after quarrelling with their father's brother, seek asylum among the Geats. Their uncle attacks them there, killing one of them, along with Heardred, Beowulf's preferred cousin. Beowulf then becomes king, having earlier turned the kingship down in favour of Heardred. He helps the surviving Swedish prince regain the Swedish throne. Beowulf then apparently rules uneventfully for fifty years, until an ancient, fire-breathing dragon comes.

The dragon has been aroused by an exile who has stolen a cup from its treasure hoard – the buried armour and wealth of an extinguished people, whose last survivor eloquently lamented the treasure he buried. The dragon tracks the thief, whom Beowulf has befriended because of the cup proferred in exchange for asylum, and begins to ravage the kingdom. In the last third of the poem Beowulf fatally confronts the dragon, aided crucially at one moment by the only brave retainer out of twelve, a young Wægmunding named Wiglaf, Beowulf's last relative among the Geats. Both Beowulf and the dragon receive mortal wounds. Wiglaf gives heroic aid, and the childless Beowulf now considers him especially dear. Beowulf seems to pass on the right of succession to him by giving Wiglaf his golden necklace, golden helmet, and corselet. He does this after Wiglaf, directed by Beowulf, retrieved some of the treasure from the dragon's mound. The sight of that treasure gives Beowulf some peace of mind. He thinks that his people might use this wealth for which he is now, in effect, dying.

As the poem winds down to the funeral observances, both Wiglaf and his messenger expect renewed strife from various quarters – from Swedes, Franks, and Merovingians especially – once news of Beowulf's death goes abroad. The poem ends on a scene of mourning for the great king, now dead and immolated on his funeral pyre. He is then buried in a mound with the great treasure that had been taken from the dragon. Noble Geats ride around the mound and declare that Beowulf was, of worldly kings, the most generous of men, the most given to kindred kindness and gentle honouring of others, and the most eager for note-worthy fame.

From this sketch we can readily observe the salient importance of kinship feeling and protection, lordship, loyalty, gift giving, and revenge, feud settlement, and matters of succession. For the Anglo-Saxon world generally, kinship and lordship can be understood by working from Francis and Joseph Gies's admirable overview of middle and late Anglo-Saxon society.

> Like the other Germanic peoples, the Anglo-Saxons brought with them a form of society in which the dominant element was the larger kinship group. This group was not the territorial clan (a corporate body with a territorial base, tracing its origin to a common ancestor) but the kindred (an ego-focused group consisting of each individual's close relatives). This network of overlapping clusters of parents, grandparents, siblings, aunts, uncles, and cousins exercised important social, economic, and juridical functions. It determined the status of its members, negotiated marriages, and arbitrated inheritance. It exercised a degree of control over individual behavior, lent protection to its members, pursued vengeance for them, and paid or exacted compensation ... the Anglo-Saxon kindred's juridical authority was eroded by the rival power of lords and kings ... Yet kinship retained social importance, determining a man's (or woman's) prestige and even identity.
>
> Like the *Sippe*, the Anglo-Saxon kindred was bilateral, with emphasis on the father's side of the family. Its exact extent was indeterminate. The circle of relations who could be enlisted for such aid as payment of wergeld compensation probably depended on proximity and accessibility, but every individual could rely on a basic group of close kin that scholars have concluded from analysis of Old English terminology always included the conjugal family plus a few collaterals ... The most commonly used terms for uncles, aunts, nephews, and nieces specified the side of the family: father's sister was *fathu*; mother's sister, *moddrige*; father's brother, *faedera*; mother's brother, *eam*. Broth-

er's and sister's sons and daughters were likewise distinguished. No specific terms existed, however, for different kinds of cousins, indicating that such distinctions were not significant.

Despite the male bias of the kinship system, marriage did not change a woman's status. She retained the wergeld she was born with and did not take her husband's. Although her children assumed their father's status, she kept that of her own father ... women shared in inheritance, along with children and close kin ... Surviving Anglo-Saxon wills show no strong preference for sons over daughters or for elder over younger sons in the inheritance of land ... Land was willed to a wide range of relatives, many of them female: mothers, fathers, sons, daughters and sons-in-law, brothers and sisters-in-law, grandsons and granddaughters on both the male and female side, nephews and nieces on both sides, even stepchildren, godchildren, and foster relations ... Royal succession, however, was limited to males, and the ancestry of kings was traced agnatically (through the male line) ... Until the late tenth century, the Anglo-Saxon kings commonly employed a unique form of succession. The kingdoms were ... transmitted intact from brother to brother.[8]

According to Lorraine Lancaster, bilateral or cognatic kinship systems are those in which, in simplest terms, 'descent from ancestors and affiliation to a set of kinsmen may be traced through both females and males ... each sibling group has affiliations with a different set of cognatic kin. If relationships by affinity are taken into account ... every person may have his own range of relationships, which coincides exactly with no other in the society. Evidently, bilateral sets of consanguineal kin centred on Ego, the focal relative, have no structural persistence over generations ...[9] One immediate consequence of this for 'ego,' for any individual with an immediate and extended family on both the mother's and father's sides, is that these blood relationships create a wide 'range of choice for the application of an individual's rights, claims, and affiliations.'[10] This notably distinguishes bilateral kindred from clans and lineages, which are descent groups focused on an ancestor; indeed Alexander C. Murray is justified in calling the cognatic or bilateral kindred a personal group, 'even though strictly speaking it cannot be corporate and permanent, but is rather a category of cognates out of which groups can be recruited from time to time.'[11] Thus care must be taken when speaking loosely of kinships, kindreds, rights, and obligations. These are work-a-day terms with little or no clear-cut meaning in themselves. Some anthropologists have noted how empty they in fact can be, especially when we consider that 'kinship' in bilateral societies can involve, besides blood ties, such ties as one might produce through fosterage, adoption, in-law relationships, vicinage (cf. kith and kin), spiritual brotherhood, and legal friendship.[12] The issue of recruitment and mutual involvement should be emphasized: indeed, because bilateral societies have no permanent, corporate groups, the groups that form as 'kinsmen' in particular agricultural, hunting and fishing, craft-related, and feud or war-making circumstances may well involve some people who have no blood ties to each other. This situation is documented in the bilateral world of Konkama Lapps as well as of some Polynesian peoples.[13] Hrothgar has at least a Wendel among his Danes, yet he calls his retainers a *sibbegedriht*, a kinsmen band (a term also applied to Beowulf's Geats). Moreover, even if residence patterns show wives moving in with their husbands and their husbands' families, as in the aristocratic world of *Beowulf*, individuals can still move around; they may have consanguineous kinsmen in many places – a possibility, say, in the case of Ecgtheow, Beowulf's father, who leaves his people and seeks refuge among the Danes. They have entrée into other groups; and groups through the advents of births, marriages, and deaths continue to change.

The overlay of war-band and lord-retainer relationships on blood ties, and the aristocratic, that is, agnatic milieu of *Beowulf* of course give the poem's world some features that have not been emphasized so far. These features indeed de-emphasize the ties of local groups (other than those of the *comitatus*) as well as the ties of an extended kindred. The poem recommends amity among close relatives – amity that should hold (but does not always) between fathers and sons, brothers, cousins, uncles and nephews, daughters and potential suitors.[14] In this connection, the violent and niggardly king (Heremod) is a powerful image, as is dynastic strife: whether among the Swedes (between uncle and nephews, who are brother's not sister's sons) or among the Danes (in possible future rivalry between Hrothulf and Hrothgar's sons). But the poem also mainly emphasizes right behaviour for retainers, lords, and kings, with kinship especially noted if also involving the lord-retainer relationship. Thus we err in loosely supposing that lordship ties override or else simply replace kinship ties.

The obligations to one's kindred, other than those involving inheritance and guardianship, and the duties to one's lord are often invoked as a general explanation for conflicts. One such conflict is that between Cynewulf and Cyneheard in the Parker chronicle, entered for the year 755, although Cynewulf dies in 786. The episode involves a lethal attack on King Cynewulf (who at the time is visiting his mistress) by Cyneheard and Cyneheard's retainers; in response some of Cynewulf's men come to avenge their lord and are offered terms. They refuse these terms and so they are killed. Then the rest of King Cynewulf's army appears and surrounds Cyneheard and his men, who offer terms if Cynewulf's men will acknowledge Cyneheard as king, pointing out that kinsmen are on both sides. They are refused but Cynewulf's men offer safety to their kinsmen, who refuse in their turn to leave their lord and so die in the ensuing battle, during which only Cyneheard's godson is spared.

All of this spurs Charles Plummer (1899, rept. 1965, p. 46) to speculate that *comitatus* loyalties supersede kinship ties, although we do not know how close the kinship ties were in this case or how typical the episode is (Cynewulf became king after slaying Cyneheard's brother). Possibly the dramatic form of the entry reflects a new, monastically or politically inspired sense of loyalty to groups or to a lord outside the kindred (it may not be merely coincidental that the story is inserted thirty years too soon at year 755 – a mistake for 757, the date King Æthelbald is murdered by his own retainers). However, we do know that, as stated in various law codes, one could pay wergeld to the appropriate lord, rather than keep the matter exclusively for settlement by the near-kindred or the immediate family. This does suggest the overlay of the lord-retainer relationship upon kinship in Anglo-Saxon kingdoms.

But Beowulf's lord is also his kinsman – his maternal uncle in Hygelac's case, and his maternal cousin in Heardred's. This is true also for his loyal retainer, Wiglaf, who is Beowulf's kinsman on his father's peoples's side. However, support for lordship over kinship might come from Heorot: Hrothgar has retainers who are not Danes, most notably his herald and high officer, Wulfgar (who is a Wendel). These matters need careful scrutiny rather than simple acceptance (and not least because the Old English vocabulary for kinship relations is small, focusing at most on two or three generations in the immediate family of parents, siblings, and offspring). Evidence for the relationship between kinship ties and *comitatus* ties and how they affect feud and exchange needs to be evaluated in some analytical way. At present our understanding of these matters is vague, rather than particular and focused.

The dramatic and literary interests of *Beowulf* scholars are, however, only partly responsible for this hapless state of things. The lack of extensive historical records and of field reports on ancient, Germanic peoples is also responsible. Yet here there is often more for our attention than cursory summaries entertain. We can, for example, think of Tacitus' heterogeneous account of the Germanic peoples as a valuable source, even given its exhortative discovery of freedom and noble valour or warlike vigour in these barbarians.[15] Among many other things, Tacitus reports on marriage customs and on matters of communal law especially; the husband brings gifts of livestock and weapons to his wife while she brings weapons to him, and the wife must hand on her husband-dowry to her son's wife undiminished. This custom among a gift-giving people, if credited, would precede the Anglo-Saxon custom of gifts to the wife's immediate kindred, the 'weotuma' or bride-price, and would be a direct source for some of the personal wealth of a queen like Wealhtheow. It is reflected among the Anglo-Saxons in the so-called 'morning gift' the husband gives his wife on the day after the marriage (William Holdsworth takes this phrase from the laws of Æthelbert, capitulary 81);[16] reciprocally, one presumes, the wife brings her connubial and domestic services, but she keeps the morning gift and any other personal property in cases of separation that are not tied to charges of fornication.

In matters of criminal punishment, Tacitus reports a distinction between death for traitors and death for cowards and perverts: 'ignavos et imbelles et corpore infames coeno et pallude injecta insuper crate megrunt' (chap. 12) 'cowards, shirkers, and sodomites are pressed down under a wicker hurdle, into the slime of a bog' (Mattingly, 1948; revised by Handford, 1970). The decision is made by the armed assembly of the tribe, with appointed officials presiding over wergeld for less than capital offences. Law becomes a group decision, with kinship groups no doubt exerting pressure for particular settlements, even in cases of homicide. Contrary to the view of many scholars and older legal historians like William Holdsworth and Frederick William Maitland, compensation (rather than continuing blood feud) is not a relatively recent development: Tacitus notes that a fixed number of cattle or sheep, paid to the aggrieved family, can atone for homicide. Presumably Grendel could have made such an atonement but simply would not; and clearly enough in *Beowulf* a violent act, far from merely continuing a line of violence, can settle the matter legally, as in Beowulf's meeting with Grendel. But, apart from the uncle-sister's son tie, Tacitus does not elaborate Germanic kinship values nor does he have much information on the economy of gifts, despite such tantalizing hints as the continual demand young warriors make on the generosity of their lord (a process that can impoverish chiefs or great men even today).

These are fruitful matters to explore, although we do not have Anglo-Saxon witnessing to them in great detail. We often assume too much when we look at exceptional, especially Scandinavian and continental law codes, for example, and note the distribution of wergeld and the responsibility of different parts of the kindred.[17] Indeed, the Anglo-Saxon law codes in general do not support a wide-spread distribution of wergeld payment or obligation: the payment burden falls upon the responsible man or woman or, in his or her absence, upon the perpetrator's (probably near) paternal kindred in greater proportion (two-thirds to one-third) than on the maternal kindred. Moreover, the law codes may, in many cases, state hoped-for arrangements rather than customary ones, while probably not recording accepted practices comprehensively. The secondary burden of some of the codes seems to be to extend customary lordship rights, feud settlements (hence monastic 'kin' rights), and taxation or tribute rights to the clergy and to the church.[18]

Finding both modern and historically proximate (that is, European) societies with features similar to those we can document for the Anglo-Saxons is the best way to proceed analogically, even though no close parallels in all respects are likely. We need only consider the evolution of lordship and of law codes as examples. But identity is not important; rather we can profit from the insights and possibilities that analogy opens up. In Icelandic sagas we hear of raids and unsociable seizures but they are distinguished from theft, and though they may invite reprisals they are not necessarily without honour.[19] These raids may dismay *us* but they are not necessarily heinous or darkly piratical among the Germanic peoples.[20] Subduing one's neighbours by dragging off their mead-benches and striking terror in their hearts is something good that Scyld does, although the poet is not happy with generalized belligerence between peoples; he considers some strife (such as Swedish attacks on Geats after Hrethel's death) as simply lawless.

Comparative ethnology – the study of primitive economic and social systems – can also easily redeem the early, unfortunate confusions in *Beowulf* studies between nature myth and anthropology and restore empirical validity to what we can call an anthropological approach to the world depicted in the poem. Indeed, comparative ethnology is the most promising way of bringing out of obscurity the shared organization of those groups in the poem upon whom the *Beowulf* poet founded his heroic world and the Anglo-Saxon people to whom, in his own (unknown) time and place, he addressed his poem. We do have at least a few literary and other documentary hints for this kind of comparison.

This point of shared organization should be emphasized. The organization of Danes, Geats, and Swedes is not described as quaint or antique or different from the organization of groups in the poet's present. The poet's occasional sense of difference is moral or spiritual, rather than social or temporal. And even here the poet strongly implies a continuity between past and present through God's governance. For example, when he remarks on the heathen hope of some of Hrothgar's counsellors he says unequivocally in the voice of the present, 'Woe be to those who, driven by terrible affliction, would thrust their souls into the fire's embrace' (ll. 183b-185a). Here one can easily imagine him looking out at assembled lords and warriors, not to mention a few clergy, knowing that some of them may well revert to heathen practices if tried at all severely by pestilence, famine, or disaster in battle. But it will not be the burden of this study to locate the poet or the poem in an historical, Anglo-Saxon milieu, in a social world out of which the poem comes. Concentrating on the social world depicted *in* the poem is as far as ambition goes.[21]

In turning from *Beowulf* to comparative ethnology and then back to *Beowulf* again, one admittedly works by analogy, but the analogy offers many points for observation and comparison. The adage that 'analogy proves nothing' is true if the analogy is all; but that adage is false if analogy is a structure of thought leading to efforts at verification through observation and empirical investigation. Both thought experiments and controlled, laboratory experiments have an analogical spine, as it were, historically owing much to Aristotle's development of the formal analogy, whereby an 'unknown' is compared with a 'known': if there are two points of identity or significant likeness, then one may suppose that other facets of the known have their counterparts and their mutual relationships in the unknown – counterparts for which one then looks (not being entitled simply to assume them).

To work otherwise than by careful analogy from comparative studies, for a little-documented people who are now beyond direct study, is to arrive at either an impasse of understanding or an intellectual arrogation that takes these ancient peoples as really very much like ourselves. One result of the latter approach has been to find the prototype of social and economic communism, or democracy, or even rugged individualism in the Germanic peoples. It has led to the imposition of modern ideas of political institutions, such as monarchical kingship, onto Germanic kingship, not to mention middle-class evaluations of drinking, wealth, and feuds.

An equally abysmal alternative approach is to concentrate on the archaic character of Germanic societies. This effectively ends investigation: these ancient peoples and their traces – their law codes, charters, and wills, their poetry, proverbs, superstitions, and myths – are held to be alien, more completely other than we have hitherto suspected. If this great difference from us is real, and we have no analytical recourse to comparative studies of people similarly organized, then our investigation of social system – of the institutions of bilateral, but agnatically biased kinship and feud, of gift exchange, and the warband – will end in vague, somewhat inscrutable generalizations. An anthropology of *Beowulf* would then be a brief and unsatisfying affair. Frederick Klaeber noted that the poem has an 'edifying character' in need of explanation. Kenneth Sisam does not think, however, that we need to seek some Anglo-Saxon key to understand the poem, although Anglo-Saxon tastes no doubt differed from ours.[22] In part, I agree – there is no 'key.' But the wrangle in *Beowulf* studies over the poem's covert religious character, for instance, reflects Klaeber's uneasiness – as he responds to Beowulf's nobility and actions without an adequate, moral framework.

That framework, I think, is in the poem and becomes clear when illuminated ethnologically. Beowulf's world is a face-to-face one, characterized by bilateral kinship; morality is probably tied first to familial, then to lord-retainer, and then to group relations. In this world violent settlement is part of the institution of the feud (which in turn has a customary, juridical heart); grand gift giving has complex social dimensions; time is a matter of cycle and kin-line (or patriline), not clock time or historical measurement; and God is both in heaven and in the life and death events of this world, effectually underwriting the customary values of revenge as settlement, of amity between kinsmen, and of loyalty between lord and retainer.

Thus I am convinced that the impasse mentioned above is far from inevitable. We can undertake a significant anthropology of the social world reflected in *Beowulf*. When we draw ethnological information from contemporary people with similar institutions, we can formulate questions and suggestions about the relationships of these social institutions to those in ancient, Germanic contexts. Then we can look for either evidence overlooked by others or confirming indications from old evidence hitherto only partially understood.[23] Sometimes no confirmation is forthcoming, in which case we are not entitled to assume the presence of a given institution or custom, simply because it is there for other people similarly organized. Lorraine Lancaster (1958, p. 372) in effect offers a salutary warning in this connection when she disagrees with P. Vinogradoff's interpretation of Anglo-Saxon society as being a 'loosely constituted,' patrilineal one; he drew upon his knowledge of similar but quite differently framed kin-groups in the Greek and Roman worlds.

Social systems are heterogeneous and internally varied in some sense. Different customs can fulfil similar functions, thus occupying similar places in the relational system; and similar customs can indeed have different functions in different systems. Thus they can evolve into quite different expressions of such matters as gift exchange, much as potlatch differs considerably from the continuing, reciprocal system of gifts and services within the *comitatus*. As much as possible, we need to compare both point to point likenesses and the systems in which they are embedded, which functionally organize and relate them. The analytical traffic can go both ways after a while, for no 'known' in an analogical structure is completely and deeply known. But mainly the traffic, in the case of *Beowulf*, goes from ethnological studies to the poem. Ethnological observations can increase the depth of our understanding and illuminate the social and dramatic coherence of the poem. Those observations, of course, should include evidence of Anglo-Saxon kinship and legal customs, along with a background awareness of ideas about ancient Germanic customs (see Phillpotts [1971], Seebohm [1911], Lancaster [1958], Diamond [1971], and Loyn [1974; also 1984]). The following chapters give the results of forays from relevant ethnological literature into the Anglo-Saxon epic.

As those forays become attuned to the nuances within and dramatic moments in the poem, they reveal the possibilities for manipulation and ambiguity in otherwise generalized or even idealized social roles, and character interactions. The chapter on the economic world of *Beowulf*, for example, provides ample evidence for the dramatic complexity of gift giving both in Heorot and in Hygelac's hall; the chapter on law initially focuses on the social difficulties Beowulf must pass through before he can receive special status as Heorot's guardian against Grendel. Indeed, wherever we turn in *Beowulf* we find a subtle contextualizing of social roles and of otherwise idealized interactions within the poem. This reflects much that is currently exciting in ethnological studies of various cultures today.[24]

Certain points about kinship can be suggested now that might result from ethnological speculation. Perhaps Beowulf's father, Ecgtheow, goes to Hrothgar for help in settling a feud because he can claim kinship among the Danes on his mother's side (which would make Beow either his great-grandfather or great uncle once removed and Beowulf becomes Beow's namesake); perhaps Hrothgar's offer to adopt Beowulf as a 'son' is conceptually appropriate and even common when kinship can include such a relationship and when both adoption and fosterage are practised in the poet's world. If Ecgtheow is Hrothgar's nephew and sister's-son, then Beowulf, although firmly identifying himself as a man of the Geats and Hygelac's hearth-retainer, is like a great-grandson or nephew once removed – well within the normal bounds of extended kinship (three removes or degrees away). Hrothgar's attempted adoption of Beowulf after the Grendel fight would not then be merely a figurative offer (his command 'heald forð tela / niwe sibbe' 'henceforth hold well this new kinship,' ll. 948b–949a, urges a rightful even sacred possession and custodianship of this new relationship). Given the highly formulaic, half-line placement of 'tela,' Hrothgar here is voicing ritual speech, by which he would move Beowulf closer, perhaps directly into the line of succession.[25] That is why Wealhtheow takes Hrothgar's words seriously and why she pointedly urges Hrothgar to leave the people and kingdom to his sons. Beowulf, a Wægmunding on his father's side and a Geat on his mother's, is the chief warrior among the Geats, but not necessarily committed to staying among them. His relationship to the Geats and especially to Hygelac is one he reaffirms later in the poem, implicitly disavowing any loyalty or any kinship to anyone else (those who exchange gifts become friends and may even consider each other kin, especially where kinship between earlier generations may have existed). Such an affirmation would be odd if no other relationship were possible, especially considering such ties as are reflected in Beowulf's father's oath to Hrothgar, Beowulf's services to Hrothgar, and Hrothgar's gifts to him.[26]

These are interesting possibilities, more so in fact if we assume their ethnological plausibility; indeed, in a world like Beowulf's, recruitment of a total stranger may be relatively rare, if not unthinkable. Even if Germanic war-bands could fluctuate greatly in their composition, taking in skilled recruits as needed, could a warrior simply enlist in any war-band in a settled area of competing groups? Powerful and successful war-band leaders may well have attracted recruits from outside their immediate families and domains; perhaps this could occur for warriors outlawed from their homelands (a status that would probably be noted); no doubt warriors might also enlist in the service of notable foreign princes, but in *Beowulf* we hear of nobody with that status. Beowulf accepts his retainers from among the Geats (and of course Wiglaf is a Wægmunding kinsman); and Hrothgar, while clearly embracing men like Wulfgar, who is a Wendel, is not necessarily recruiting outside of cross-group connections. Indeed, ethnologically considered, we may suppose just the opposite for anyone mentioned as part of Hrothgar's hall-troop, given the enclosed, inter-connected character of this northern world. And we may well wonder why Hrothgar, a great and powerful king, would trouble to *settle* a feud on Ecgtheow's behalf if Ecgtheow is not embraceable as kin in some way;[27] could he settle it with a people, like the Wylfingas, who are not in some receptive relationship to him? The poet does not comment on the relationship between Hrothgar and Ecgtheow or on Hrothgar's attempt to adopt Beowulf. No explicit kinship links are claimed between Hrothgar and Ecgtheow, but perhaps that is because such links are assumed. In a world of happily or unhappily linked peoples, recruiting a stranger and resolving a feud on his behalf might seem simply outlandish.

The poem contains other feud issues that are just as important and just as much in need of an anthropological reviewing. For example, two cases of failed peace, based on marriage between previously hostile groups, have often struck readers as evidence for a general critique of revenge. These cases certainly involve considerable disquiet, but, as I discuss in the next chapter, they primarily involve other matters – a jural sense of the world especially, of just revenge in Hildeburh's case (the Finn episode), and of too little time having passed for hatred to weaken after the fall of princes in Freawaru's case.

To bring this introduction to a close, I think it important to indicate the different view of the heroic world we gain through comparative ethnology – especially in relationship to earlier accounts of that world in its literary incarnations. Many of the assumptions still guiding scholarly commentary have their roots in that older set of views, views in fact owing something to the anthropological climate of the early twentieth century. In this connection a review of the most comprehensive of those discussions is ideal.

H. Munro Chadwick is the most significant forefather for any comprehensive account of the social world in *Beowulf*. In *The Heroic Age* (1926) he notices much and, at least at the level of motif and background reference, is monumentally comprehensive. His preoccupation with comparative study, particularly between Germanic, Celtic, and Greek heroic ages, sets an agenda that only recently has come to fulfil itself in notable studies of heroic behaviour, speech, and poem-making. But that expansive preoccupation restricts him, paradoxically, because he looks for typologically fixed elements rather than for contextual conflict and movement; this mode of thought also accounts for his tendency to read dramatic action and speech as aspects of conventional scenes rather than as socially subtle gesture. Perhaps the best way to see this is to consider a number of Chadwick's organizing points about heroic society, government and religion.

Generally, Chadwick thinks that the evidence we have of Teutonic social life reveals a shift away from cognation and perhaps even matriliny to the agnatic and away from the importance of the extended kindred to that of the 'primitive sanctity' of the family, and from the family to that of the *comitatus*. Aside from suggesting that a precondition for these changes is a revolt from the power of the kindred and the bonds of tribal law, he attempts neither historical nor evolutionary analyses of these changes. He does not define 'kindred' or discuss to what extent we can legitimately infer general Teutonic practice from the various codes of law.[28] He does not even tie any given code to actual, customary practice in its region and time.

When he turns to the literature, especially to *Beowulf*, he finds evidence for many of these generalizations. He cites the importance of lord to retainer allegiance, but does not note that kinship ties are also present (and seem in Beowulf's case to inform the highest ideal of kingship); he asserts that customarily the sons of noblemen entered the king's service at an early age, but this does not sufficiently consider the kinship tie in grandson and nephew fosterage in Beowulf's case (as Hrethel's daughter's son and as Hygelac's sister's son) and also makes this seem more feudal than it was; he notes the paramount importance of kingly generosity, but not as something that defines morality, nobility, and fame; he assumes that the 'knight' should give whatever he gains by his own exploits to his lord (much as Beowulf renders up gifts to Hygelac and to Hygd), but he does not consider either why this should be so or the dramatic context of this giving; he uses historical records to suggest that kings commonly gave land when retainers reached manhood, citing Hygelac's gift to Beowulf of seven thousand hides, but this of course misses the dramatic context of that gift and supposes that Beowulf's meeting with Grendel is mainly a manhood test. According to Chadwick, Beowulf's final giving of goods to Wiglaf becomes yet another instance of the alienation of familial inheritance through the lord to retainer relationship. Again, the context of Beowulf's behaviour is not discussed because the general point – the weakening of kinship bonds – governs the use of adduced material in all of these examples. Rather than give an anthropologically informed account of *Beowulf*, as a kind of ethnography, let us say, he uses material from the poem (because *Beowulf* and all heroic poetry in the north are late) as evidence for anthropologically presumed change.

Thus the complex in *Beowulf* of kinship amity, kingly generosity, warband leadership, and combat rage is not understood as expressive of interrelated aspects of warrior-king life and social reciprocity; nor is warfare seen as positive and jural. Chadwick cannot see the non-linear sense of time and social relationships expressed by royal genealogies. Nor does he read heroic narratives as complex fabrics that in themselves reveal socially coherent attitudes, values, and beliefs. *Beowulf* does this in the interplay of action and speech, interpreting the drama of which is this study's burden, as informed by the inspirations of comparative ethnology.

CHAPTER ONE

Feud Settlements in *Beowulf*

Much of the commentary on feud and revenge in *Beowulf* confuses raiding behaviour with feud relationships. It also overlooks successful settlements, such as Hrothgar's on Ecgtheow's behalf, while focusing on the supposedly terrible lessons of revenge feud. Supposedly such feud is interminable, bringing everything to grief; even hoped-for settlements through marriage are not immune to disaster; indeed, they may well be especially vulnerable to ongoing blood-revenge. Thus the marriage alliances, more than anything else, become symbols of terrible pathos and are seen as implicitly anchoring the poet's social critique of the heroic world. Yet one can understand the complexity of feud and especially the outbreaks of violence between in-laws quite differently.

Rather than inevitably being undermined by feud, a marriage can be a long-term alliance between two families and may also implicate their wider kindreds. A 'marriage' could also be little more than a (sometimes forced) sexual coupling with some intention of permanence (bride capture); it could begin as an asocial, consensual arrangement. In Anglo-Saxon contexts marriage could and perhaps ideally did involve a transfer of wealth from groom to bride and from groom or groom's family to the bride's family – either to her immediate blood kin or to those who raised her.[1] Presumably the bride also brought something besides herself to the marriage (a dowry of sorts, perhaps in the form of weapons early on, or so says Tacitus).[2] In political contexts this may well involve tying a previously hostile group to one's own and thus beginning something more than a tributary relationship. This process of exchange could lead, through both cognation and a system of fosterage in succeeding generations, to an enduring alliance such as the Geats and Wægmundings enjoy.

Hildeburh's case is instructive here: She is a Dane and is married to Finn, whose Frisians are known as 'giants,' apparently an epithet for them. She has a son by Finn. Years pass and her brother comes to visit. Somehow violence breaks out, perhaps instigated by these 'giants,' if not by Finn's immediate kin (the poet says that Hildeburh had no reason to praise the fidelity of 'giants'); Danes and Finn's men kill each other until so much blood has been shed by each side that neither can prevail. Barricaded in Finn's hall, the Danes offer a truce, which is accepted and sworn to as Danes and Frisians exchange oaths of peace and mutual honouring. But the winter is bitter for Hengest, who must honour his lord's slayer. One supposes the winter is also bitter for Hildeburh, who lost a son and a brother (Hnaef, Hengest's lord). She mourned that decree of fate deeply, there under the skies where she had had her greatest joy but must now gaze sadly upon murdered kinsmen. She aggressively directs their immolation, lamenting them in song.[3] 'Murder-bale' links what Hildeburh sees with what Grendel does, with what Hrothgar accordingly feels, and with terrible kin-slaying. Thus Hildeburh's grief and her bitterness about dark crime must cry for settlement, for revenge.

With spring, some Danes insist and Hengest enacts that revenge, killing Finn and all who remain with Finn, sacking Finn's hall, and carrying off royal treasures, including the Half-Dane, Hildeburh. The poet does not say so but she may now feel some relief as her consanguineal affections and legal worth remain with her father's family. The urging of revenge is by no means an unnatural act for an aggrieved woman (contradicting a notion in literary studies that women – Grendel's mother excepted – should confine themselves to peace-weaving).[4] The outcome is a Danish triumph and justice for a malicious slaughter. Hildeburh returns with her bride goods and her morning gift – no doubt part of the treasure the Danes take. Very likely she still grieves but at least she is partly compensated. Clearly the *initial* deaths of both son and brother end the possibility of cognatic ties in the next generation.

This difficult narrative emphasizes Hildeburh's sorrow but not as something wrong in the system of revenge. She sorrows deeply, as anyone would, when violent disaster ('fær') and murder befall her dearest kinsmen but, unlike Grendel's mother, or the princess Modthryth, Hildeburh does not act on her own. Thus she is a model of the noble queen, whose aggression and commanding power do not take up the spear. Yet, in effect, all ends in a just settlement, if not altogether happily. That is why this episode is recited as a *victory* song. Hildeburh reassumes a familiar and secure place in the world, brought back 'to leodum,' to her people.

The episode is long and breaks up the scenes of gift giving at Heorot. It clearly separates Wealhtheow's munificent gestures and powerful words from Hrothgar's, allowing us to focus on whatever special gestures Wealhtheow makes. If the Finn episode functions in any larger sense, it may prepare us for instability in a world of warring groups, where peace and amity between in-laws exist and might be expected to continue (although we should grant that Anglo-Saxon in-law relations are designated by very few terms, compared even to modern English). Terms such as 'sweor,' 'aðum,' 'tacor' emphasize relationship by oath and sign, making these relationships more ethical than compelling. Along with the sparseness of such terms, this could indicate the relative insignificance of in-law bonds.[5] Perhaps Hildeburh had brothers-in-law, bound by sign and oath to her and to her immediate kin, who were involved in the slaying of her blood brother, much as would then be so for Finn; both his son and his Danish brother-in-law die. This is cause for considerable sorrow but several times the passage justifies rather than indicts revenge; revenge taken is the better of two settlements, of two reassertions of order. Finn seems intent on reknitting relations by exchanging peace-oaths and by sharing gifts and halls (as though a hall held together between recently hostile parties might establish a kind of kinship).[6] I like Alan Bliss's ingenious suggestion that the 'giants' in question are Hengest's, not Finn's, mainly because the sharing of a hall between adversaries strikes him as bizarre.[7] But the force of the passage and the careful stating of oaths and of lethal sanctions suggest otherwise. Whatever Finn agrees to tie together here, for Hengest there is in the hall certainly no cup-bearing queen to reconcile the retainers to each other. The blood-letting has been so grievous that the entire arrangement in itself stings: like the ice-fetters of winter that prevent Hengest from departing, his arrangement with Finn is a bond of torture, not amity.

Another instance involves Beowulf's anticipation of revenge feud in Freawaru's case. Marriage hope and political fruition are unlikely, says Beowulf, even though the bride is good (Freawaru is both good to look upon and comes from the most notable of families among the most notable of peoples). Some kind of jural arrangement must already make possible this marriage – one by which Hrothgar hopes to settle a portion of his feud and deadly strife with the Heathobards. But, while characterizing the spear as deadly and the issue as grievous because it involves the death of princes, Beowulf emphasizes a temporal link. In the *short* run these arrangements are subject to the vaguely jural incitements of those who cannot take revenge for themselves (primarily women and old men). Full of grievance, these figures (an old warrior in this case) shame others into acting; the spear does not rest even for a short while.

The old warrior's shaming speech has many analogues in Old Icelandic contexts, especially in the legalistic world of the sagas.[8] Beowulf then gives a plausible scenario of how a grim, old, Heathobard warrior will goad others by noting how a Dane comes through the hall wearing the weapons of slain Heathobards, his forefathers. All of this speaks to Beowulf's wisdom about the world's affairs, especially to his jural sense of how the subordinate or the relatively disenfranchised can think and gain a cold-hearted hearing. He notes that the old warrior will be grim and sorrowful of mind and he will urge a son of the sword's previous possessor to meditate upon the sword that should by right be the son's (wartime) counsel ('rædan') and should be in his control. Repeatedly the old warrior will urge the young one so that eventually, unlooked for by the Danes in question, a violence will break out that will likely bring the anguished Ingeld to think less well of his wife, Hrothgar's hope for kindred-like peace ('friðusib,' 'peace-kinship'). For their part, the Danes do not seem to think about the grief their captured weapons would incite. It is as though Beowulf imagines them as innocently displaying their warrior honour. One can speculate that the old warrior's urgings also reflect a subconscious darkness in the minds of Danes, who wear captured swords to the wedding where their princess will eventually be bedded by their former enemy, Ingeld.[9] Thus Beowulf does not look for fast friendship between Danes and Heathobards and that, I think, is the centre of his point and the poet's. Not, isn't revenge awful, but rather, how does a firm friendship develop between feuding peoples? In this connection, we have totally overlooked the extent to which *Beowulf* is a poem about settling feuds, about successful and unsuccessful efforts to establish peaceful and secure arrangements.

Clearly a good peace arrangement and reciprocal visits are necessary. The noble bride as 'peace-kin' is a good beginning. But Beowulf might well say that Danes and Heathobards also need time and regular visits, as well as gift exchange, before mutual and even dependent relationships can form. (This includes ties with Hrothgar's grandchildren – the cohort for fosterage.) Beowulf has already established continuing exchange and support between Geats and Danes, who once exchanged only enmities. A good bride and time would help. But until enough time has passed perhaps one should not count on marriage alone. Perhaps one should maintain an armed and diplomatic wariness (being careful not to wear the arms of the wrong enemies, such as weapons taken from slain kinsmen of one's in-laws) until the memories of old warriors dim and the hearts of the wedded grow fond. I suggest armed wariness because Beowulf moves from the Heathobard scenerio to tell Hygelac about Grendel and about how he repaid that evil creature. This connects Grendel for a moment with the grim warrior, the old Heathobard, and suggests the will toward definitive settlement – something the old Heathobard seems to want, although his dark-mindedness seems to undermine it. We too easily forget that even bitter feuds can be brought to a private and binding close.[10]

With ferocity and will – that is how one settles particular moments of violence. With a good bride, reciprocal visits, armed wariness, and time – that is how one forms a fast friendship between previously warring parties. Perhaps just such a friendship formed between Frisians and Half-Danes over the years during which Hildeburh's son grew into a young warrior. Finn's serious efforts at first accepting and then adjudicating a peace between Danes and Frisians speaks, perhaps, to his grief over the bitter rupture. The poet might be implying, moreover, that friendship may not survive the enmities of others (giants, literally or metaphorically, in this case) and that one should look well to the hatreds of one's mixed troop and not presume too much about the 'kinship' of the hall. Perhaps, even where friendship lasts, a wise wariness is best if one would have peace and good order continue.

I submit that we have either underread or misread these episodes because we think of blood revenge as inexorably baleful rather than as a settlement that can last. We think of revenge as something extralegal, as something to be replaced by systems of payment or some other form of non-lethal settlement, such as outlawing the offending person or party. But many societies, including Germanic societies, do not see revenge in exactly these ways; nor does the *Beowulf* poet in the world he dramatizes for us.

Acts of revenge can be good and jurally definitive; when urged by an old, grim-hearted warrior they may have jural respectability. The just-minded Beowulf does not condemn the old Heathobard. Of course the poet is ambivalent about violent exchanges; this is clear from his focus on Hildeburh's grief and from his later comment that when Grendel's mother slew Æschere both sides had to pay with the lives of friends (ll. 1305–6): that exchange was not good. But here the *situation* is bad mainly because Beowulf's slaying of Grendel was not definitive. Indeed, it is the value of friends which links this passage with Beowulf's later maxim stating that, rather than mourn much, one should avenge slain friends. His vow to seek Grendel's mother wherever she might go meets with Hrothgar's joyful approval, and we are told that even God takes his revenge upon those who warred against him. A critique of revenge is not in question here; more important is the task of establishing a fast friendship between either tenuously reconciled foes or established in-laws whose allied retainers may not be the best of friends.[11]

We have gone now from an instance of feud-settlement, to one of disaster and horrible murder, calling for revenge, to an anticipated case of failed peace-kinship, and on to Beowulf's maxim concerning the good of revenge. Our perspective has widened in the process of reevaluation, but now we need to expand virtually to the horizons of revenge feud seen globally. Here modern, comparative ethnology can clarify possibilities only briefly glimpsed, for example, in ancient, Frankish records where, in cases of failed or insufficient compensation, the guilty party is given to the aggrieved, perhaps to be killed.[12]

Working in Africa, and in the tradition of E.E. Evans-Pritchard, Max Gluckman has formulated what he calls the 'peace in the feud.' By this he means that in long-settled areas, with much intermarriage between groups as well as close working arrangements between neighbours (which may create a quasi-kinship), nearly everyone will be related in some way to nearly everyone else. This limits the taste for prosecuting feuds and increases pressure for and the likelihood of peaceful settlements that 'attempt to reconcile parties in permanent relationships.'[13] Gluckman's work on actual deliberations among the Barotse does not include juridical reviews of cases involving manslaughter or murder; moreover, the people reviewed by Evans-Pritchard and by Gluckman are characterized as unilineal rather than as bilateral in their kinship systems and in their group formations. Yet this idea of pressure for settlement short of violence (or at least of runaway violence) between feuding people is a valuable one generally, for even manslaughter might lead only to limited reprisal, and in small and isolated bilateral societies, the pressure for a settlement other than blood-taking may even be greater given the many ways in which anyone's near kindred can overlap with anyone else's. Of course the effects on overlapping kinship of warring and perhaps expansionist groups organized around the lord-retainer relationship can vary greatly from Gluckman's view of the matter. The Danes, beginning with Scyld and no doubt continuing through to Hrothgar, established both their frontiers (note the frontier guard) and tributary relationships with subdued peoples (Scyld having 'carried off' their mead-benches).

That famous but problematic entry in the Anglo-Saxon chronicle about Cynewulf and Cyneheard concerns acknowledged kinsmen facing the prospect of fighting each other rather than abandoning loyalty to their lord. To understand this event anthropologically we need to know the particular conditions of the feud, the society, the kinds of groups, and any extended community involvement. For example, because feud can hardly be maintained within a close kindred, expiation through ritual or through payment within the close group might be the solution to homicide. Feuds between groups including in-laws might exclude those in-laws (although in-laws slay each other in the Finn episode). Finally, the issue of exact settlement and of group solidarity, as well as of apportioned responsibility, will operate differently in different personal, social, and economic circumstances. Norman war-bands, for example, were kinship groups in a bilateral context, with deliberate recruitment taking place through marriage alliances. Feuds within the group tended to be suppressed and feuds between competing groups of Northmen could be settled through compensation as well as marriage, especially if a lord's centipetal influence was powerful. But feuds with outsiders (Franks, for example) were prosecuted lethally or else, through a combination of war and marriage, involved the absorption of those outsiders.[14]

William I. Miller masterfully explicates blood-taking and peacemaking in Icelandic society as filtered through the sagas. This is a literary world in which community involvement and pressure for nonviolent solutions seem weak. Perhaps this is so because the literary world reflects an Icelandic society that is a congeries of scattered farmsteads and dependencies, with little hierarchy, no large settlements, and something like an ethos of aggressive individualism, sensitive to slights, quick to take advantage, and eager for ways to enhance or to preserve honour and status. Even so, pressure for settlement short of runaway violence exists; even those recruited in support of a particular individual's grievance may vary in some ambivalent way in their eagerness for violence (as may the aggrieved party;[15] and if the disputants go to the 'All-Thing,' an annual gathering for settling disputes, then a wide circle of interested onlookers, uninvolved or 'peripherally involved free farmers and chieftains,' can come into play. Substantial 'segments of the community usually desired some kind of reconciliation,' we are told, 'if for no other reason than to avoid the vexations of being expected to separate combating disputants, of suffering the depredations of outlaws on their livestock, or of having the outlaw's dependents become a charge on the district.'[16]

Probably Max Gluckman is more hopeful than absolutely right about the peace in the feud in most societies where feuds occur. Yet the runaway feud is probably an aberration – the result in literature of an interest in melodrama or, in life, either of irreconcilable hostility between groups and their clientele (who do not recognize mutual kinship) or of something akin to insanity and the monstrous. Such balefulness appears in *Beowulf* in Grendel's feud against the Danes and in Onela's and Ohtere's attacks on Geats.) Large, interrelated groups of close relatives, friends, and supportive neighbours – of kinspeople, in effect – have a vested interest in contained settlements of even lethal acts, crimes, and accidents (especially in subsistence economies where periodic scarcity is a persistent threat and where interdependence enhances the chances for survival).

In the last twenty years, several studies have attempted a global view of feuds in stateless societies. They have found that feud is generally different from activities we easily confuse with it, such as raiding and warfare. In feuds, coherent groups are often involved in direct competition with each other. When feuds involve homicide, the exchanges are limited in scope and may not involve just anyone in the opposing group as a suitable victim (especially if an opportune victim does not even the score).

However, *Beowulf* does not clearly distinguish between warfare (battle) and feud. Feud, of course, involves individual battles, either one on one or group against group; and feuds in principle can be settled through compensation unless spawned as criminal or malicious. Feud and crime ('fæhðe ond fyrene') characterize Grendel's attack on Heorot, Sigemund's and Fitela's werewolf-like deeds, and Swedish attacks on Geats (which culminate in a final, Geat-led reprisal at Ravenswood). Raids are not feuds, although feud reprisal may take the form of a raid – when Geats attack Swedes who ambushed them, seizing Ongentheow's queen and her riches, and are then surrounded in turn by an enraged Ongentheow until the morning brings Hygelac and Geatish reinforcements, who kill Ongentheow. Hygelac does not attempt to settle any portion of this feud further, at least not through marriage (he marries his daughter, not to a Swede, but to the warrior who kills Ongentheow). And a raid, as when Hygelac sweeps fatefully into Frankish territory, can turn into an occasion for revenge – as when Beowulf avenges Hygelac's death by killing everyone in Dæghrefn's war-band, including Dæghrefn, whom he crushes to death.

Some anthropologists think that blood feuds are in effect interminable, even if a given feud series is compromised through compensation. The blood debt is never quite even, as no two groups are perfectly balanced in prestige and power, and the psychology of debt looks for repayment with interest. Others consider that any feud is in principle resolvable, given the shifting compositions of the groups involved over time.[17]

This dispute seems to founder over priorities. Is feud some definable state that in turn defines groups? Or do competing groups fall into a feuding relationship that is susceptible to changes in the constitution of the groups and the climate of competition? I incline to the latter view although *Beowulf* does not say much about this directly. Indirectly, in its underwriting of just revenge through divinity, king, and hero, *Beowulf* clearly countenances the good of violence in situations where one seeks a justifiable settlement rather than dark pleasures. And directly, in the alliance Beowulf announces between Geats and Danes, the poem shows that groups who once exchanged hostilities – whether called feuds or not – can put that behind in an arrangement of mutual support.

Near the poem's end, a Geatish messenger from Wiglaf expects a time of war ('orleghwile') with the Franks when they hear of Beowulf's death. Although not in a state of feud, neither are the Geats at peace with the Franks (with whom they do not exchange gifts). Their relationship is one of opportunistic raiding, each upon the other.[18] But with the Swedes a different relationship seems to have formed. At least during Beowulf's tenure as king, the Geats and the Swedes have been in a state of trust and kinship-like amity (negatively indicated by the 'sib' and 'treow' the messenger no longer expects). The messenger implies this will end when Beowulf's fall becomes widely known. Rather than continuing friendship, the messenger predicts feud and hatred because the Swedes will probably now act on memories of slain kinsmen in the very battle during which Beowulf avenged Hygelac's son, Heardred, and helped Eadgils, Onela's nephew, to Onela's throne. In this case feud between Swedes and

Geats seems nearly interminable; but even that could change in time and feud itself is not judged here. The messenger dwells upon consequent suffering and sorrow – grief to be sure, but not in any necessary way a judgment upon feud as something lawless and deeply poisoned. His lament, and perhaps the larger, darker mood that overtakes parts of the second half of *Beowulf*, is less for a world of sometimes hostile peoples than for one's vulnerability in that world when a powerful lord dies. After all, consistently in *Beowulf*, possible revenge and defence are occasions for joy, as when Hrothgar leaps thankfully to his feet following Beowulf's vow to seek Grendel's mother.

It is somewhat surprising that the poet nowhere states the extent of involvement of a kinship group in any given act of feud. Kinsmen should avenge each other – the general point is well known – and perhaps the recruitment of a group for revenge is too familiar a practice for comment (although the unusual may not be, as when a non-agnate proposes vengeance). When Hrothgar loses Æschere to Grendel's mother's revenge (she seems satisfied with any Dane grabbed blindly from among the kinship band) Beowulf takes up the responsibility for revenge and phrases his justification in general terms: it is better to avenge the death of a friend than to mourn much. Such a deed is praiseworthy; given that we each die, it is best that each retainer seek approbation before death. His speech is gnomic and unmotivated by personal ties of kinship or retainership. Could the poet be implying through Beowulf's formality that the revenge case needs to be made general and abstract?

One can only look to the immediate context. Clearly we have Beowulf implying here that revenge is a glorious way to deal with mourning and perhaps it is a way to gain deep relief and satisfaction. This is a relief that the Geat, Hrethel, does not have when one son accidently slays another – in *Beowulf* there can be no feud or compensation within the family – and it is a relief denied the miserable, old father whose young son is hanged because there can be no revenge or compensation for the death of an outlaw. Beowulf broods over these and other ideas after the dragon's initial, revengeful terror, but unlike either Hrethel or the old father, Beowulf always has recourse to laudable action. He assumes responsibility for avenging Aeschere even though he has not responded to Hrothgar's offer of adoption. Perhaps he is implying that 'friendship' ties him to the Danes in this affair and this apparently allows him to accept their injury as his own.

But more is involved. Hrothgar has already tried to implicate Beowulf in this matter. He notes pointedly how Grendel's mother avenged the death of her son whom Beowulf killed, even though Grendel had for a very long time diminished Hrothgar's band. This does not oblige Beowulf to act, but it might dispose him to. Hrothgar also says that Beowulf's is the only advice he can rely on in this terrible affair (the counsel he wishes to hear is Beowulf's vow to act). Thus does Hrothgar beseech Beowulf: a plea and a recruitment that succeed. Beowulf solemnly vows to pursue Grendel's mother no matter where she might go upon the earth's expanse, through mountain forests or to ocean's bottom. Unlike Grendel's mother, whose motives are sound insofar as she would avenge a son's death, Beowulf's here are neither self-interested nor dark-minded. For his mother to be righteous, Grendel could not be an outlaw; for her revenge to be pure, she would have to be willing to accept either compensation or a circumscribed, if violent settlement, rather than intend as much bloody-minded slaughter as possible. To be sure, there are ambiguous, psychological issues here, about which the poet seems deeply troubled - as he is over instances of feud characterized as strange or as criminal. But the general status of revenge has jural dimensions and is not under critique: only malignant instances fall under the poet's implicit scrutiny, as reflected in his characterizations of them.[19]

I have claimed that Hengest's settlement with Finn and his mixed troop of Frisians and Jutes is a jural one and that the old Heathobard's urging of revenge is also jural or at least tentatively so. One might say that, in many cases, instances of feud are hardly extra-legal; they do not occur outside of customary notions of what is lawful in the sense of rights and obligations. This idea has troubled many literary, historical, and anthropological scholars. I take just one response as an example that may clarify the issues.

In his analysis of law and societal structure among the bilateral Nunamiut Inuit, Leopold Pospisil distinguishes between processes of law and reconciliation within the autonomous hunting band. This is a community of subgroups that moved down through extended and polygamous families to the nuclear family. At the band level one might perceive factions that betoken later fission of the band but disputes within the band were usually settled in some legal fashion, discouraging interband feud.

These deliberations in ancient times probably did not involve applied codes or rules. Some procedure using a combination of general value and immediate practice probably negotiated the dispute to a right outcome. But between autonomous bands long-lasting and bitter feuds could occur, primarily because there was no customary law for violent disputes at this level. Rival bands could be at war with each other. Thus Pospisil can say, in this context, that feuds occur in the absence of or outside of the law.[20] In part this is correct, if by feud we mean a state of warfare between rival groups, and if by law we mean a process of adjudication, taking of evidence, weighing accounts, seeking reconciliations, and assessing an abiding outcome (such as ostracism in the case of murder). But in part this position is disingenuous: feuds between groups are not easily or quickly settled but they are not seen as in themselves a state of war or as criminal. They are also subject to negotiation, and to the peacemaking possible through marriage between groups (although the Danes' prospects in wife-making kin-peace do not hearten Beowulf in one case and do not last sufficiently into the second generation in the other).

In non-centralized, face-to-face societies, one rarely steps beyond law into some lawless zone when one avenges one's kinsmen and friends (Black-Michaud does consider vendetta as revenge outside of group support). Indeed, the right to do so would inform a group's council in its decisions about feuds. Such a right is something Pospisil does not discuss, yet I think it a distinct likelihood. Before Beowulf sets out to counsel Hrothgar and the Danes against Grendel, for example, he receives good omens from wisemen among the Geats – presumably a council that thinks there is right in his intentions. And when he comes to Heorot, he comes to speak and give advice in an open council about what he hopes to do against Grendel, the creature who wars against right, because he offers no compensation for his crimes nor would he in any way end his feud with the Danes. Perhaps there is a crucial distinction here: ongoing blood feud is jural but not a part of jural adjudication; an act of requital in response to violence waged against one is as 'legal' as it is right (even in the case of vendetta, defined as revenge without solidarity, without a group of obligated avengers).

There is nothing intrinsically malignant, lawless, or viciously extended about Beowulf's violent dealing with Grendel (any more than there is in the poet's note that God, presumably by means of the flood, requited those giants and others who warred against Him). Indeed, we can see Beowulf, who does not give laws, as nevertheless inherently a 'legislator' figure of sorts. Or perhaps we should think of him as a juristic warrior: he brings to the Danes the efficacy of the sworn, strong, and purging hand of law, something they have tried but failed to assert successfully for themselves (cf. Latin *jus* and its derivative *jurare* – to swear by ritual formula – with Beowulf's promises, vows, and resolvings of mind). Thus violent requital and even war can be right and, in that jural sense, a legal response.

That response may well involve right, just, and proper behaviour that includes appropriate deliberation or council in the hall and aims for settlement. In chapter 3, I discuss such jural action, its appropriate vocabulary, and its mythological background through Beowulf's movement from uninvited stranger to an especially entrusted guardian of Heorot. To see the jural dimensions of Beowulf's progress in the poem is a deep gain in our re-viewing of the poem's social world, for we then move decisively away from the usual accounts of Beowulf's early journey as a simple undertaking on the part of a hero-adventurer bent on cutting his teeth against an especially formidable creature. Beowulf's motives include winning honour and perhaps renown but those are not his primary aims. He comes to assert what is right against an unimaginably savage creature who, by literally cannibalizing the warriors he finds in the hall, attacks the soul of the community and occupies its 'bone-house.' Beowulf comes as purgator; he comes to enact the law out of friendly, honourable feelings toward Hrothgar and the Danes, an enactment deeply validated (as I show in chapter 3) by ancient myth and deity. These are the twin, one might even say the formal and material, justifications not only for revenge and feud settlement but also for every other social value expressed in the poem.

CHAPTER TWO

The Temporal World in *Beowulf*

God underwrites revenge in the requital he takes against giants who warred against him, presumably by drowning them in Noah's flood. Grendel bears the mark of God's wrath and Hrothgar sees Beowulf as quite literally a god-send in his feud against Grendel. In these and many other respects, Beowulf's social world is far from demythologized; it is neither a world of mechanical relationships and automatic duties nor one simply arranged between existential humans who make their meanings and establish their values as they go along. Thus we might do well to leave our considerations of revenge and proceed with a summary of some of the large-scale ways in which myth and the sense of past and present can operate in a primitive culture.

Malinowski states that 'myth' comes from the past; it is what illustrious forbears have done, not what immediate ancestors have achieved (in this sense Scyld Scefing is more mythical than is Hrothgar's father). He notes that in the live relation of myth to a people, the past is inherently more important than the present and carries enormous social weight.

> The stories of important past events are hallowed because they belong to the great mythical generations and because they are generally accepted as truth, for everybody knows and tells them. They bear the sanction of righteousness and propriety in virtue of these two qualities of preterity and universality.
>
> Thus, through the operation of what might be called the elementary law of sociology, myth possesses the normative power of fixing custom, of sanctioning modes of behavior, of giving dignity and importance to an institution ... This is what we could call the normative influence of myth on custom.[1]

For Malinowski's Melanesians, mythical tales of great luck, strength, and magic show that it lies 'in the hands of man to bring this luck on himself, provided he acquires the necessary magical lord.' Consider in this connection Beowulf's sense that if one is not fated, and one has courage and strength, then one may prevail. Another feature of Melanesian myths is that they involve certain places occupied by local groups who thus have a special but not exclusive ownership of the myth and who presume to know it in its greatest, unadulterated detail.[2] That presumption is the dynamic issue here; just as genealogies can be adjusted to reflect changing political environments (especially with bilateral groups) so can myths or narratives that overtly sustain cultural values. Such myths are open to wholesale appropriation in the world of Beowulf, perhaps reflecting a pan-Germanic and Mercian or West Saxon hegemony. Because social myths are narrated under public and even authoritative conditions, they may even, if we go far afield for a moment in Jack Goody's extrapolated view from a particular Lo Dagaa clan myth, confer through recitation various medical, ritual, and social benefits upon their audiences.[3]

But more to the point for the poet's world in *Beowulf* is the use of myth (legend and heroic story) to say who one is and how one is that way. Kirsten Hastrup (1990) discusses a similar world in Iceland in terms of the old virtues promoted in the sagas. 'As a myth of the past, the sagas provided a permanent image of the Icelanders in the past tense, as it were. The mirror provided by these stories showed the people that things had changed; but no new literature was created which could have produced a contemporary imagery of moral values ... Instead the old cultural models were reproduced' (p. 193). This assessment may overstate the degree of deviation between the values of the saga world and those of the twelfth and thirteenth centuries when the sagas were written down. But it suggests the incorporating moral force of myth, even in the face of acknowledged historical change. Icelanders saw themselves in terms of a past world of moral values. *Beowulf* can easily be seen as myth in this sense. With its pan-Germanism and its blend of theistic pagans and basic Christianity *Beowulf* can also be seen as myth formed in terms of an authorizing past as the poet's Anglo-Saxon society defined values to itself. In this way, perhaps, it 'maintained its equilibrium through strategic adaptations during a period of major change (the West Saxon hegemony achieved by Alfred the Great's brothers, especially Athelstan)' (Niles, 1993, p.79).

The world in *Beowulf* is demonstrably not the West Saxon kingdom, or any Anglo-Saxon kingdom. It is, however, an ancestral world the West Saxons and Mercians can especially own when we consider the Anglian and partially Mercian West Saxon royal genealogy ascending to Sceaf and beyond. We might place *Beowulf* at some stage in its development within the provenance of that much expanded, early tenth-century kingdom. Thus to understand *Beowulf* as myth is in some sense to see it as an incorporating force for the society that produced it. Malinowski's terms provide a fruitful way to understand that incorporation, even though his Trobriand islanders live in matrilineal clans. The incorporation he notes is reflected in Indo-European societies both on the grand level – if Dumézil is correct in his theory of tri-partite functions (where the roles of gods are mirrored in the social functions of Indo-Iranian and Germanic kings, warriors, and priests) – and on the small, as Hastrup and others (Miller especially) have noted for the Icelanders and their saga worlds.

The *Beowulf* poet looks back to an heroic past that is mythic. He seamlessly establishes a basic continuity with that past. Indeed, he asserts a fundamental *sameness* of values and reality that frames his moderate sense of difference in some customs and in the theistic scope his noble characters express. He inveighs strongly against heathen worship and he clearly establishes a double perspective in the poem – speaking to his audience about things his noble characters do not know (such as Grendel's associative, genealogical link with Cain). But that perspective does not put him or his audience into an ironic and dismissive relationship with the past. The poet and the poem assert the 'normative' relationship of that past to the (unspecified) Anglo-Saxon present; the poet does not alienate that past from himself and his writerly present. In many ways his temporal sense is less historical than simply continuous (e.g. 'hwil,' 'tid,' missera' or half-years, also equated with the passing of winters). That duration is time within which emotional, or fateful, or victorious events happen.

This emphasis on Beowulf's heroic world as socially functional myth opposes a strong line of interpretation, going back to J.R.R. Tolkien, who argued essentially that the Christian poet of *Beowulf* looks back with some regret to a doomed past from which he distances himself. That interpretive lineage takes in nearly every allegorical or neo-patristic approach, excepting those few readings of Beowulf as a Christ-figure. It also embraces many non-allegorical efforts to find something tragically flawed in Beowulf's world of heroic values, exchanges, and feuds, or else in Beowulf himself, especially in his fateful (and to some either greedy or vainglorious) decision to meet the dragon at the end of the narrative. But those readers who see the poet looking back more or less approvingly, and who see Beowulf's world as that of the 'noble pagan,' can find ethnological justification in Malinowski's account of mythical narratives and in the emphases of this chapter. Their efforts at historical justification – such as citing Anglo-Saxon missions to continental, Germanic pagans or Celtic Christian views of noble ancestors – are interesting and no doubt germane, but they are more free floating and ad hoc in character than convincing. I believe that an ethnological approach not only supports the perceptive intuitions of such readers, but it can also ground those intuitions deeply and coherently.

The themes involved in this chapter all concern the issue of continuity, of essential connection with the past created large in *Beowulf*. Continuity shows through in such major frameworks as the poem's time scheme, its concern for genealogical connections and identities, and its valuing of customs. The poet thinks of objects and of social relationships as having identity through time, essentially as being what they are only in virtue of their entire history or, if applicable, of their cycle: consider swords as identical with their histories; think of Heorot as identical with its history, first of towering liberality, then of savage, night-time incursion, along with day-time greatness and splendour, then of lawful purgation, and, eventually, of defence and hateful fire during in-law strife (the attack of the Heathobards); consider also Hrothgar's friendship with Hrothulf as identical with its (to us) inscrutably full history, and Modthryth's history as identical with her full transformation from terror-princess to noble queen. In this connection the poet's sense of time is crucially linear. His tie to the heroic past of Danes and Geats is essentially inclusive; his sense of real time then is structural and concerned with sameness. He is neither impressed by a sense of deep and distancing continuum in the past nor aware of profound change.

We can see this in the short kin-lines he gives to his noble and ignoble characters alike. Grendel is linked to Cain, through quick association, not down a great distance back into a mysteriously remote past. The main action of combats and purgations occurs in the sons' (or nephews') generation but the fathers and grandfathers are regularly invoked and are part of the present. Beowulf is his father's son (we know his father's name but not his mother's); Hygelac is his maternal uncle ('eam'), lord, and great kinsman; Hrethel is like both a father and a grandfather – he treats Beowulf as a son and Beowulf places himself in protective, near equality with Hrethel's grandson; Hrothgar's immediate line is born from his grandfather, Beow, and encompasses his own sons. Kenneth Sisam has noted this effective tie of three to four generations in the context of likely historical memory for pre-literate Anglo-Saxons – thus casting doubt on the depth of living memory as well as on the historical accuracy of extensive genealogies.[4] This is exactly right for non-centralized face-to-face groups today. Genealogies are not historically understood; rather they are a kind of mnemonic for social arrangements and structures. The older ones, unless the society has specialists to remember and pronounce long lines, rarely go back more than ten or eleven generations. The focus on a near kin-line of three or four generations is also inherently functional socially, today as it was then. This generational triad can even be the matrix for upward mobility in Anglo-Saxon England: the prosperous son of a prosperous 'ceorl' cannot join the 'gesith'; but his prosperous grandson can.[5]

The Danish family tree emphasizes four generations, from Scyld Scefing to Hrothgar, but Hrothgar has sons and presumably Heremod ruled the Danes sometime after Sheaf, but before Scyld arrived, thus giving us the longest genealogy – seven generations – in the poem. (Heremod's renegade status implies the dying out of his immediate line, making any list above Scyld essentially a king list, rather than an agnatic line; and it is impossible to determine where to fit Hoc, Hnaef, Hildeburh, and all the Half-Danes.) The nucleus of the genealogy is Beow, Healfdene, and Hrothgar's generation, in that Scyld's funeral ship separates the second 'founder' from those who are born from his son.[6] Presumably this cycle of from three to four generations will recur, much as it does in some non-centralized societies today, creating a repeating structure of family relationships that could dominate political relationships based upon the entire genealogy of eleven to twelve generations, which also seems to cycle. For many groups the genealogical depth remains constant across time: social relationships, which change and involve adjustments in the official genealogy, do not increase its depth greatly among those peoples who trace incorporating genealogies back to a founding ancestor.[7] What this means is that measures of near and far kinship, and thus of rights and duties, extend no further than can be linked back patrilineally to the eleventh and founding generation. The *Beowulf* poet, working within a bilateral social world rather than a unilineal one, does not go into this for Hrothgar and the Danes, concentrating instead on the aristocratic family in each case – and there only on the immediate siblings and offspring within an agnatic line of descent. He does this for Danes, Geats, and Swedes. No doubt how one claimed aristocratic and even kingly rights was a flexible business in Anglo-Saxon times, before either primogeniture or a fixed father-to-son rule became general. But, as already noted, Beowulf's is a bilateral kinship world with an agnatic bias, perhaps idealized in relation to Anglo-Saxon historical realities, yet clearly insisted upon.

The three-generation cycle is apparent if we consider Hrothgar's relationship to Hrothulf. Should Hrothgar die, Wealhtheow wants Hrothulf (Hrothgar's brother's son) to take Hrothgar's place in the generational triad, becoming 'father' and protector to her and Hrothgar's boys (each a young 'swor' or cousin to Hrothulf). Wealhtheow insists upon this in her commanding speech to Beowulf, Hrothgar, and the assembled retainers. Hrothulf functions therefore as 'son' and heir to his grandfather (no longer just to Hrothgar's brother). Perhaps she would have Hrothgar add affection (as though to a sister's son) to the amity and trust he shows Hrothulf. This, then, may be the significance of such precise but compacted compounds as 'suhtergefæderan' applied to Hrothgar and Hrothulf in their kindred, noble peace together: the 'father's-brother's son' can become a 'father' (dropping the 'son' from Hrethric's or Hrothmund's place and point of view in the generational triad; and he can become 'son' to his 'eald fæder,' his father's father (moving functionally both up and across in the family tree).[8] 'Fædera' can name Hrothgar's position in relation to Hrothulf, whose sons could be called Hrothgar's brother's grandsons or 'nephews' ('nefa') especially if Hrothgar were alive at the time. This implies a figurative taking up of the 'son's' wife as a sister, which could also, in some sense, raise the position of the agnatic nephew, the 'son' to whom one stands in a father's position.[9] Perhaps in his effort to adopt Beowulf, and by giving Beowulf Heorogar's corselet (Heorogar being the brother and king before Hrothgar and of whom Hrothgar says 'he was better than I'), Hrothgar essentially invites Beowulf into the line of succession, at the level of son to Healfdene and father to Hrothgar's boys.

Aside from the eponymous Scylf somewhere at a fourth generational point, the Swedes also come to us as a generational triad – Ongentheow, then Onela and Ohtere, then Eanmund and Eadgils (seemingly Beowulf's generation). However, the Swedish triad is coloured by its penchant for strife, perhaps echoing the kind of kinship conflict that can occur given competing obligations to immediate and less near kin. Eanmund and Eadgils, Ohtere's sons, are part of a minimal kin-line which is separate from the minimal line Onela establishes (one presumes). Moreover, Eanmund and Eadgils are not 'sister's-sons' to Onela and so he and they would not exchange any special tenderness.[10] Presumably the poet and his audience have some knowledge of this story; indeed the poet's frequent allusiveness assumes considerable knowledge of many heroic stories, and thus an audience engaged with, rather than dismissive of, old heroics and feuds. In the Swedish family Onela becomes king after Ohtere and meets with opposition from his nephews, who may well rebel because they see their father's uncle blocking their way in the succession. Ohtere, their father, is spiritually his father's son more than Onela is (Ongentheow is fierce; the name Ohtere implies 'army-terror' or something like that). However, the poet implicitly disapproves of their rebellion; he expresses high praise for Onela, protector of the Scylfings, the best of sea-kings who distributed treasure in the land of Swedish warriors (ll. 2381b–2383).[11] Behind these triads are vaguely historical, vaguely mythical figures, such as Heremod, Sigemund, and Weland, who 'live' in the present of action through various associations, parallels, and warnings. Those figures are not expressive of a deep, receding history.

An assertion of sameness is also apparent in the poet's numerous, approving remarks concerning heroic behaviour and results, with an overarching continuity expressed most clearly in statements of divine governance ('God ruled over all, as He still does now'). By stating such things, the poet does indicate a sense of past and present, of then and now, and of 'those days' in this life (he speaks of Beowulf as being of men the strongest in might in those days of this life). Clearly the poet does not believe in an unchanging, temporal present, and he can countenance large numbers of years as brief, characterizing details (50-year reigns; a 300-year-old dragon; a 1,000-year-like corrosion of the treasure); but he frequently asserts shared values and God's continuing rule then, now, and on to doomsday. Beowulf's great strength is always mentioned in auspicious contexts, with approval of 'se goda' and with horror of his criminal adversary, Grendel, who is God's adversary too.

When people construe time within a kin-line system, they see a structural relationship, not a continuum, between two points. For the aristocratic families in *Beowulf* this would involve 'the first and last persons in a line of agnatic descent (or "awakenings," to use the poet's word).' The line of descent differs for the matrilineal group, but the sense of time is the same, as it is also for a bilateral structure. However here, without countervailing factors, even the identity of strongly formed kin-groups would break up or become hopelessly diffused after a few generations, and need to be reformed at recurring intervals, perhaps every three generations or so.[12] This is a shallow sense of time, involving no more than four generations inhabiting virtually the same world of values and institutions (such as gift exchange, feud, and the reciprocal favourings and loyalties of the *comitatus*). This is reflected closely in the explicitly connected genealogies of *Beowulf*. Such connected genealogies appear even in Bede when he cites from three to four generational forbears for kings he especially notes, and they are generally indicative of northern peoples, whether Germanic or Celtic, according to Frederic Seebohm.[13]

Across many face-to-face cultures in the twentieth century, African anthropologists have found a genealogical depth of eleven to twelve generations, even for groups studied for over a century. In many groups, however, only the bottom four or five generations reflect actual relations between men, the rest being a perpetual arrangement used to rationalize the hostilities and allegiances imposed upon people of mixed descent from related but different groups, usually from the point of view of the dominant or aristocratic family in a given group of clans.[14] Although organized not for clans but for people given to a greater dissolution of group structure and thus of clear connection across generations, Anglo-Saxon genealogies also reflect some of these uses. The Mercian genealogy, for example, in Chronicle A at the date 626 (although composed much later) goes back from Penda eleven generations to Woden, and at the date 755 goes back four generations from Offa, connecting there with Penda's generation.[15] The latter entry is affixed to the dramatic account of strife (thirty years too early) in which the West Saxon Cyneheard slays Cynewulf, and which features the absolute loyalty of Cynewulf's *comitatus* (reciprocal loyalty to the king is thus given a double sanction – that of the narrative's implicit approval and that provided by the weight of ancestry, which we are told goes back to Cerdic).

The importance of the Mercian ancestry in this year may relate to the notable slaying of Æthelbald and then Offa's eventual accession to kingship. The giving of Offa's line could be seen as both a clarification and a justification for the shift between parallel lines of the families descended from Eawa's sons. Something of what may be going on in various Anglo-Saxon genealogies, especially in mixed lists (such as Mercian and West Saxon), might be clarified by looking at a similar society, ancient Hawaii. As Marshall Sahlins (1987, p. 20) tells us, the ancient Hawaiians, like the Anglo-Saxons, had chiefly aristocracies, were warlike, had gift exchange, and lacked 'the segmentary polity of descent groups known to cognate Polynesian peoples' (that is, landholdings did not reflect an organization of lineages, with corresponding ancestral cults, property rights, and chiefly titles tied to genealogical privilegings within the common group). Although their genealogies at the upper end reflected dynastic priorities and thus fixed dynastic relations between the islands, the 'historical dynamism of the system is in the east, among Maui and Hawai'i chiefs, who are able to differentiate themselves from local competitors, or even from their own dynastic predecessors, by appropriating ancestry from the ancient western sources of legitimacy.' Sahlins calls this a genealogical game that makes lineage more an argument than a structure, as Hawaiians trace ascent more than descent, picking their way upward 'by a path that notably includes female ancestors, to a connection with some ancient ruling line' (p. 20). Although some of the great royal genealogies are nine hundred generations deep (and remembered by genealogical adepts attached to high chiefs), 'the immediate male and female ancestors of the chief are attached' usually at some point within the last ten or twelve generations (p. 20, n. 18).

Whatever the unique sexual and political consequences of this for Hawaiian chiefly politics, especially given the parallel lines of male and female ancestry, we can see significant likenesses regarding the Anglo-Saxon world. There too the genealogical lists, especially the more elaborate ones and all that go back to Woden, are probably 'arguments' of incorporation, priority, and succession all at once. This is a compelling reason for looking carefully at the variations between Anglo-Saxon genealogies across time, rather than at our own construction of composite genealogies, drawn from different sources for particular kingdoms.

Kenneth Sisam has authoritatively noted the composite and constructed character of Anglo-Saxon royal genealogies, putting them down to dynastic manoeuvring and self-glorification.[16] Doubtless this is true enough, but ethnological comparisons suggest the viability of a deeper motive. These genealogies, which are less corporate lines of descent than asserted, prestige-making lines of ascent, assert continuity and sameness while absorbing competing political or social arrangements. They assert an embracing corporate structure where one probably does not in fact exist, given the dispersive tendencies of bilateral kinship and the persistence until after Alfred of violently contested successions.

When can different and perhaps overlapping groups of men (warriors and clerks, Anglo-Saxons and Danes) accommodate themselves to a common ancestry and a common set of social and institutional values? The eighth-century has been proposed because it encompasses Anglo-Saxon missions in contact with pagan but redeemable Saxons on the continent. However, a more likely argument anthropologically looks to the late ninth and tenth centuries and sees increasing accommodations between Anglo-Saxons and Danes, especially the conversion and political ascendency of the Danes.[17] John Niles thinks that political conditions were favourable between West Saxons and Danes more or less from the accession of Athelstan in 924 to some time after 970, and so poems like *Beowulf* might have been composed or else refurbished within the milieu of the 'united Anglo-Scandinavian kingdom of the post-Viking age.'[18]

The West Saxon genealogy shows such Beowulfian names as Sceaf, Heremod, Beowi, Beaw, Sceldwa, Geat, and Finn in the ancient, fixed past (following Noah and his ten-generation lineage) – a good place for them if they are also Danish ancestors. From that position they can reinforce mutual religious and social values – such as the good of reciprocal oaths – without raising conflict over particular issues and unstable settlements associated with such tenth-century kings as Eadwig, Eadward, and Æthelred.[19] By looking to his ancestors and to the ancestors of his patron, the *Beowulf* poet – probably composing with an aristocratic audience in mind – would reflect an anthropological law: one's ancestors are as one is; one's relationship to them is that of continuity, of time as a coherent structure of asserted values and similar social structures. As social relations change, so do details of the genealogy, breaking into levels even in the Anglo-Saxon hands of grafting clerks. These clerks would link group ancestry to Noah's genealogy and, through that, to universal history. But then a new equilibrium of sorts would be reached, perhaps evident in some of the variations and omissions in the West Saxon genealogical gathering; for example, if we break the compilation into segments, we have ten generations for Noah's line, and from thirteen to twelve generations – given variations among the two A Chronicles – between Noah and Woden, with ten generations encompassing Woden and Cerdic. In each segment down to, but not through, historical time the rough generational depth is maintained: the genealogy insists upon a chronology and layers what is probably a combination king list and a family genealogy to fill universal time structurally. Thus the community of monks and religious becomes as West Saxon (perhaps even asserting priority and breadth) as the community of lords and retainers, in spite of the actual social relationships among the families descending from Æthelwulf.

What this enormous gathering means (this culmination, as Kenneth Sisam nicely puts it, of the genealogist's art) is an open question but with several parts. Clearly a rough depth of ten generations controls the strings of names from Adam to Noah, from Noah to Geat (or on to Woden for fifteen generations), and from Woden to Cerdic; there are nine generations from Cerdic to Ingild (or seventeen from Woden to Ingild).[20] Sisam finds a rough standard of fourteen generations for Anglo-Saxon genealogies somewhat suspicious, but that length is not far from an anthropological average even today. At some point part of the Bernician genealogy for Ida is annexed to the West Saxon, with both strings going beyond Woden to Geat. And above Geat a further string appears for the West Saxon genealogy that embraces the heroic past of poetry and legend before connecting with Noah. That Æthelwulf died a pious king of a powerful, although temporarily divided Wessex, may have earned him this ultimate signature of nobility for his pilgrimage year, 855, in the Chronicle. That West Saxon names appear in the Northumbrian genealogy and Bernician names in the West Saxon could mark several different political affiliations between the two kingdoms, say from Ecgbryht's day (829) to Edward the Elder's (920).[21] We do not know when the Bernician names first appeared above Cerdic, and so we do not know what affiliation could be involved, assuming no clerical mistake.

Ethnologically there is probably no mistake here; rather this list is quite likely a political and social statement, reflecting some kind of asserted kinship between West Saxon and Northumbrian, from the West Saxon perspective. The addition of names from heroic legend, above Woden, suggests an effort to enclose the heroic past and the West Saxon present within one world, continuous and inclusive. Additionally, this subtly de-emphasizes the Wodenesque character of Woden-sprung kings, without eliminating that sacral issue; indeed, the sacral issue is given extension and recharacterization through heroic legend and an Old Testament ethos. Such a continuity and embrace is very much like what we see in *Beowulf*. Furthermore, a close internal search of *Beowulf* shows that this compelling 'law of kin' holds for our Anglo-Saxon epic in small ways as well as in large.[22]

In her masterful essay on the poet's sense of history, Roberta Frank essentially counters readings of *Beowulf* that take a neo-patristic and implicitly dismissive point of view (dismissive, that is, of Beowulf's world and its values). Instead, she looks to the poem and to historical moments for the appropriateness of the poet's insistence on both the pagan and virtuous nature of such characters as Hrothgar and Beowulf. She sees Beowulf himself as resorting to arms almost from the world of good, Christian knighthood: 'Beowulf resorts to arms out of concern for the defenseless and for the common good, not exclusively out of lust for conquest, ambition, or vengefulness. He is heroic and pious, a pagan prince of peace.'[23] This overstates a truth, however sound it is in spirit: Beowulf defends his people but they are not inherently defenceless; the Danes could do nothing against Grendel, but they have a strong frontier guard or coast watch; and Beowulf fiercely avenges Hygelac's death and supports Eadgils in a feud that brings Eanmund and Onela to grief, although Beowulf hardly acts out of unrelieved bloodlust.

If not a 'prince of peace,' Beowulf is certainly a strong hand for lawful, just settlement. Roberta Frank wants to see the accommodation between heroic values and monastic culture from the monastic side – a perspective she plausibly articulates by looking to the continent, citing such synthesizers as Odo of Cluny; she also notes that English 'religious sculpture after the Danish invasions' could draw upon pagan myth and heroic legend.[24] But one needs less agility if one looks at the matter from the perspective of a royal patron, a battle-king who sees honour and a continuity of social and ethical values in his ancestry. In any Christian, Anglo-Saxon century, from the warlord's perspective, joy and gifts in the hall and oaths of fidelity to one's (Christian) warlord would be wholeheartedly embraced. Even churchmen could find it hard not to approve when revenge is taken for the murder of a Christian king. And warlord as well as monk would decry treachery, manslaughter, and perversion within the *comitatus* or among kinsmen.

This perspective seems unassailably sound. However, there are many dissident voices in *Beowulf* studies – voices, moreover, of considerable stature, beginning with J.R.R. Tolkien, who says that the *Beowulf* poet surveys a doomed world from an enlightened present, a perspective detaching the poet as Christian from the pagan world he labours, and sometimes lovingly so, into being.[25] Other prominent scholars have emphasized a dismissive strand in the tone of regret Tolkien hears. Quite recently Fred C. Robinson has taken a related and occasionally deeply perceptive approach, inspired by what he calls

Beowulf's appositive style and acutely attentive to theistic collocations that have been overread in Christian directions. In doing so he argues for the poet's mastery of lexical ambiguity, by which the poet creates an admirable, although poignantly doomed world of virtuous pagans.[26]

For contemporary *Beowulf* criticism, Robinson has made himself the formidable standard-bearer of Tolkien's point of view, up-dated and highly sophisticated in its stylistic attention to lexical distinctions in the poem. His observations and arguments require particular replies, in appropriate places later in this chapter. In arguing, not for sameness given some difference, but for profound difference framing some shared values and pieties, Robinson and others do not argue an inherently impossible position for a poet looking back at a related but alien world not his own. If a devout monk living in a community of similarly devout souls is concerned about the threats of heathen burial practices, worship, curses, witchcraft, and spells, he might well consign the world of Ingeld – the world of heroic life – to damnation (although he might share some of that world's values, such as reciprocal loyalties, friendships, and exchange). But it is highly unlikely that he would labour for 3,182 lines to re-create it. Nowhere in the history of great, poetic narrative (at least in the West) can we find a clear instance of any past, heroic, or 'golden' world created in what we might call a disutopic, if tender, spirit. If anything, the great evocation of a noble past is inevitably a prologue to one's sense of one's present, whether it be a sense of decline or of prophetic greatness or justification. In *Beowulf* the poet recreates or recalls something not understood as fictive invention or as a benighted past, but as a great past that justifies insistence on the same values and social relations highlighted there. This is narrative as myth in Malinowski's sense. It is not 'a fictitious story, nor an account of a dead past; it is a statement of a bigger reality still partially alive. It is alive in that its precedent, its law, its moral, still rule the social life ... [27] Robinson and Tolkien, to invoke this line of criticism point to point, know that creative effort requires an investment, a connection with one's subject, not simply a dismissive separation. Thus they emphasize the poet's sympathies and shared values regarding his noble characters, but they also need to sustain the argument for separation and distance – managed essentially by historical assumption and textual buttressing wherever possible.

Robinson rests his argument for the poet's historical perspective on ideological grounds. He assumes that the poet would see his 'pagan' characters as pitiable because not redeemed in fact. For example, he notices that 'the virtues of Beowulfian heroes are extolled ... while at the same time the poet never loses sight of the hard fact that these are pagans, and pagans, say the churchmen, are damned.'[28] The use of appositive style, of compounded and collocated terms that have both old and 'renovated,' that is, Christian meanings, presumably allows the poet to suggest both Christian connotation in pagan settings and Christian difference from pagan perception and feeling (they did not know where the noble dead go, but we do; they might invoke a great measurer, but we know the true King of Victories, and so on). This is a seductive approach, especially when Robinson rightly observes that the poet reserves for his own use a few, clearly Christian references to God (built on uses of 'sylf,' soð,' and 'heofon' in relation to deity) and when he astutely indicates the less-than-doomsday meaning of Beowulf's references to a judging God. But in pursuing the distance argument, he would have the poet jog the audience's sense of pagan connotation by using such words as 'metodsceaft' in conjunction with 'wyrd,' and giving them to Beowulf or Wealhtheow. This and other pieces of evidence, however, overemphasize only a handful of words or compounds, often scattered hundreds or even a thousand or more lines apart. Moreover the poet uses 'geosceaft' himself, a compound boasting a good, pagan pedigree. Robinson also lapses occasionally into unjustifiable assumptions of indirect discourse; he assumes that some of the poet's narrator voice is really spoken on behalf of the 'pagan consciousness' of, say, Beowulf. He also assumes, as have many others, that 'pagan' and 'heathen' have risable connotations for any Anglo-Saxon Christian and are interchangeable.

The poet never uses the word 'pagan.' While thinking of Grendel – the outlaw, the creature outside society – as heathen, he certainly does not think of his noble characters as particularly 'heathen,' although some among them, out of desperation, ignorance, and blind custom do a heathen thing (which he vigorously condemns when it comes down to heathen prayer). In other 'pagan' matters, he simply observes such events as a ship burial or a funeral pyre, emphasizing the drama of each moment, not the mode of interment or funeral.[29] Moreover, Robinson assumes that the Germanic setting in the past automatically galvanizes pagan meanings in the poet's theistic vocabulary (much of which he clearly shares with his characters, although he 'knows' they were not Christian). He establishes a semantic domain of shared extension and reserves an area for himself and his audience of connotation as well as information about such things as Grendel's Cain-like status and the destination of his soul. Had he been, say, of Alcuin's persuasion and threatened by heathenish possibilities, he almost certainly would have reversed the logic of his approach, delineating much difference and little sameness. There is much to be admired in Robinson's attention to the lexical reality of various passages, but here and there, in a regrettably tendentious way, he weakens his argument by seeking to glimpse an implied pantheon of gods (paganism revived). This can be seen in several of his translations, such as the inscrutable phrase concerning Hrethel, who left this life, choosing 'godes leoht.'[30] I am sorry to see this connotatively translated as 'sought out the realm of a god.'

I do not see the poet insisting anywhere that his noble characters (aside from some desperate, nameless Danes, and then only once) are after all *pagans*. Even Beowulf gives thanks to the Lord, the King of Glory, the Eternal 'Drihtne' (l. 2796b). Even if we read 'ece' in this context as 'long lasting' rather than 'eternal' (and I am not convinced), we must agree that Beowulf is given quite a prayer; here certainly his pagan status is not insisted upon (Robinson's examples of 'ece' as 'long-lasting' are almost persuasive, concerning as they do material objects or worldly renown, until one notices that he has not found a collocation of 'ece' and deity that can support his case). Moreover, we simply do not know what the poet as Christian thought of himself; we do know that he approves repeatedly of events and behaviours in the world he depicts.

I think a nearer approach to the poet's sense of time and continuity is still that of Edward Irving, Jr. He denies any Christian separation in the poet's sense of time and sees part 2 (after Beowulf's return to Hygelac) as forming part of a general attitude, an 'austere seriousness about the real place of man in the endless stream of time.' He finds that present, past, and future tend to impinge upon each other and that characters in part 2 tend to 'reflect on their past and search it for meanings.'[31] Irving does evoke the image of man's life as an island of light in a drifting darkness – a captivating image for many medievalists, drawn from Bede's account of the sparrow emerging from darkness, flying through the bright and comfortable hall, then exiting to darkness. However, he overlooks 'the real place of man' as presented by the poet – a place that requires seeing the poem as framed within a perspective of continuity through time (along with a location of significant values in mundane time) rather than controlled by a sharply artificial division (part 1, time present; part 2, reflection on time).[32] The poet does not view time as a stream or as a deep continuum: he has a sense of past and present, of deeper past and nearer past, and he notes the eventuality of doomsday. But his is not yet that high medieval world from within which Chaucer can worry about the strangeness of old stories and the great differences that language, custom, and time can make. Chaucer projects an unelaborated, but cosmic perspective for his constant if embittered Troilus, a pagan whose love and pain were worth recreating, along with Criseyde's shifting fears and complexities and Pandarus's polyannish perversities. Both Chaucer and the *Beowulf* poet find values in the recreated past – values that assert connection and essential sameness in the *Beowulf* poet's case, notwithstanding 'pagan colouring.'

Without characterizing the past as antique, the poet initially constructs a framework that suggests the clarity of what we know about events in the past, of what a good king is, and of what shape our lives have. We live days of valorous achievement bounded by the unknown. We have heard of the might of the spear-Danes and of how they performed brave deeds. Especially we know about Scyld Scefing's frequent forays against many people and his seizing of their mead-benches since first he was found, destitute, lacking treasures ('feasceaft funden,' l. 7a). He received comfort for that, growing up to become mighty and much honoured by surrounding kingdoms. He did well: 'þæt wæs god cyning' (l. 11). Apparently, although a destitute babe, his virtues are such that he is given success in war and honour, as well as a noble son. There is here a kind of reciprocity between a deserving man and worldly rewards, overseen implicitly by the Life-Lord, the Ruler of Glory, the God who sent a son to comfort the people and who gave that son worldly favour, 'woroldare,' with 'ar' being a term of reciprocal favouring drawing from the ethical vocabulary of the *comitatus*.[33] God favours the Danes because he perceives the distress they suffered before Scyld Scefing arrived. Thus the good battle-king receives not only material rewards and the honour and approbation of men, but also the gift of continuity, of dynastic health and prosperity. His son, Beowulf of the Danes, becomes famous also and assembles a worthy war-band through a splendid or martial dispensing of treasures ('fromum feohgiftum,' l. 21a), thus embodying a world of martial ethics on behalf of the Danes that meets with explicit approval. The poet says that 'so should a young man do,' while his father is still alive (stressing the need a kingdom has for continuity and strong succession); he needs to accomplish good through a martial dispensing of treasure, so that when war comes his comrades and people will stand fast with him. Praiseworthy deeds shall, among peoples everywhere, profit a man.

We look back, then, to days when kings and princes of the spear-Danes were worthy, when one could say emphatically that they were good. We look back, not to a far distant heroic world, but into our world's familiar, heroic past to see what kings in general should do in the service of themselves and their people; they win personal fame, attract a strong cohort of warriors, treat them well, expand and protect the kingdom, and through liberal behaviour look to a strong succession. Thus they achieve worldly honour, the means granted by God but the achievement left to their courage and prowess. When Scyld dies, his magnificent funeral marks the auspiciousness of succession: he voyages out, regally honoured by golden banners and prestige burial goods, while the Danes continue on in Beow's protection, from whom arises yet another war-band leader and powerful king. The difference between the poem's opening funeral (Scyld's) and its closing one (Beowulf's) is largely a difference of auspicious context natural to the changes and reversals of the heroic world.[34]

Along with its focus on good battle-kings in days past, the Exordium contains the notion that a man's life has a fateful shape, 'to gescæphwile' (l. 26b). We all reach our death-fate, our previously shaped space of time, the whole of which we should use well. The life span of each warrior or warrior-king, bound at each end by the unknown, is a time of unfatedness, of heroic energy shaped to the curve of an appropriately vigorous life.[35] Both Beowulf – in speaking of 'metodsceaft' (rule of fate) – and Wiglaf – in speaking of Beowulf's 'heahgesceap' (high destiny) – express similar notions and mean nothing particularly gloomy or fearful.[36] These are pre-Christian notions but not marked as particularly heathenish, and they are ones the poet shares in his own voice (casually speaking of Grendel's mother as coming according to an 'ancient shaping'). Of course he could express common notions of 'fate' as we still do and still somewhere subsume such notions within an idea of Christian providence. But he only tells us of an afterlife in the Father's keeping or protection – a keeping we cannot be sure of, although we may seek it (as Beowulf's soul may be said to do) and be granted it after doomsday. His notion of the Father's keeping is hardly a clear notion of providence.[37]

The poet shares a great deal with his noble characters (thus expressing considerable sameness with little difference). He has Wiglaf say that the dead Beowulf will long remain in the Ruler's protection and he has Beowulf express notions of death judgment for Grendel (ll. 975–79). Fred C. Robinson is acutely perceptive when he hears those lines Beowulf speaks, along with others concerning God's determining of outcome in battle, as much less than they have seemed to many readers. They certainly are not indications on Beowulf's part of a last judgment (eschatologically understood). What Robinson hears in these lines is the echo of an ancient *topos* concerning the Germanic god of war as law; this language was originally applied to Tiu, Tyr, or *Tiwaz and taken up by Christian Anglo-Saxons into expressions for the Christian godhead most likely to appeal to battle-kings and war-band leaders. However, the presence of Tiu is only conceptual here, not a palpable paganism; moreover, Robinson, because he is unfamiliar with Tiu as a mythological sovereign fulfilling the functions of a 'legislator,' seeks a dark paganism and would read those lines as invoking norns or deciders of fate in some general Germanic sense.[38] Beowulf faces the possibility of death in a just and clear-minded way; he knows that God, the holy lord, will assign fame (essentially give the law in this battle [ll. 685–7]). His theism is certain and his language is unequivocal, just as it is when the poet tells us that the Measurer ('metod') would not allow Grendel to enter Heorot on Beowulf's night and then draw off happily into the shadows. Both Beowulf and the poet use the same epithets for God, whom they describe as mighty, holy, and Judge of Deeds. Indeed, the poet shares so much with his noble characters that he effectively gives them his sense of life and his theism (insofar as we can judge this matter empirically) while largely reserving an overview perspective and what we might call a comparatively precise theism for himself and his audience (evident in language Robinson also cites – those collocations of 'soð,' 'sylf,' and 'heofon' with the deity).[39] But all that we can decide deductively from *Beowulf* is that the poet as narrator does not profess even the rudiments of Triune faith, although his theism accords well with God the Father's status in (Old Testament) Christianity. When we look to Old English poetry apart from *Beowulf* for anything like a similar, monotheistic devotion, the *Maxims I* and *II* come to mind for their rudimentary expressions of faith tied up with secular values, necessities, and sententiousness.

The poet's statements about God's rule apply to fateful moments, to life and death decisions (involving Grendel in the first third of the poem and Beowulf in the last). God's rule of mankind in this matter is what is important, not some pagan difference the poet's noble characters might suggest to him were he to ponder the matter. Without breaking the past-tense framework of his narrative, the poet repeatedly asserts the continuity of time, indeed of a kind of presentness of value and social relations, between past and present; the narrative steadily moves from a four-generational past to those anticipations of a violent future near the poem's end (anticipations that necessarily encroach upon any literal present from which the heroic past is invoked). Even the seasons conspire in these expressions of continuity: 'oþðæt oþer com [spring] / gear in geardas, swa nu gyt deð" until spring came / yearly, as it still does' (ll. 1133b–1134). God, the True Measurer, of course rules the seasons and times just as he rules mankind (l. 1611a). Interestingly, in each case of seasonal rule, a victory after bitter feud is achieved: Hengest slays Finn, settling their bitter relationship, and Beowulf has just beheaded Grendel's corpse. This value, then, concerning the good of violent settlement for wrongs, is strongly underwritten in the poet's theism. Looked at in this way, the heroic world can be seen as the poet's past and near-past arena for depicting his sense of value, experience, man's life, fate, time, and man's relationship to God's rule. As such the heroic world is the only one the poet realizes for us.

If in essential respects the heroic world is our world, what then do we make of its apparent fatefulness in the last third of the narrative? Initially, the poet concerns himself with dark moments that befall us in their own good time fatefully. We are reminded that such moments can follow bright ones: Heorot arose in a time of communal cooperation, not yet the time of in-law enmity; the great banquet was a splendid occasion, occurring at a time when kinsmen were still loyal to each other; and Grendel comes after hall-joy, in the course of a day, approaching with the advance of darkness. The poet, then, seems to have a temporal notion of fate. Some events follow others as part of the history of an object or a place, a slice of time being all that he narrates concerning Heorot, for example. But the identity of the hall is tied up in its full history, and therefore future strife is mentioned (not necessarily as apocalyptic foreshadowing). The hall is great in its essential self, in its full, temporal history. A slice of that history may be benign, another malignant – neither has priority. In this sense fate does not colour the world: some events end our lives; some seem shaped in a sequence ('geosceaft'); some involve victories.

I suspect the poet holds to several moods here in answer to his sense of events in time – as impending, then coming to fullness (whether fateful or otherwise) in all their local character, and then moving on. This happens in such a way that we are not conscious of acting out an ancient decree (a retrospective notion in his use of it). When we place ourselves in the sweep of events, we have only intuitions of impending possibility, without knowledge of particular fates taking shape around particular influences, which often emerge in sudden ways. In this sense, the poet's conception of an event unfolding requires something like a notion of indeterminacy. The sweep of events, then, can be said to be determined only in its fated close. Much of our trouble with concepts of fate in *Beowulf* – whether 'wyrd' is an agency, whether man can alter his fate, whether God can change a 'decree of fate' – and much of our unwillingness to accept any view that would have us embrace a world seemingly ruled by dark fates (a world that many readers have seen as both fateful and doomed) may stem from a failure to recognize that in itself the sweep of events, as with events themselves, is treated as unpredictable, made up of variables that render an ongoing series of actions as an indeterminate process.[40]

Let us look at one example. After Grendel's mother comes, her revenge seems to be inevitable, her arrival clearly anticipated by the poet. But the sequence of actions, including the accidents of her foray and the defence of the hall, is a surprise. Fate is revealed in the event, a mystery not in fact fully realized until the event comes to a close with all its complexity and even its uniqueness. This is as true for events fatal to otherwise favoured men as for ones in which men, through courage, strength, and God's help, triumph over monster-criminals or lawless feuders. Even Beowulf's fight with the dragon, despite his forebodings and spiritual restlessness, is an entry into the unknown, into an event that proves much more complex than we could have anticipated, given Beowulf's other monster fights. Beowulf does not enter the event certain he will die, or knowing the moment or manner of his death; he does not know how many times the dragon will attack, nor does he know whether or not Wiglaf will come to his assistance; finally he does not know how the dragon will in fact be dispatched. Indeterminancy has the great consequence of opening up room for human action and courage, for the influence of physical events and accidents, for whatever finally does occur.

Thus we need not see the heroic world as inexorably fatal. Rather, we do well to see it as a changeable world in which men can act purposefully and over which God rules. Moreover, as an arena for the poet's depiction of values, that world holds both good and great crime. We have noted various beliefs shared by the poet with his noble characters and we have noted his assertion of God's continuing rule. We should now examine his major statements of unqualified good or moral truth. These statements, when taken together with his theism, complete a fabric of shared values by which the poet culturally authenticates the temporal continuity he asserts between himself, his audience, and Beowulfian ancestors in those illustrious days of this life.

When the Geats bury Beowulf's gold with him, they of course act in the past. But the effect of their action, a simultaneous honouring of Beowulf and a rendering useless of the gold, survives them down to our present (the present of any reading or narration of the poem). Beowulf has paid with his life for the treasure he thinks of as wergeld. Obviously God has broken the old, warlord's curse on the treasure, as Beowulf's soul seeks the 'dom' of the truly firm, and is not bound in hell-bonds. But the sense of terrible misfortune the Geats feel is real enough. Only the poet notes that the curse 'explains' not the manner of Beowulf's death, but the sheer, fatal fact itself, this loss of their protecting king and warlord. Neither Beowulf's living nor dying is a cursed business. His people, no longer blessed with a great and powerful lord, feel somehow overcome, but this happens repeatedly in the heroic world down to any present hinted at: Scyld Scefing came to a people who had suffered at Heremod's hands; Beowulf comes to help the Danes terrorized by Grendel; and now the Geats Wiglaf organizes (exclusive of the cowards, upon whom Beowulf threw away his gifts) can expect a near-future of strife (although annihilation is not predicted).

Moreover, like fitting behaviour, the reburying of treasure also cycles – it will be found again. After the treasure is buried, we are told that 'then around the barrow rode the brave in battle.' That 'then' takes us immediately back, or forward, actually both: forward from the useless, if now honorific, past of the treasure, and back from our present.[41] Focused on the Geats, the phrase reports their sorrow. Their moment, fixed between a past antedating them and our present, entails a future they will never see. The scheme inherent here is one of continuity. Crucially, it is here, in the last fourteen lines, that the poet places his last statement of moral value:

swa hit gedefe bið,
þæt mon his winedryhten wordum herge,
ferhðum freoge, þonne he forð scile
of lichaman læded weorðan. (ll. 3174b–3177)

so it is fitting that a man praise his friendly lord in words, love him in mind, when he forth shall out of the body be led.

So the loyal, although untested people of the Geats, hearth-retainers, mourned their lord's fall. The poet approves of what they did in that moment fixed in a space between their past and our present. His approval indicates that more than interred gold survives from that past; conceptions of fitting behaviour, tied to particular moments, survive as well. The Geats acted properly, in accord with a timeless propriety: in a funeral observance, praise of one's friendly lord is fitting.

The poet's first statement of moral good follows his approval of Scyld Scefing's kingdom-building warfare. This warfare leads to tribute ('gombe') from surrounding peoples, no doubt something of a burden to those paying it (cf. the people of Sodom and their disastrous refusal to continue paying tribute in *Genesis A*, ll. 1976b–2017). The past stresses the good of various continuities – father to son and war-band to war-band – as he concentrates on Beowulf the Dane's giving of gifts and his assembling of a loyal troop. His remark that praiseworthy deeds 'shall prosper' a man among any peoples is free of temporal qualification, true for every place and time. Immediately linked to Beowulf the Dane's actions, it makes those actions totally praiseworthy, although not ruling out the possibility that other actions could be as praiseworthy in other times. Through comments such as these, joined with a scheme of continuity, the poet directly asserts his support of Scyld's world; to put it differently, he approves of heroic virtues for all suitable places and times.[42]

Such independent statements, however, are rare in *Beowulf*. More frequently, the poet applies a general truth to particular occasions. Most characteristically, he asserts a relationship between himself and the world he creates through his use of 'gehyrde ic' 'I heard' or 'mine gefræge' 'as I have heard' constructions. They tend to distance us from the gesture or event concerned, while simultaneously communicating the splendour, the comparative worth, or the destructiveness of that event or gesture. Here the heroic past becomes an arena for virtues, to which the poet may add a moral injunction:

Hyrde ic þæt þam frætwum feower mearas,
lungre, gelice last weardode,
æppelfealuwe; he him est geteah
meara ond maðma. – Swa sceal mæg don. (ll. 2163-6)

> I heard further that from that treasure four horses remained all alike,
> apple-brown; he unto him with favour rendered horses and treasure.
> So shall a kinsman do.

This honouring or favouring ('est') of the inferior rendered unto the superior kinsman is exemplary, in the poet's opinion. In similar ways he stresses moral value or indicates action superlative in its splendour as well as in its propriety: 'Ne gefrægn ic freondlicor feower madmas' 'I never heard of four treasures [given] in a more friendly way' (l. 1027); 'ealles moncynnes minne gefræge / 'þone selestan' 'of all mankind as I have heard / the best' (ll. 1955 – 1956a); 'Ne hyrde ic cymlicor ceol gegyrwan' 'nor heard I of a more splendid ship made ready' (l. 38). In their immediate contexts, these phrases imply his approval of aspects of the heroic world and they indicate the usefulness of that world for him: Scenes of the heroic past offer him a setting for various events, gestures, and virtues written large. Through them he can directly or indirectly assert the good of splendid, friendly bestowal of treasures, of Offa's justifiable renown (for gifts, war, and his battle-boldness), or of the Danes' splendid readying of Scyld's funeral ship (in effect their return gift to him, as is the hoard Beowulf wins, which his Geats honorifically inter with him). Moreover, the poet shares those values with several of his characters. And, on one occasion, he even shares his use of the past with Hrothgar. Hrothgar also looks back and invokes old customs. He even uses the 'ne hyrde ic' formula, 'ne hyrde ic snotorlicor / on swa geongum feore guman þingian' 'never heard I / anything more prudently said by so young a man' (ll. 1842b–1843) to moral purpose immediately after Beowulf offers a continuing alliance and exchange between Danes and Geats.

The poet is, however, silent about what might be splendid today and about the particular help God might give now, or the crimes he might prevent, or the deeds he would rule. That silence might permit praise of one's friendly lord, for example, in terms other than those used by the Geats. It might permit God's rule of deeds very different from those he is said to have ruled in the past. But what terms and what deeds? We are never told. Instead, God's relationship to the poet's characters, and to their actions and fates, is generalized to mankind at large. Hence, to turn these remarks around, only in terms of the heroic world does the poet elaborate his conception of God's relationship to man and the values men should hold in their affairs with each other. He founds those conceptions in the generations before Scyld (given Heremod as an anti-type) and brings them forward four generations into Beowulf's time, projecting them into an unnarrated 'future' as Wiglaf reorganizes those Geats still fit to be called 'battle-brave.'

As God judges and rules then as he does now, and as values are shared, we do not leave the heroic world behind; instead we begin to see our world in it. But if, as I have argued throughout, the poet asserts a temporal and cultural continuity between days long past and his present, what is he doing in the last third of the poem, with its terrible facts of violence, feud, and gloomy moods? Clearly the succession of days and years shows that the heroic world easily extends beyond the vigorous lives of its best kings. It is an unstable world, one in which great virtue somehow is close to or calls up great vice. But I think from a temporal perspective the poet is mainly weaving an empirical fact – the sad and awful predicament of great men facing thoughts of their imminent mortality and of a people similarly facing a threatening and less protected future. By focusing on the Geats, the poet overlooks the commonplace terror of their circumstances and invites empathy with them. He would also have us recognize Beowulf's greatness, the loss of which casts doubt on the Geats' abilities to continue in prosperity. But here he would transcend formulas of dead kings and leaderless people. He would evoke the pathos of a people burying their ring-lord while anticipating raids and revenge-feud on three sides. Finally and movingly, if somewhat enigmatically, the poet observes failure, death, and fitting ritual while noting mortality and worldly vicissitude. As with heroes, so with particular peoples: they come and go, eventually leaving only their treasure in the ground. Can we reconcile this great fact of mortality – along with the misfortune it often entails – with the True Measurer's rule through time? Bede would invoke ideas of sublunar mutability, of change and fate, and of over-arching providence. The *Beowulf* poet does not. He implies only that something like a curse might explain great misfortune in the Geats' case, while God as True King of Victories can undo even the most powerful curse – that of a chieftain or a lord.[43] Life has its bitter misfortunes, but the true God, the just God of Victories, can either undo or reverse them. That is all we get here. We must do what we can in the face of these observations. The poet will not give us a detailed guide: within general constraints and recommendations, he leaves us to our own judgments of what is fitting in the moment. But we must never forget that God – 'sigora soðcyning' 'the true king of victories' (l. 3055a) in the poet's last formulation (applied to the power to unwind the curse) – governed the deeds of all mankind, then as now.[44] When applying God's power to the chant-curse wound around the treasure I think the poet mainly implies that we should not put ultimate faith in man's powers. As it turns out, none of the poet's noble characters do; Beowulf, for example, thanks the Lord of all, the Glory-King, the Eternal Lord before he dies. Nor do any of the major characters suppose that human will alone can perpetuate either worldly honour or dynastic success. Hrothgar learns this when he becomes Grendel's victim. Beowulf is always well aware of it, refusing to predict the future; Wealhtheow, Hrothgar, and Hygelac thank God on various occasions for good things that have happened in part through Beowulf's great agency and promise. We can, of course, speculate further on the poet's motives for reserving a few epithets for God to himself. Minimally they may mark his sense of difference in time from the poem's world of action. But within that difference he marks out a great sameness of values, of events to rejoice in, of hopes to entertain, through which the heroic past becomes an arena for noble depictions and for man's relationship to God – depictions to emulate as we will, given our societal circumstances and fates.

CHAPTER THREE

The Jural World in *Beowulf*

Although Beowulf is not a law-code giver in the sense that kings in the seventh to ninth centuries were in Anglo-Saxon times, he is nevertheless a juridical figure in that his combats and activities occur within expressly acknowledged jural and ethical contexts of what is right and of what one is obliged to do. Those contexts have been almost entirely overlooked by *Beowulf*'s readers; we have seen Beowulf only as an oddly extra-social warrior-adventurer, like Sigemund, or else as kind of culture hero, a warrior-saviour who somehow operates outside the networks created by such overlapping social institutions as the feud, the kinship system, and the ties of the warband.[1]

Both the great editor, Frederick Klaeber, and E.G. Stanley, a masterful assesser of diction and meaning, have commented on some legalistic diction in *Beowulf*, but each insists on seeing that diction as merely figurative, not as part of a quickening social context for the poem's main drama of monster fights. Another reader, Morton Bloomfield, has come closer in noting that Beowulf's fight with Grendel can be seen as analogous to the *judicium Dei*, although Beowulf also simply tells Wealhtheow that he will work the will of the Danes alone or else die (his solemn, mead-sanctified 'beot').[2] Beowulf both defers to God and, in the appropriate ritual and social moments, stresses his own valour and determination. But Beowulf is not simply a bold warrior, generously volunteering to try his luck: quintessentially, he is an ethically conscious figure of just, rightful action, of warfare as law; his approach to Heorot is more than diplomatic and more than an 'epic' occasion for a set of courtly speeches (the usual way of construing Beowulf's encounters in the course of his movement from the Danish shores to a trusted position in Heorot).

We need to appreciate more deeply the difficult social context into which Beowulf arrives uninvited. Within this social context he is vigorously challenged twice and Wulfgar suggests that bands such as his could be marauders. This social context involves a mixed vocabulary we have too often either overlooked or under-translated. That vocabulary speaks of reciprocal favouring ('hold,' 'ar'), counsel ('ræd'), urgent petition ('ben,' 'ne forwyrne'), juridical meeting and settlement ('meþelword,' 'sacu,' 'þing,' 'þingian'), law in the sense of rights or of what is right ('riht'), entrusting ('alyfan'), and special office ('sundornytt'). In the course of the poem, Beowulf reveals his jural state of mind; he is indeed the kind of hero who much later in the poem will naturally assume that he has somehow mysteriously offended the eternal Lord, over 'ealde riht,' when first set upon by the night-scorching dragon.[3] Neither an adventurer nor a Germanic bounty hunter, Beowulf is, finally, a hero whose ghostly, mythological sanction is not the battlefield terror and general duplicity of Woden, the god of war most often mentioned by Anglo-Saxonists when discussing genealogies. Woden is a terrifying presence on the field of slaughter, as signified by such carrion beasts as wolves and ravens. But Beowulf is neither Woden-sprung nor Woden-inspired (no matter how fierce in actual combat). Rather he embodies the jural sanction of Tyr (also known as Tiu), the Germanic god of war as law, as settlement and the establishing of boundaries.[4]

When Beowulf comes to the Danes, uninvited and unlooked for, his sudden arrival and his progress into Heorot meet with challenge and interpretation, much as his arrival needs to be questioned and interpreted by us, not just accepted as an heroic given. But before undertaking an explication of Beowulf's jural progress from uninvited stranger to special guardian of Heorot, I want to step back and indicate the associative cluster of originally mythological functions that sanction the role of the Germanic warrior as legal force – functions not well understood by most *Beowulf* scholars any more than they were understood by Tacitus 1700 years ago.

Because we know so little about Tiu as the sovereign who presides over lawful war, I will begin with the boldest speculation about Tiu – that of Georges Dumézil – and then move towards increasingly English contexts through a constellation of associated terms that I think give evidence of a topos that once applied to Tiu. With that background in place we can then better appreciate the resonance of such details in *Beowulf* as the language of glory, of life and death decision, of binding and unbinding, and – perhaps the most uncanny analogue of all – the seeming sacrifice of one 'Hondscio' (read handshoe or glove) before Beowulf definitively restrains Grendel. These last details are functionally analogous to Tiu's loss of his hand in the wolf Fenrir's mouth, a loss that enables the gods to bind the terrible, and quickly growing, cosmic wolf.[5]

Working within a comparative, Indo-European context, Georges Dumézil comments on Tiu's loss of his hand in relation to Odin's loss of an eye and formulates what he calls 'the two mutilations, clearly symbolic, [which] first create and later manifest the lasting quality of each of the gods, the paralysing visionary and the chief of legal procedure.' These mutilations, he adds, are the

> palpable expression of the theologeme that is the basis of the coexistence of the two highest gods, namely that the sovereign administration of the world is divided into two great provinces, that of inspiration and prestige, that of contract and chicanery, in other words, magic and law. This theologeme is, among the Germanic peoples, no more than a faithfully preserved inheritance from the time of the Indo-European unity, for it is found, with all the desirable extensions and commentary, in Vedic religion, where the binder magician Varuna, and Mitra, the contract personified, form a ruling pair at the head of the world of gods.[6]

Dumézil goes on to say that through an excessive development of a military aspect, the god of law began to lose his reason for being and descended into the less disquieting rank occupied by Thor (although Odin also may absorb some of Tiu's original functions, among them fertility and all-father roles). However, a close look at warfare as settlement and the establishing of boundaries in Old English poetry might have brought Dumézil to less gloomy reflections, to a sense that Tiu's functions are not necessarily absorbed into, and therefore distorted by, the frenetic cult of Woden, on the one hand, or into the more agrarian and domestic world of Thor on the other.[7] The sense of contract and of law presided over by Tiu remains a powerful sanction for fruitful battle.

That battlefield function is reflected in at least two other heroic poems in Old English. In *Widsith* we hear praise of the fourth-century Offa, who is also mentioned in *Beowulf*: no one in youth gained a greater kingdom, says Widsith; by his single sword, Offa marked the boundary against the Myrgings at Fifeldore ('Ane sweorde / merce gemærde wiþ Myrgingum / bi Fifeldore,' ll. 41b–43a). In *Beowulf* Offa's 'legislative' fame is implicit in the praise accorded him and in his sublime marriage. By marrying him, the terror-making princess, Modthryth, is transformed into a noble queen, one who rules in 'high love' (l. 1954a) with the best of men between the two seas. Offa, we are told, was widely honoured for his gift giving and his warfare as he ruled his realm in wisdom. In *The Battle of Brunanburh* Athelstan and Eadmund win long-lasting glory with the edges of their swords ('ealdorlangne tir' and 'sweorda ecgum,' ll. 3b, 4b). *Brunanburh* is a patriotic poem that seems to do little more than celebrate an English victory; yet the victory is just, a settlement, a protection of the realm, and accordingly the language is that of glory through the sword.

The use of 'tir,' a word derived from Tiu, is exactly appropriate in this context. Councils made decisions on war as a rightful settlement; therefore the battle boast made in the hall is not merely a reflection of hubris or personal turbulence. If spoken seriously in the assembly, then such vows must be acted upon on the battlefield, which then becomes a meeting place of arms, of spears and swords. (In the Finn episode, 'meðelstede' is used of the battleground, l. 1082b. Offa rebukes the cowards in *Maldon* on ethical grounds: he had told Byrthnoth some time before that in the hall when he had an assembly – 'meðelstede' and 'gemot' – many would speak bravely who would not be firm in time of need, ll. 199–201.) As the mythological sovereign presiding over lawful war, as the pledge-giver who sacrifices his hand, Tiu essentially oversees war as the binding of that which is terrible or else the unbinding of reigns of terror.[8] This language of bonds and unbinding is at the heart of Tiu's actions.

However, none of this should be construed as an argument for the palpable, living presence of Tiu as mythological sanction in *Beowulf* or anywhere else in Old English heroic poetry. Paganism, however alive in tenuous conversations and in times of Anglo-Saxon apostasy, is not alive in Old English poetry, as E.G. Stanley has shown in *The Search for Anglo-Saxon Paganism* (1975). But Christian meanings have not erased either the history or the conceptual weight of Old English pagan vocabulary, especially in the heroic poems, and *Beowulf* does indeed look back to heathen times within a social and cultural world still structured deeply by Germanic concepts of reciprocity, loyalty, and law. The details of pagan practices have been largely extirpated (even when generally recalled, as in ship funerals and temple worship).[9] However, even though we do not have pagan remains sustained through time by some vitalistic spirit, we may yet see the deep, conceptual structure of pagan thought, at least in part. Indeed, Christian conceptions may thrive or not insofar as they fit into that deep structure (a point that differs from Gregory's well-known instructions to Augustine about accommodations wherever possible between pagan practices and Christianity). Pagan warrior-kings and their retinues will change to stay the same. Does the new God fit in with their system of loyalties, settlements, and exchanges?[10] Can this Christian God bring battlefield victory? Can He step into the shoes (or stirrups) of Tiu, that resplendent guarantor of pledges, binder of terror, and presider over the Thing or law court, and over war as settlement, who may also have had an original status as All-Ruler, All-Father, and Sky-God?[11]

If Tiu had some such status in pagan times, then the appearance in Christian poetry of terms for the glorious, resplendent, heavenly divinity could well have come from language and from a religious system that once honoured Tiu especially in contexts where the Christian God performs Tiu-like functions such as in pledges, in unbinding terror, and in overseeing warfare as settlement.[12] D.H. Green has suggested that the Anglo-Saxons were inclined to apply warlike vocabulary from the *comitatus* to the Christian deity ('drihten' in particular, but also such terms of reciprocal favouring as 'hold' and 'mild') in an effort to link ethical behaviour (the provenance of the *comitatus*) with religion (given an original separation between Germanic religion and the *comitatus*). In addition, an interest in appropriating the warlike character of Anglo-Saxon peoples for Christian ends distinguished the Anglo-Saxon mission from, notably, Wulfila's earlier, pacifistic work among the Goths.[13] This means that even strongly pagan conceptions such as 'hæl' (the sacred luck that brings victory), 'halig,' and 'gast' could be applied or used in relation to the Christian deity.

'Halig drihten,' then, might be a syncretic, religious, and ethical phrase. Although it does not appear in *Caedmon's Hymn*, arguably the earliest application of Old English vocabulary to the Christian deity (late seventh century), the *Beowulf* poet uses it once (whereas 'halig god' appears twice, ll. 381b, 1553b). 'Halig drihten' is used along with 'witig god' and is Beowulf's phrase for the deity who will judge ('deme') the outcome of battle as it seems fit to Him. All three phrases, then, may once have applied to Tiu, although we have no evidence from early times of 'drihten' or its cognates applying to Germanic gods. But surely 'halig god' would have applied to Tiu, especially within a context of war as settlement (which it most certainly has in Beowulf's thinking about the Grendel affair, case, or Thing). In *Exodus*, 'halig god' shields the Israelites against the sun by means of a holy net ('halgan nette,' l. 74a), whereas in *Christ* the vocabulary changes partially with Christ becoming the one who loosens bonds (the fetters of sin, probably) and upon whom alone those hardbound in baleful ropes can depend for compensation: 'gebunden bealorapum. Is seo bot gelong / eal æt þe anum, ece dryhten' (ll. 365b–366). 'Ece dryhten' does appear in *Caedmon's Hymn* twice, each time connected directly to making or adorning the world and its wonders. In *Beowulf* the phrase appears four times: it is used in relation to God's vengeance (against Cain), to requital (for the giants' war against Him), to a happy decision (that Hrothgar would live long enough to see Grendel's severed head), and in association with 'ealde riht.' The phrase is also twice linked closely with 'metod' (an ancient word for 'measurer').

To measure is to limit or decide and is as good an epithet for Tiu as we are likely to suggest.[14] Moreover, Tiu must once have been 'tirmeahtig,' a term applied in *Christ* to Christ's harrowing of hell, an act that focuses the attention of all creation: the ocean particularly says that 'tirmeahtig cyning' (l. 1165) set it in place (perhaps a curious reflection of Tiu's nature background, whatever that was).[15] As establisher of the world's boundaries, this king of glorious might also uniquely beautifies and protects the Phoenix's tree against all bitterness for as long as the world endures (linked with 'metod' in *Phoenix*, ll. 175b–181). Tiu's fertility function may lurk here and appears even in his demoted status in later Norse poetry, particularly in his close association with the Vanir, Freya and Freyja. In *Christ and Satan* the devil, bound in torment, says he and his fellows are not blessed in glory, 'Nis her eadiges tir' (l. 92b), while 'eadig,' in *Beowulf* suggests battle-luck (victory, 'sigor,' and glory, 'tir'); it is applied to both the giant sword and to the man (Beowulf) who experiences reversal from slights – this man whose great strength is an ample and well-ruled gift from God (ll. 2181–9).[16] 'Tir' by itself or as a compound applies to utter victory when Beowulf brings Grendel's head into Heorot as a 'sign' or token of 'glory' in a battle during which, Beowulf says, God was a protector; as Ruler of Men he granted that Beowulf should opportunely see and wield the spectacular, giant sword. Grendel is 'tirleas,' lacking glory, when he makes a bloody, doomed retreat from Heorot – a retreat in which he is overcome with affliction and which ends in gore in his fen-refuge where he loses his life and his heathen soul, and 'hel' grasps him. In contrast, Hrothgar reflects Beowulf's great victory when, in the morning light, he steps in firm glory ('tirfæst,' l. 922a) towards Heorot. Heaven's candle, the sun, shines on victory in *Beowulf*, much as it does in *The*

Battle of Brunanburh (where it is associated with 'ece drihten,' l. 16a, and called god's candle).

Finally, 'tir' appears in close conjunction with either promised victory or a life and death choice in *Elene*. After having his dream of the cross, the still pagan Constantine, in his boar helmet, is called 'tiredig cyning' (l. 104); the wonderful vision frees him from the sorrow and terror occasioned by the approaching Huns and Goths. Later Helena, in her search for the true cross, offers Judas a life-or-death choice and in that offer she is called 'tireadig cwen' (l. 605a). Even Judas becomes 'tireadig' and 'gesælig' (ll. 945a, 955a) when, filled with the wisdom of the holy ghost, he achieves victory over the devil.

Similar associations in *Beowulf* and elsewhere in Old English poetry suggest that when terms for brightness and glory fall together with 'god,' 'drihten,' and 'metod,' within a context of judging the outcome of battle or of binding the terrible and undoing bonds of terror, then a cluster of terms and attributes appears which parallels our reconstructed sense of Tiu or Tyr as the original sky god and god of war as law, as settlement. When Judith prays to God for strength and for His vengeance, she calls him 'mihtig dryhten / torhtmod tires brytta' (ll. 92b–93a); when she urges her troops into battle upon the God-sent morning light, she tells them that the honour-firm King, the 'mihtig Dryhten,' has already doomed their enemies; the Israelites will gain fame and glory (ond ge dom agon, / tir æt tohtan, ll. 196b–197a); when the *Beowulf* poet denounces the Danes' heathen prayers, he says that while they were in these moments of prayer, mindful of hell, they did not know 'metod,' the judge of deeds, 'drihten god,' nor how to praise heaven's 'helm' (ll. 180–2); it is truly known that 'mihtig god' rules mankind by giving successful fortune in war, although that glory can be withheld no matter how good the champion in question. In *The Battle of Maldon*, 'tir' is simply fixed as glory in battle, directly linked to the fall of doomed men (ll. 104–5) and indirectly reflecting Byrthnoth's conviction that God alone knows who will rule the slaughter-place.

This god, who decides the outcome of battle as he thinks best, can be called 'witig god,' 'halig dryhten,' 'mihtig god,' 'metod,' 'halig god,' 'witig drihten' and 'rodera rædend' (the last in line 1555a). As 'ylda waldend' he grants Beowulf sight of the giant sword in the Grendel-kin's lair; as 'sigora waldend' he grants that Beowulf avenge himself upon the dragon; as 'wuldor cyning,' he receives Beowulf's thanks for sight of the hoard ('wuldor' is related to 'Ullr,' the god of kept-oaths, paired in contrast and Tiu-like with Odin in Sweden, also forming part of compound names for warriors);[17] and as 'sigora soðcyning' he would grant legal access to the hoard to whomever he would, opening it by implicitly unwinding the spell wound around it.[18] The *Beowulf* poet is surprisingly consistent about these usages in these contexts. When we come across these names for the deity, then, we are certainly in Tiu's conceptual field and we may well be reading and hearing language once applied to him.[19] We are, in Beowulf's case, clearly following a warrior (and later a king) who is of Tiu in that his combats are juristic in their context from the very beginning of his appearance in the poem.

Beowulf's progress from Hygelac's shores to Hrothgar's hall is a movement towards Hrothgar's official, legal permission to hold Heorot against Grendel. In effect, Beowulf would undertake a legal task: he would purge ('fælsian') Grendel, and therefore horrendous crime or pestilence, from Heorot. This accords with the sacral and purifying connotations of 'fælsian' in that Beowulf bears a sort of sacral sovereignty in being Tiu-like, in 'unbinding' a reign of terror, much as God unbinds the fetters of winter (an action linked by likeness to the melting of the giant's sword). Thus legal force is also sacred force, the domain of the sun god, Tiu. At another level, Beowulf fulfils three warrior functions or obligations at once: purger of disease (a 'fertility' function in that Grendel's attacks prevent the young from maturing in the hall and insofar as Beowulf's victory over Grendel's mother clears the lake of vile water monsters); punisher of outlaws; defender of his people (in this case both his personal war-troop and the Danes). Readers have long noted Beowulf's virtues – he fights to protect others and for the common good – but few have seen his combats as reflecting sacral, warrior functions, especially jural functions that make him more than just another defender of the hall, more than just another retainer willing to try his martial luck against Grendel.[20]

A hero-adventurer like Sigemund seeks renown, not legal standing. He seeks fame, not trust, and he may have been involved in crimes and malicious feuds. Beowulf, in crucial contrast, seeks neither crime nor feud but does seek renown and trust. Unfortunately the Danes' comparison of Beowulf with Sigemund and our tendency to think of analogues has lulled readers into taking Beowulf's arrival among the Danes as the arrival of an adventurer, seeking to cut his teeth, as it were, on a monster fight. Instead, Beowulf's arrival is in fact the arrival of the strong hand of law, although as an outsider to Hrothgar's *comitatus*, he must win his way into what becomes a unique guardianship of Heorot and the encounter he desires. Each step in his progress is important and involves the implications of rightful assembly. In a sense, Beowulf's unexpected arrival causes several meetings to take place and is interpreted favourably in legalistic terms.[21] The first such meeting is with the coastguard, who approaches the Geats brandishing a mighty spear, and, in words of parley ('meþelwordum,' l. 236b), challenges the uninvited stranger and his retinue to disclose themselves forthwith. Arriving without permission ('leafnesword,' l. 246b) and without the consent or agreement of kinsmen Beowulf must both identify and explain himself.[22]

He names his people and his lord, gives a tribute to his father, and finally states his friendliness and loyalty of heart ('holdne hige') toward Healfdene's son. D.H. Green has pointed out the reciprocal and even legal nature of the word 'hold' as an ethical term within the *comitatus* and as a term for oaths and contracts (citing Liebermann) where the 'huldi' of the lord is invoked as a guarantee of the truth of the statement.[23] Beowulf here uses it in an ethical sense, with its *comitatus* meaning implied: he has come in good heart, much as a loyal retainer would come to his lord, to the prince of the people. But its power as a binding word in relation to oaths is clear to Beowulf when he later invokes 'hyldo' in relation to 'aðsweord' when speaking of the likely outbreak of violence between Heathobard and Dane, despite the presence of Freawaru as peace-kin (ll. 2064a, 2067b).[24] A characteristic, late Anglo-Saxon legal use appears in the Colyton oath: the swearer vows to be 'hold and getriwe an eal lufian thæt he [his lord] lufath ... and næfre willes ne gewealdes, wordes ne weorces owiht ðon thæs him lathre bith' 'loyal and true and love all that he loves and never of one's own will or power, in words or deeds, do anything that to him is hateful.'[25] This kind of trust is contractual, albeit short-lived, in the Finn episode. Beowulf often places trust in his great strength, whereas the dragon misplaces trust in the strength of its barrow; but, crucially, Beowulf trusts appropriately in his strength as a great gift, the Measurer's favour ('hyldo'), for which he reciprocates by assigning ultimate judgment to God. To hold in favour and trust, then, is a legally bound and reciprocal relationship between people (particularly between retainer and lord) but misplaced when applied to the inanimate.

Asking the coastguard for possible clarification about a mysterious doer of hateful deeds, Beowulf further adds that he has come in largeness of spirit ('rumne sefan') to offer counsel and advice ('ræd gelæran') about how Hrothgar might overcome his enemy. Essentially,

Beowulf says that he has come in peace and in generosity of spirit (presumably without any conditions). He has come to call for and speak in a rightful assembly concerning response to the injury and slaughter Grendel has wrought – injury that the poet has expressly framed in legalistic terms, prior to Beowulf's arrival; he speaks of Grendel as contending against 'riht' (l. 144b), as engaging in continual and (implicitly) illicit strife ('singale sæce,' l. 154a), and as refusing to make peace, settle in payment, or offer compensation (ll. 154b–158a). The collocation of 'sæce' and 'sibb' (kin-like peace) is a strong mark against Grendel, indicating the lawlessness of his quarrel with the Danes.

'Sacu' and 'sæc' have legalistic connotations ('lawsuit' in Old Saxon; 'legal accusation or charge' in Bosworth and Toller). They can also mean battle as settlement against illicit or unjust strife. These are the negative and positive domains of the words. Negatively, 'Sacu' and related forms mark illicit strife whenever that strife would countenance no peace or friendship. The strife ('synn ond sacu,' l. 2472a) between Ongentheow and the Geats after Hrethel's death, or the strife Thryth treacherously prepares for unlucky men who gaze upon her (l. 1942), or the malicious strife once waged between Danes and Geats (l. 1857) are examples of 'sacu'. In response to such strife, the same word marks positively a violent settlement. Beowulf will offer to contend ('sacan,' l. 439b) against Grendel, life with life; and Hygelac much later will tell us that Beowulf resolved to seek battle ('sæcce') against Grendel. In almost half of its appearances this word applies to battle against the monsters. In direct relationship to settling ('gesette') a violent quarrel, the word appears in Beowulf's account of Hrothgar's arrangements for a peace kinship – the marriage of his daughter, Freawaru, to Ingeld of the Heathobards. Thus the word reflects either an enraged and lawless quarrel (cf. the dragon's contention with Beowulf, ll.2561b–2562a) or an attempt at settlement (a settlement like Beowulf's great deeds against Grendel and his mother). Indeed, invoking the word's negative domain, Hrothgar says that Beowulf has brought about a shared peace between Geats and Danes, an end to malicious strife ('sacu restan / inwitniþas, ll. 1857b–1858a). Associated with Beowulf's sword late in the poem, 'saec' suggests that kind of settlement which is the sword as law, albeit Nægling breaks on the dragon's head. Such settlement is exactly what Beowulf said he often achieved in battle, especially when he repaid Hygelac's gifts and kindnesses against the Frisians. Thus we are allowed to read 'sæc' as 'settlement' in such lines as Beowulf's, especially when he notes to Hunferth that Grendel kills and feasts in Heorot, expecting no 'secca' from the Danes (l. 600).

So it is that Grendel often commits many crimes ('fela fyrena') against mankind. He inhabits Heorot without permission (perhaps in the sense that he cannot approach the gift-seat),[26] and he is so powerful that in their councils the Danes have been unable to formulate good advice ('ræd') for stopping this violator of all that is 'riht.' That conjunction of 'ræd' and 'riht' is a powerfully legal one, sanctioned by the deity (cf. 'rodera Rædend hit on ryht gesced' l. 1555), and concerning victory in battle (overseen by 'halig God,' the ruler of 'wigsigor,' l. 1554a). Thus it involves the rule, at all levels, of what is right, of proper obligations and good counsel (cf. *Waldere*: 'Þeah / mæg sige syllan se ðe symle byð / recon ond rædfest ryhta gehwilces' ll. 25–26a). The efforts of many Danes in arms have been futile, as have heathen temple practices. Beowulf would, then, provide an alternative 'ræd,' the exact nature of which he does not disclose to the coastguard.

Hrothgar's coastguard – one of several warriors assigned to particular posts as evidence of Hrothgar's regal government – replies fearlessly and gnomically that a sharp shield-warrior shall be a judge, a decider of words and works, one who thinks well. That words are not deeds is not the import of this gnome; rather, the import is that brave words and good advice may not prevail when the work is undertaken. Advice ('ræd') offered must be perceptive advice. The guard does not know yet what Beowulf's counsel will be; nor does Beowulf know exactly what Grendel has done. When he finds out, he may modify the counsel he has come to give. In the meantime, the coastguard has heard Beowulf's language of loyal and oath-like reciprocity and pronounces Beowulf and his troop to be a 'hold weorod' to the lord of the Scyldings. It is for that reason that he will show them the way to Heorot, set a guard for their ship,[27] and invoke 'Fæder alwalda' to keep the Geats with 'marks of honour or favour' ('mid arstafum,' l. 317b). Both 'ar' and 'arstafas' have reciprocal connotations: Beowulf has come to offer good counsel; may God keep him and his men safe in return. This extension to the term 'ar' means that relationships with the deity are in some way reciprocal, on the side of favour or gratitude rather than demand: for kindness shown, show kindness to others; if God has favoured one, then one should favour one's retainers; freely favouring a stranger deserves God's favour in return.

When Beowulf meets Wulfgar, another exchange and a further revealing take place. But another sign of tension is raised and implicitly put to rest first: Wulfgar, identifying himself as a high officer in Hrothgar's court, notes the Geats' resplendent battle-ready appearance before concluding that the Geats have come out of high spirits and not as marauders. From the coastguard to Wulfgar, and later in Heorot itself, there is implicit challenge in response to possible threat. At a surface level this is easily dealt with when Beowulf requests an audience with Hrothgar, the great king – a request Wulfgar interprets as a petition or boon, although Beowulf is not a petitioner for some injury or injustice against himself. Soon enough, after speaking with Hrothgar and receiving permission, Wulfgar invites the Geats to an 'outcome of words' ('worda geþinges,' l. 398b).

But at this moment we might consider a large pattern that has occupied *Beowulf* critics in many ways. There is a clear contrast between Beowulf as an active, powerful leader and Hrothgar as one who just sits and suffers in the Grendel affair and yet is wise. The opposition inherent here has been posed as a variously framed, but always doubled, kingship ideal – strength and wisdom; fortitude and sapience; youthful energy and aged reflectiveness; and so on. At a mythic level it suggests something like the opposition between terrifying warrior and calm legislator (say a singular Odin and a refined Tiu); at the level of cross-cultural patterns it might be thought of as an opposition between *celeritas* and *gravitas*, the combination of the two producing a third term, 'a sovereign power, itself a dual combination of the war function and the peace function, king and priest, will and law' (Sahlins, 1987, p. 90).

This duality of sovereignty suggests an ideal mix of any approximate version of the opposed or sharply distinguished characteristics. But when the opposition here is put into dynamic action, strength, fortitude, youthful vigour, and *celeritas* become aggressive and threatening in relation to the sitting king – Hrothgar and his court in this case, Fijian chiefs and their territories in Sahlins's. Sahlins suggests that in Polynesian as much as in ancient Indo-European worlds the sovereign is able to rule, that is, mediate between these antitheses, insofar as he partakes of the nature of the opposition itself. *Celeritas* 'refers to the youthful, active, disorderly, magical, and creative violence of conquering princes; *gravitas*, to the venerable, staid, judicious, priestly, peaceful, and productive dispositions of an established people. In the initial moment of their combination *celeritas* prevails over *gravitas*, as the invaders capture the reproductive powers of the land to found their kingdom' (p. 90).

In Polynesia, an invader may eventually be accepted and given the daughters of the conquered chief as wives; the invader's sons then become sisters'-sons to the invaded (and in partaking of the woman's side, partake of the settled, the sitting). In fact, Sahlins adds, the warrior functions of the new ruling chief 'devolve as soon as possible upon a youthful heir, a son whose roving, killing and womanizing prowess is a cultural prescription' (p. 90). But this or some other splitting of the duality is not the key point; rather it is the duality itself as an always ambiguous, unstable, 'complementary and cyclical opposition of the two natures of kingship' (p. 90).

In *Beowulf* this duality appears prominently in the alternation within the Danish line itself between aggressive kings like Scyld and Healfdene and more legislative kings like Beow and Hrothgar. When we consider the threat inherent in Beowulf's uninvited arrival with armed forces, we should keep Sahlins (who is inspired by Dumézil) in mind and note parallel details. Hrothgar, of course, sits helplessly against the Grendel terror but is wise, generous, and legislative; Beowulf when active is fierce, terrifying, and hugely strong. When not fighting in Heorot, Beowulf sits, receives gifts, and hears advice from Wealhtheow. Her offer of a necklace that reminds the poet of the famous and sexually salacious, legendary necklace of the Brisings may be a subliminal offer of herself if Beowulf will simply fade away, refuse the conqueror's role, and reject Hrothgar's effort to adopt him. By joining the renewed drinking after Wealhtheow's words, Beowulf seems wisely to accept them (*gravitas*). On the other side, *celeritas*, Beowulf vigorously pursues violent and seemingly definitive settlement (against the Grendel-kin, against Hygelac's presumed killer, Dæghrefn and his entire warband, and against Swedes). As an active hero, moreover, he does not embody just *celeritas*. He largely brings the two terms together in his role as lawful purger of the hall and the Grendel-kin's mere and as wise offerer of continuing alliance between Geats and Danes. Thus he is both juridical (the strong hand of the law) and judicious. Beowulf's central role in the poem as the immensely powerful, strong hand of law is the one within which he turns aside any suggestions that he might be something else. Thus he confidently requests the meetings he does.

As Wulfgar escorts Beowulf into Heorot, a second council is about to form, during which Beowulf will refer to the Grendel affair, 'Grendles þing,' which he would settle. 'Þing' in *Beowulf*, I submit, usually carries something of its formal meaning as an assembly in which matters of right and obligation are decided. Thus the connotation for 'Grendles þing' would be ironic – Grendel's criminal meeting with Danes in Heorot, during which the horrific orality of cannibalism takes the place of speech, resulting in wrongful death, not a decision to act or a rightful judgment. Beowulf goes on to say that his arrival is not mere, high-spirited impulse; he held council in his own country with wisemen, who advised him to seek out Hrothgar, and to settle this 'thing' with the giant Grendel, alone. They saw how he destroyed water monsters who had afflicted the Geats. In this context, þing can only mean a rightful settlement, in and through combat – a course of action advised in council by wise, old men (perhaps the sense of 'snotere ceorlas,' l. 416b).[28] Having stated what he was advised to come and do, Beowulf now requests this boon from Hrothgar: permission for him and his retainers to try to purge Heorot. He formally urges that Hrothgar not 'refuse' him ('forwyrnan'). The intensified form of 'wyrnan' appears in *Beowulf* only here and in the Finn episode, where we are told that Hengest did not refuse the awful settlement implied by Hunlafing's laying of the 'best of swords' in Hengest's lap.[29] That particular settlement of feud, of revenge for injury, is called a 'torngemot' (l. 1140a), a 'hostile meeting' (much later Beowulf will refer to his combat with Grendel as a 'gemeting' or 'meeting' known to many men). The parallel between the Finn episode and Beowulf's proposed combat with Grendel is enhanced by the bitterness of the Danish ordeal in each case, by the juridical character of each episode, and by a retainer's wartime counsel and the possibility of revenge.[30] The meeting Beowulf proposed with Grendel in Heorot will be a trial of the criminal in unarmed combat, the outcome of which is properly in God's judgment ('Dryhtnes dome,' l. 441a). And so Beowulf will settle this thing with Grendel or else death will take him. If he is killed, Beowulf asks that Hrothgar send his corselet to Hygelac. Fourteen hundred lines later, when speaking to Hygelac, Beowulf mockingly says that Grendel thought to 'try' Beowulf ('costian'), as though in a trial and as though to taste him.

In face-to-face response, Hrothgar interprets Beowulf's arrival and proposal as a reciprocal settlement, a return for Hrothgar's earlier settlement of a great feud on Beowulf's father's behalf.[31] Essentially Hrothgar invokes the reciprocity of one rightful settlement for another – something the Danes could never expect from the terrible Grendel. Hrothgar further underlines reciprocity by suggesting that Beowulf has come out of 'arstafum' ('marks of favour or kindness,' l. 458a), 'ar' being part of the reciprocal, ethical vocabulary of the *comitatus* – favour given for favour received (as with 'hold').[32] Hrothgar then tells of the slaughter brought about in the past by Grendel's warfare, and of how, in the light of day, the bench planks steamed with blood. Given this cautionary scenerio, Hrothgar now invites Beowulf to a banquet where he might disclose or unwind his thoughts (implying the unravelling of a rope). Having now been informed of Grendel's bloody prowess, perhaps Beowulf's resolve will change during the banqueting, which is separated from the outcome of words through which we have just passed.

Thus the scenes in Heorot can evolve from meetings where advice is given and heard to banqueting, where impromptu meetings might well take place as further 'disclosures of mind' are made ('onsæl meoto,' l. 489b, suggests its opposite, the evil winding of secret thought, which the legislator hero would naturally oppose).[33] To draw out Beowulf's thoughts and the quality of his resolve is Hunferth's essential function. His battle-speech has too often struck modern readers as an expression of jealousy, rather than as the highly competitive, albeit contentious counsel-speech it is. It is true that the poet attributes displeasure or vexation to Hunferth ('æfþunca'); he is one who would not wish or grant ('uþe,' a form of giving) that any other man should achieve, perform ('gehegan'), or perhaps desire (MS. 'ge/hedde,' l. 505) more of glories on middle-earth under the heavens than himself.[34] Beowulf has come with a counsel – an offer to perform ('gehegan,' l. 425) a settlement with Grendel that no Dane has offered for twelve years. Indeed, we can suppose that the Danish abandonment of Heorot at night is a counsel Hunferth might have given, which the Danes have followed and which, among other matters (not least being Hunferth's status as the possessor of a spectacular sword), makes Hunferth a chief counsellor at Hrothgar's knee. Counsel in gift giving contexts may well turn into a competitive arena where one can lose or gain status.

Hunferth's is a challenge-speech that instantly turns banqueting back into a meeting, into an 'outcome of words' ('worda geþinges'). Hunferth's eloquence gives his speech a formal stature. Consider his invocation of that great stream of water, the ocean, that Beowulf and Breca foolishly thought to measure ('mæton') with their arms, to traverse and weave together with their hands (ll. 513–515a). They thought they could legislate over the waves, so foolhardy were they (implicitly berserk)! Implicitly, Grendel's terror is like that ocean, not to be measured or embraced lightly by one giving a boast that may well reflect a foolish frenzy. Hunferth's rhetoric finally comes down to this judgmental point: if Beowulf is indeed the Beowulf of Hunferth's Breca story, then Beowulf's attempted settlement with Grendel will be worse than was dealt to Beowulf in that foolish episode with Breca ('wyrsan geþingea,' l. 525b).

Hunferth expresses not only his own displeasure, however; he voices both Danish ambivalence towards this powerful stranger and group pride.[35] At the group level, Hunferth's challenge-speech sustains for the moment a sense of identity by accusing Beowulf and the Geats of misrepresentation, essentially of having a past deed – the ostensible loss to Breca – betray present boasts as hollow. Implicitly, no Dane would state hollow boasts – a boost to their self-esteem – and no outsider can come into Heorot and say whatever he wants. (A sense of group is thus reinforced for the Danes, for whom direct aggression against Grendel has proven disastrous, and for whom no other alternative, such as leaving Hrothgar's court, is attractive.)[36] At a personal level, Hunferth would destroy Beowulf verbally by feasting on Beowulf's reputation.

In his crushing reply, closing with an indictment of Hunferth's character, righteousness, and valour, Beowulf departs from his customary deference to the decision of God. Essentially, he predicts a 'sunny' outcome in the morning light, virtually under the same heavens where Hunferth would not be outshone; in effect the son of Ecglaf will be thoroughly silenced. Thus he reverses the gory scenerio Hrothgar sketched earlier and suggests a Tiu-like sanction, that of the Sky-God. The shining of God's candle often marks victories, even in the underground battle with Grendel's mother. Moreover, Beowulf spoke of combats with sea-creatures who thought to dine on him (a physical analogue to Hunferth's oral aggression) and of his dispatching of them 'fittingly' ('saw hit gedefe wæs,' l. 561b). This sense of the fitting is potentially juridical, as in a rightful judgment.[37] Beowulf will use the same phrase after returning from the mere and announcing that he avenged criminal deeds, the death-slaughter of Danes. Consequently, we are told that Hrothgar now counts on Beowulf's 'firmly resolved thought' ('fæstrædne geþoht,' l. 610b). Although involving a shift from his usual deference to the God of Victory, Beowulf's words are neither hollow nor foolish; informed about Grendel's prowess and challenged by Hunferth, Beowulf comes out firm, with loyal counsel and with resolved, steady thought concerning brave deeds in the service of what is fitting and right.

Wealhtheow then approaches Beowulf within the context of renewed banqueting, laughter, good cheer, and pleasant words. She presents a 'ful' first to Hrothgar and then to other retainers and youths before coming to Beowulf. In her round through the hall she commands joy and beer-drinking, which is to say festivity and community, with beer-drinking understood as a preamble to serious speech (should occasion arise for speech). It is, perhaps, in this sense that Beowulf earlier referred to Hunferth's beer-drinking: beer-drinking is constructive, even potentially solemn in the midst of joy, even though Hunferth's words are fiercer than his appetite for battle.[38]

The ring-adorned queen bears a cup full of mead to Beowulf and says in wise and firm words, as reported indirectly, that she thanks God that now her will has come to pass and she can count on a man for solace against crime. Her word, 'gelyfan,' is related to Gothic 'ga-laubjan,' a word for trust, praise, and approval. D.H. Green traces the word back to Gothic legal vocabulary, through Wulfila's uses of it.[39] Wealhtheow's trust, then, is a special kind of 'counting upon' or faith, as in assent to the rightness or efficacy of a praiseworthy proposal put forth at an assembly (cf. Tacitus' observations of Germanic assemblies: 'Si displicuit sententia, fremitu aspernantur; sin placuit, frameas concutiunt: honoratissimum adsensus genus est armis laudare,' 'if the advice is displeasing, they groan; if it pleases, they violently shake their spears. The greatest mark of respectful assent is this martial praise,' *Germania*, chap. 11). As Jan de Vries would have it: 'from the Germanic point of view, there is no contradiction between the concepts "god of War" and "god of Law".'[40]

Wealhtheow's trust and Beowulf's receiving of the 'ful' require an oath or solemn vow in response; this is exactly what Beowulf now gives. He says that while setting out to sea he resolved to work the will of the Danes or else die in the slaughter, firm in the enemy's grasp. He adds that he will perform a noble deed or else end his days in this meadhall. Wealhtheow likes his boast-words – a vow that Beowulf fulfils in the event, accomplishing not only his boast but also rightful remedy and settlement ('gebetan,' l. 830b) against an outlaw creature from whom the Danes could never expect 'beorhtre bote' (l. 158b). The outcome of Wealhtheow's words and her offering of the cup has been a noble vow added to Beowulf's earlier, praiseworthy proposal.[41] Banqueting resumes and all partake of mead-hall joy, until it is time for evening rest.

Hrothgar turns to Beowulf and effectively completes Beowulf's progress from uninvited stranger at the Danish shore to especially trusted warrior in this matter of Grendel's crimes. Hrothgar says that never, since he could raise hand and shield, has he entrusted the best of houses to any man, except now to Beowulf. 'Entrusted' is carried by the word 'alyfde' and seems to mean more than special hope and more than just leaving the hall to yet another, brave retainer or would-be defender (which he did repeatedly after Grendel's first raid). 'Alyfan' is related to 'permission,' and to 'praise' (cf. Ger. 'erlauben'). It implies proper possession of the hall, as though Hrothgar were leaving Heorot to Beowulf in trust, to be not just its defender, but its rightful possessor for the night (cf. an O.E. adverbial form, 'alifedlice,' glossed as 'allowably,' 'legally' by Toller and Campbell, *Supplement*). This Hrothgar has never done before, which is why he formally urges Beowulf now to have and rule the best of houses, to be its guardian in Hrothgar's place ('Hafa nu ond geheald husa selest,' l. 658).

The Danes depart and the Geats bed down for the night. Hrothgar, fit to be the most glorious of kings ('kyninga wuldor,' l. 665b, especially with 'wuldor' related to oath-keeping), has set a guardian of the hall against Grendel; that guardianship is a special office or service ('sundornytte,' l. 667b; cf. the court office held by a cup-bearing Dane: 'Þegn nytte beheold, / se þe on handa bær hroden ealowæge,' ll. 494b–495).[42] In this he may be repeating the special honour his ancestors showed their friendly Scyld Scefing, by setting ('asetton') a golden banner high over his head. Likewise, Beowulf's possession of the hall is a special, official one, pointing towards an unknown, life-or-death outcome, and made fully jural by the processes of words, assembly, and permission gained. He will now await his fierce meeting with Grendel, the trial by combat against a creature the poet calls God's adversary, a creature who bears God's anger. Beowulf, we are told, firmly trusted in his courageous might, in the Measurer's 'hyldo' – a reciprocal 'favouring' that implies mutual trust: Beowulf in the Measurer's power; the Measurer in Beowulf's strength and will. 'Trust' here can also have legal connotations, as 'getruwian' emphatically has in Old English. Thus Beowulf's 'trust' in his God-given gift, his courageous might, has both juridical and sacral connotations that probably predate the Christian period and which hold Beowulf in good stead here and in the second fight, as well as later, although severely qualified, in his meeting with the dragon.[43] In the course of their eventual struggle, we are told that Beowulf, the protector of nobles, would not by any means ('æniga þinga,' l. 791b) let the death-comer leave alive. Here 'þing' can easily recall prior agreements or resolutions, with 'agreement' or 'compact' being its meaning in the Finn episode (l. 1085): the protector of nobles would not by any means, according to any agreements, let that creature flee. But Grendel does break away, although he leaves his grisly arm as a token, a clear sign – of Beowulf's victory, of justice done, of vow fulfilled, and all distress remedied ('ealle gebette,' l. 830b).

Because the outlaw monster would in no way settle his feud with the Danes, Beowulf has now exacted 'bot' and speaks of Grendel as having been 'captured' and 'jailed' in effect, as the sin-drenched one awaits in pernicious bonds the great judgment of the resplendent Measurer (ll. 975–9). Although not fully enacted as Beowulf had hoped ('Ic hine hrædlice heardan clammum / on wælbedde wriþan þohte' ll. 963–4), the right of the strong hand, of the juridical warrior who unbinds reigns of terror and binds up the doers of terror, has sufficiently prevailed. The mythological sanction for Beowulf's role in Heorot is clearly Tiu's act on the gods' behalf against the wolf Fenrir: Tiu left his hand in the wolf's mouth, enabling the gods to bind this ever-growing, cosmic terror. Tiu loses his hand much as Beowulf loses a valued retainer named, appropriately enough, Hondscioh (Klaeber compares the name to Handscuh, 'glove'). To save his life momentarily, Grendel left behind his hand, arm, and shoulder. For Beowulf the loss of a hand (Hondscioh) is a prelude to victory; for Grendel, the loss of a hand is prelude to defeat – an ironic parallel to the kind of counsel Grendel would have held had he not had his expectations surprised by Beowulf's restraining grip. In both Tiu's case and Beowulf's the loss of a 'hand' marks victory; in both Fenrir's case and Grendel's the swallowing of a 'hand' (Tiu's and Beowulf's retainer, respectively) marks defeat. Thus the analogue I see for Beowulf's heroic action is acutely, if elastically, appropriate – in each case the terror is bound and a potential reign of terror undone.

Later, when Beowulf descends into the mere and is granted use of the giant's sword, another unbinding occurs as the sword's blade melts in the heat of Grendel's blood. The sword diminishes like a 'battle icicle,' like the unwinding of frost fetters, which the Father who has rule of seasons and times unloosens. The giant's sword of victory suggests Tiu or Tyr for a moment, but then its opposite, the unravelling of giants and terror, while the function of loosening the bonds of terror has a divine analogue in the loosening of winter frost and the coming of spring and fertility.[44] In a feud context that coming is a matter of revenge and victory, closely associated with the ending of winter's icy bonds in the Finn episode, and here with the slaying of Grendel's mother before a beheading of dead

Grendel. The juridical-warrior undoes the bonds of terror much as the True Measurer undoes the bonds of winter and later unwinds the chant curse placed on the hoard.[45]

After munificent banqueting and the receiving of gifts, Beowulf sleeps elsewhere than in the hall. Having purged Heorot of Grendel's night-time crimes (which include illegal possession), Beowulf has returned rightful use of the hall to the Danes. Unfortunately, another creature still lives and comes to avenge her son's death.

Hrothgar grieves that he has lost Æschere, his exemplary knower of runes ('runwita'), bearer of right counsel ('rædbora'), and equal battle companion (thus a counsellor in arms). He tells Beowulf that a restless slaughter-spirit killed Æschere to avenge that feud in which 'you, Beowulf' killed Grendel. But he then moves away from an implied obligation concerning injury to an individualizing plea related to kinship by remarking that Beowulf is now the Danes' only giver of promising advice (note 'ræd gelang,' l. 1376b), his mighty action the only course they might rely on with hope.

'Gelang' strongly implies a formal dependency within the *comitatus* and the kin group; Beowulf uses it when summing up his dependence upon Hygelac, his only superior kinsman and lord. The Danes now utterly depend upon Beowulf's counsel in the Grendel business, but Beowulf does not take that dependency in any stronger way than in friendly fosterage: rather than mourn much, one should avenge one's 'freond.' Having received a special status in Heorot for purging the great hall, Beowulf might now respond to Hrothgar's invitation of a special kinship (ll. 946b–949a: 'Now I will love you, Beowulf, in heart as a son; henceforth hold well this new kinship'). However, he is not willing to compromise his loyalty toward Hygelac and so he accepts an obligation to protect the Danes that is as neutral as possible (invoking an abstract principle of protective friendship, for which fitting reward is promised). He volunteers no motive now that would have him act on the Danes' behalf in any personal and compromising sense: he will seek Grendel's mother to win fame and not to do the will of the Danes (which is what he vowed earlier in his 'beot' to Wealhtheow). He does, however, take up Hrothgar's invitation to kinship in one sense: should he die, then Hrothgar might act in a father's place toward the Geats, be a protector or advocate for them ('mundbora,' l. 1480a) and, in that capacity, dispose properly of Beowulf's treasures by sending them on to Hygelac and returning Hrunting to Hunferth. This part of Beowulf's speech is something like a last will and testament, testifying to the legal and ethical character of his entire relationship with the Danes generally and with Hrothgar in particular. After Beowulf's final speech offering a continuing alliance between Geats and Danes, Hrothgar tearfully thinks that he will not see the best of 'þegns,' courageous in council ('modige on meþle,' l. 1876a) again.

When Beowulf returns to Hygelac, following the banqueting after his second monster fight, Hygelac greets him with wonder, thankfulness, and questions. These questions reveal how Hygelac understood his great retainer's mission to Heorot. Did Beowulf go merely for adventure – a Sigemund-like wayfaring on his own, seeking fame and profit? Apparently Hygelac does not think so for he says that Beowulf suddenly resolved to seek a battle or settlement ('sæcce,' l. 1989) in Heorot. This is not opportunistic adventuring but a particular, localized purpose. Hygelac wants to know to what extent Beowulf has improved or settled Hrothgar's widely known sorrow ('widcuðne wean wihte gebettest,' l. 1991). To do this Beowulf sought a particular combat to meet and violently greet the slaughter-spirit who was oppressing the South-Danes. Having not trusted that meeting, and having entreated Beowulf not to go, Hygelac thanks God that he now sees him safe and healthy.

Hygelac apparently understands Beowulf's voyage as a juridical journey to settle a widely known sorrow and not as a marauder-adventurer's search for fame and profit. Beowulf's journey was not a Sigemund's, although his mighty deed is worth comparing to Sigemund's dragon slaying. Beowulf's combat in Heorot is a work of law, leaving Heorot purged, the monster slain, and crime settled. In this sense war accomplishes something – a settlement. Warfare leaves people on the field of slaughter, presided over by carrion beasts, but slaughter, sheer terror, and death are not the point. Rather, war as law is a settlement, a drawing of boundaries, a taking of land – a work, an 'ellenweorc' performed, Beowulf says, within the kinship-like ethics of temporary service ('estum miclum,' l. 957).[46] This same work, *The Battle of Brunanburh* poet tells us, is one the Angles and Saxons performed when they came across the seas, now in a *comitatus* context ('ar'), obtained the land. Thus warfare as settlement is a jural matter. In Beowulf's world a war-band leader does well to gain the tribute-rendering attention of surrounding peoples. Thus violence is not in itself deplorable and even raiding can be respectable. In these matters, warfare in the world of *Beowulf* is more like violence in the world of the Tausug (Kiefer, 1972): their epic poetry does not celebrate violence as such; rather it presents 'an image of man which expresses itself most clearly in violence,' an image that includes such aspects of character as 'bravado, honor, masculinity, and even magnanimity' (p. 83).

For his part, Beowulf clearly understands the sense of heroic action and of gestures in the heroic world as settlements, whether of particular crimes or of an ongoing, feud relationship. He tells Hygelac that Hrothgar implored ('healsode') him to seek the mother, almost as though that act would be an exorcism of the terrible creature from both the hall and the mere. 'Healsian' suggests a sacral function, one that when invoked cannot rightly be refused. Beowulf further indicates his juridical sense of settlement when speculating about Hrothgar's use of Freawaru as a peace-kin and he refers to the combat with Grendel as a meeting well known to many men. Finally, Beowulf gives nearly all of his treasures to Hygelac, and states that everything in his life still depends entirely on Hygelac, his great kinsman and lord. In return, Hygelac gives Beowulf a subkingship and vast landholdings – a reciprocal gesture that ties Beowulf to him in honour as well as service. That giving is done ceremonially and rightfully: Hrethel's sword is laid on Beowulf's lap (perhaps implying Beowulf's place in the immediate succession) and the poet comments that both Beowulf and Hygelac now hold land by ancestral right. Throughout his encounters and actions, Beowulf's behaviour and speech have been honouring, ethical, and jural – rightful beyond question and in no way criminal, treacherous, or murderous. The poet devoutly approves: 'Swa sceal mæg don / nealles inwitnet oðrum bregdon / dyrnum cræfte, deað ren(ian) / hondgesteallan. Hygelace wæs / niðe heardum nefa swyðe hold' 'So shall a kinsman do / not at all lock the other in a net of malice / in secret craft prepare death / for a close comrade. Hygelac was / severe in enmity, his nephew very loyal' (ll. 2166b-2170).

CHAPTER FOUR

The Economy of Honour in *Beowulf*

This chapter shows the surprising and complex ways in which *Beowulf* is a drama of exchange, in terms of both violent settlement and gift giving. With an appropriate focus, this drama becomes evident in formal speeches and celebrations; these in turn become more than they have seemed to us as the poet delineates complex gestures and establishes the dynamic character and variable scope of aristocratic gift giving.

Others have seen something of this and have even looked beyond the combats of the poem to the many ways in which the poem emphasizes such non-martial social activities as feasting, gift exchange, and ceremonial speeches. Considering these materials especially, and with a theme of community in mind, John Niles questions the appropriateness of such thematic formulations for *Beowulf* as Robert Kaske's *sapientia et fortitudo*, or any other variation that emphasizes a generalized notion of heroism and the heroic.[1] That most of the poem contains material only indirectly concerned with the hero in action has suggested a non-hero-centred theme to at least a few readers; Kathryn Hume, for one, has argued that revenge and war, seen as threatening and problematic in heroic society, form the poem's overall theme.[2]

While we can value Hume's focus on threats to the social order, we need to focus on both social activity within the hall and political friendship or continuing exchange between peoples. Anthropology can provide insight through a careful approach to the social and cultural world depicted in the poem. We need to understand the poem's social world in its own terms, as a system of values and reciprocities in a face-to-face, small group society. Beowulf's world is one in which gift exchange and feud are central; law (or what is right) is reasserted through combat; and revenge or requital are unquestioned by all the noble characters. Indeed, they are the very reason why gifts of land, weapons, and armour are exchanged. Good acts of revenge are also sanctioned by God. The battle-king does not give weapons away; they are shared in common and meant to be used on his behalf in his time of need or in requital for his injury or death.

We saw that a legalistic context framed Hrothgar's reception of Beowulf and informed the ways in which he interpreted his arrival. Before turning Heorot over to Beowulf, Hrothgar promises that Beowulf will not lack anything desirable if he survives that work of valour ('ellenweorc,' l. 661a, the violent settlement against Grendel). This promise of reward is nothing like wage payment in a modern sense: it is the central, honorific contract of the *comitatus* – rewards for services rendered or rewards (rings, weapons, mailshirts) for services that might fall due in the future when war comes. Moreover, such rewards are better thought of as 'gifts' in one sense and 'loans' in another.[3] Rewards look for a return, even as they confer both honour and worth on the parties to the exchange in any gift-giving culture, whether we look to face-to-face societies in contemporary Africa, South America, Indonesia, Melanesia, and Alaska or in the historical past, among the Germanic peoples.[4] Especially in *Beowulf* this giving of gifts is at the heart of ethical life, of lawful and right behaviour in the hall, and of continuing alliance and reciprocity among men. Certainly one gives so that one will receive, be it the support of armed men in times of war or the esteem of allies. Moreover, through military prowess in the service of law and settlement one earns glory and prosperity for one's people; through liberality in the hall one earns praise and fame (with liberality opposed not only to niggardliness but to everything treacherous or murderous, especially the slaying of retainers and kinsmen). Noble status can be won and lost in most gift-giving societies: to be generous is to be noble; to be noble is to be generous.[5] Thus to seek glory, praise, and fame (as Beowulf does) is to aspire to the highest good through war as settlement and through liberality in the hall.[6]

To give gifts is rarely, if ever, a simple, straightforward affair: exchange is a continuing social act between parties who are friends, who otherwise would be at war, or who, in some astonishing sense, remain indifferent to each other.[7] As a social act, exchange can carry many meanings almost simultaneously, depending in *Beowulf* on what is said, by whom, and to whom. In the Yanomami's Venezuelan forest culture, because social status is always involved, there is always both subtlety and peril, and the potential for both esteem and insult in matrimonial and economic exchanges.[8] A highly developed level of subtlety and peril, involving a kind of status warfare, is also apparent in the potlatch competitions, exchanges, and myriad networks of loans and repayments documented for the enclosed and status-obsessed Pacific Northwest Kwakiutls.[9] The world of potlatch differs in many ways from the gift giving we see in *Beowulf* and from the character of Germanic exhortations, but as there is near equality within a warrior aristocracy, we might also suppose subtlety and some danger regarding exchange in the world of *Beowulf*. Freawaru's marriage to Ingeld is a fragile alliance; the poet's comments on the rightfulness of Beowulf's gift giving to Hygelac suggest its opposite. The poet's approving 'so should a kinsman do, not behave treacherously' suggests that a holding back is possible as is perhaps a giving of gifts without intending a lasting friendship. And of course the retainers who do not come to Beowulf's aid against the dragon late in the poem lose glory and gain infamy for accepting Beowulf's splendid gifts and then in effect making it seem that he just threw them away. As for the subtle in gift giving, this is seen in Hrothgar's munificence after the Grendel fight, although it reaches dramatic levels in Wealhtheow's parallel giving when she attempts to counter a worrisome hope or offer imbedded in Hrothgar's words and gifts to Beowulf.

In fact the drama of gift giving in Heorot continues on into Beowulf's second service on the Dane's behalf, into his offer of friendship and military alliance, into Hrothgar's announcement of firm friendship and continuing exchange, and then past Beowulf's departure and on to his giving up of most of his treasures to Hygelac. In this and in other ethical matters, it is fair to say that *Beowulf* is much less a story about monster slaying than it is a sophisticated social drama about what is best to do in this violent and changeable world.

Fifty years ago, L.L. Schücking noticed that Wealhtheow's speeches in Heorot during the great banquet scene in part express her worry that Hrothgar might adopt Beowulf more in fact than in spirit. He might designate Beowulf as heir or successor to the Danish kingship.[10] Given Hrothgar's legislator role as protector of his people, such an effort would indeed be commendable: how better to tie this magnificent warrior to himself and to the Danes than by an attempted adoption? But if we credit Wealhtheow's worry, we need to reexamine her speeches to Hrothgar and to Beowulf, along with the scene of gift giving following Hrothgar's adoption speech. That in turn requires a general reassessment of the banquet scenes, both in Heorot and in Hygelac's hall. Those scenes become, in consequence, more portentous than *Beowulf* scholars have usually allowed. As we shall see, Hrothgar does more than fulfil his promise to reward Beowulf; implicitly he does offer some leading place in the Danish succession and thus through his unparalleled giving he creates a kind of debt. Wealhtheow also seizes the occasion, fulfilling her role as queen but doing more than is customary (characters in *Beowulf* do not just fulfil social roles: they manipulate and expand those roles as well). This aggressive, gold-adorned queen (suggesting the might of Valkyries)[11] counters Hrothgar's offer. And Beowulf, although silent during the banquet scene, apparently understands the significance of gestures. He ignores the adoption words (perhaps reflecting them only in his statement of kindred-like good will, 'est,' towards the Danes and Hrothgar and in his eventual offer of a continuing alliance between the famous Danes and the powerful Geats); but he reaffirms his proper relationship later when he returns to Hygelac. He clears himself of any suspicion that he may have compromised himself in performing a *continuing* service (one fight after another) for Hrothgar and in accepting what we learn are dynastic gifts. He did not become Hrothgar's sworn retainer after either banquet scene in Heorot. In short, gift giving is always 'embedded in social relations'; acts of giving and receiving, or not doing so, can either reaffirm or change, and even change drastically given the desires, fears, and motives of the participants.[12]

Commentators have long noted the commonplace functions of gift giving in *Beowulf*. Gift giving, as we have already stated, establishes an important, continuing reciprocity: gifts, trust, and honour on the lord's part for service, honour, and loyalty on the retainer's part. Moreover, the lord's generosity may indicate either the value of services performed or the quality of service looked for. For example, we might expect something special from Wiglaf because, as we discover, his father has given him a special sword, Beowulf has given him a legal and rich share of Wægmunding land, and later Beowulf seems to pass on a kind of leadership in giving Wiglaf his necklace, helmet, and corselet.[13]

Once begun, exchange cannot easily end, short of war. The peoples in *Beowulf* are often in a warlike state characterized by periodic raiding, if not actually in full-scale war with each other, when they withhold reciprocal favour. The Franks and Frisians have this relationship to the Geats (ll. 2920b–2921): 'Us wæs a syððan / Merewioingas milts ungyfeðe' 'ever since has the generosity of the Merovingians been withheld from us' has 'milts' denoting the possibility of reciprocity between powerful equals in this case and 'syððan' indicating that before Hygelac's raid that possibility was greater than in the fifty years since.[14] Only fear of Beowulf's war prowess has kept the Franks from raiding the Geats (Beowulf served Hygelac well by avenging his death on the bodies of thirty Frankish warriors, thus destroying Dæghrefn and probably Dæghrefn's personal retinue).

The lord gives rings, weapons, or armour in anticipation of promised services; he then rewards or repays service by gifts, through which he again, while honouring his retainers, places them in a temporary debt and affirms the heroic contract between himself and them.[15] More than a bond, that affirmation underlines an entire system of reciprocal relationships between equals and unequals, with some relationships being more stable than others. But continuing exchange relations between groups also seem to involve temporary inequalities; where accounts are even, and where grievances may still remain, the bond formed through exchange will be weak and the force of grievance perhaps too strong, at least in the short run, for the relationship to continue. In a sense the grievance could be seen as buying out the relationship where there is no temporary inequality (and therefore dependence) between the two parties.[16] Perhaps this or something like it occurs in that proposed marriage alliance between Danes and Heathobards, previously feuding parties – a bond that is initially fragile. Beowulf's words imply as much: 'Oft seldan hwær / æfter leodhryre lytle hwile / bongar bugeð, þeah seo bryd duge' (ll. 2029b–2031), which I render as: 'Seldom, for the short run, does the deadly spear bend or rest after the slaughter of a prince, no matter how good the bride.' (Most editors take 'lytle hwile' to mean that deadly spears do not rest for long.) We can think that by marrying his daughter to Ingeld, Hrothgar hopes to settle his portion of deadly slaughter between Danes and Heathobards, but not enough time will elapse for continuing reciprocity and its temporary asymmetries to be established here. Nor does one party pay tribute to the other (unlike some of the people Scyld Scefing long ago subjugated).

The same observations might apply to the treaty between Hengest and Finn in the Finn episode. Oaths were sworn and absolute equality established between both sides ('ac hig him geþingo budon, / þæt hie him oðer flet eal gerymdon, / healle ond heahsetl, þæt hie healfre geweald / wið Eotena bearn agan moston' 'but they to them offered a peace meeting, a truce / such that they would clear for them another floor / a hall and high seat, that they each should rule half / with the sons of Giants, be allowed to possess the hall,' ll. 1085b–1088). This equality especially includes Finn's gift giving (he would treat his former enemies exactly as he would his own retainers), but the peace does not outlast the spring because neither party depends upon the other and Hengest's grief is so bitter. We need to attend closely to these matters in the poem, and not take one set of relationships or dangers for all, lumping everything under some rubric such as 'the heroic code' and arguing that this 'code' is either internally flawed or simply too narrow to accommodate stable relations between sometimes warring groups.[17]

Beowulf's wisdom concerning Freawaru as a peace-kin reflects his mature sense of good, firm relationships between peoples: indeed, the poem's ideal group-to-group relationship is the one Beowulf establishes between the Geats and the Danes, beginning with his words of alliance as he prepares to leave Hrothgar's presence.[18] He says that the Geats have been properly honoured, attended to, and well praised: 'Wæron her tela, / willum bewenede; þu us wel dohtest' (ll. 1820b–1821). Implicitly this has been done nobly and on such a scale that Beowulf offers a continuing readiness in return (although not the relationship Hrothgar tries to get). If Beowulf hears that he might gain yet more of Hrothgar's affection than he already has, he will soon be ready to gain that affection militarily. Moreover, if he hears that neighbouring peoples are threatening terror against the Danes, as they have done in the past, then he will come with a thousand warriors. Beowulf is sure that Hygelac will approve of this form of honouring and supporting Hrothgar – this bearing of a forest of spears should Hrothgar have need of men. This is a firm friendship that Beowulf offers – a martial and legislative one against the advent of terror; a continuing relationship such that Hrothgar's son, Hrethric, may come to the Geats and find many friends (distant lands are well sought by he who honours himself, 'þæm þe him selfa deah,' l. 1839b). By this action, Beowulf does well, although who can prevent future strife? Moreover, his gnome complements his earlier remarks about it being better to avenge the death of a friend than to mourn much. Here 'dugan' has reciprocal connotations: the Geats were well honoured in Heorot ('þu us wel dohtest') and so the Danes honoured themselves; thus the young Hrethric can be the continuing link between Danes and Geats in this relationship of exchange.

Hrothgar responds by extolling Beowulf's wisdom – a greater wisdom he has never heard from so young a warrior in speech making and counsel.[19] Hrothgar is sure that if grim battle should take Hygelac, the Geats could choose no one better than Beowulf, if Beowulf wished to rule the kingdom; Beowulf has a most pleasing mind and character, shown by the mutuality of shared peace between Geats and Danes ('sib gemæne, l. 1857a) that he has brought about. This peace has put past strife to rest and will involve continuing exchange of treasures, gifts, and tokens of esteem for as long as Hrothgar rules the wide kingdom. This political happiness between the two peoples receives a generalized phrasing from Hrothgar: 'Ic þa leode wat / ge wið feond ge wið freond fæste geworhte, / æghwæs untæle ealde wisan (ll. 1863b–1865). Hrothgar, having clearly abandoned his effort to adopt and thus recruit Beowulf, will nevertheless do his part in this greater and more complex arrangement, entrusting that relationship to the force of well-known, ancient custom governing firm postures toward friends as well as foes. This is a perfectly good relationship between peoples who have exchanged enmities in the past.

Unlike the short-lived bond between Danes and Heathobards, the Geat-Dane alliance is, for as long as Hrothgar lives and for as long as people observe the old customs, firm and good. Moreover, it is so because of Danish dependency upon Geatish military might. The poet no doubt understands this very well; thus we can review all of his observations on relationships between peoples and construct an implicit definition of the good: open warfare and terrible slaughter are malicious; battle prowess that ends active hostilities but not the possibility of periodic strife is acceptable, although worrisome, if the war-band leader dies; the subduing of neighbouring peoples and the establishing of tribute relationships is good; the annihilation of a terror-making group is a definitive good; the marriage bond between groups is noble but fragile in the short run, and even if affines become consanguineous in the next generation (as happens between Half-Danes and Frisians), the bond may still fall victim to disaster; the peace bonds and friendships manifested by continuing exchange between unequal peoples are best.

In those contexts, it is not mutability or revenge violence or sudden change that the poet eventually laments: he laments the end of exchange, stability, order, and joy among peoples. Indeed, his passages concerning resurgent strife strike me as parts of a meditation on just how order can be established and made to endure – the first note of which would then be the early, slice-of-time reference to Heorot and in-law strife. This reference has too often automatically been taken as reflecting a critique of revenge or else as sounding the first notes of an apocalyptic view of the heroic world. Within a few hundred lines of Beowulf's return to Hygelac, the poet will give us the so-called 'lament of the last survivor,' stating that the giving up of life is a giving up of joys in the hall, that centre of reciprocity, martial loyalty, splendour, song, and delightful motion. The end of these is lamented because they are desired as good in themselves and as continuing arrangements.

Marcel Mauss has given us a global view of exchange in archaic societies. With this we can invest the system of gift exchange and gifts for services in *Beowulf* and other Germanic texts with an anthropological reality. Similar systems exist in modern societies. Furthermore, Mauss briefly reviews Germanic societies, asserting that ancient Germanic systems of gift exchange, despite slim evidence, appear to be typical. This is borne out by Vilhelm Grønbech, who has enlarged our sense of Germanic gift exchange as a bond for and a concomitant of friendship.[20] Germanic exchange could approach 'potlatch,' a premonetary system of exchange between families and between groups in which one must give, receive, and return gifts. The system is competitive and there is an obligation to return the gift, although not necessarily right away or in equal kind (especially within large families with many dependency relationships).

If service is involved, a reward may end one round of exchange, as it does when Hrothgar rewards Beowulf, but continuing exchange between Danes and Geats obviously does not end (although it might have if Beowulf had simply accepted his treasures and gone home). But aristocratic exchange is something that neither Marcel Mauss nor Vilhelm Grønbech focuses on in his review of ancient Germanic exchange. Both rely heavily on the *Hávamál*, and neither examines the scenes of gift giving in *Beowulf*. This is a pity because, had Mauss done so, he might have concluded that more than a few traces of Germanic gift giving survive and he might have expanded his sense of the social purposes Germanic gift giving can serve.

The *Hávamál* is an invaluable source for Germanic attitudes toward the gift. It focuses on gift giving between equals, essentially between folk and friends. Friendship requires an exchange of gifts, which forms the bond for a relationship – the identification of friend to friend. A gift always looks for a return.[21] The advice here is general, even gnomic in its formulation (although some of it is manipulative). Doubtless it would resonate well in any Germanic context. However, it is neither particularly Anglo-Saxon nor aristocratic. As evident in different themes woven through and around gifts, Germanic literature does not exploit the gift all in the same way; different cultures and different audiences must have responded to different aspects of gift giving and the gift. Old Icelandic poetry, for example, often focuses on the darkly portentous or tainted gift (especially in the Sigurth cycle) and on sardonic liberality (as in the Atli cycle showing Gudrun's liberality with both her husband's treasury and the lives of his sons).

When commenting on gifts, the Old English *Maxims I* and *II* focus on aristocratic liberality as an unalloyed good, a necessary and proper state of things.[22]Elsewhere, munificence in a king is also praiseworthy – whether the king is important for his humility (in Bede) or for his patronage (in *Widsith*).[23] Exchange between unequals, as a good and wonderful affair testifying to the inferior's deserts, is something approved of in *Widsith*, as is the liberality of gold-adorned queens. We can concluded that liberality is good and natural, the heart of noble behaviour in the hall. Through liberality kings and queens confirm their worthiness, establish the *comitatus*, and support their kin. Against that background, gift giving in *Beowulf* comes into particular focus, both for its commonplace and its unusual features.

The giver's intentions appear either in the nature of the object given or in the effect attributable to the giving. Marcel Mauss notes the former for all archaic exchanges whereas the *Beowulf* poet clarifies the latter.[24] The first mention of gift giving occurs in the Exordium, in a hortatory passage. It establishes a familiar function for giving: a young warrior does well, the poet says, by a 'splendid' dispensing of treasure ('fromum feohgiftum,' l. 21a) so that later on when war comes dear retainers in turn will stay with him. His generosity has a purpose: 'I give so that you will stand by me in time of war.' The effect of giving reveals the purpose. Therefore, the functional meaning of 'fromum feohgiftum' is not 'splendid' dispensing of treasure – that, essentially, is an editorial comment – but a 'martial' one (from 'from,' meaning 'strenuous,' 'bold,' 'brave').

The next mention of gift giving concerns Hrothgar's munificence. He would share ('gedælan') all that God gave him among young and old alike (excluding the people's land and the lives of men). His sharing, however, will occur in a great hall, which he will build. Hrothgar's munificence, then, complements the dynastic fame of the great hall and justifies it. Here we can see sharing as the consummate gesture of one possessing power, honour, and fame, someone who has achieved success and glory in battle – indeed the fourth to have done so in a noble, agnatic line (Hrothgar directly succeeds his brother). His reciprocal gesture is in kind with his appropriate sense of dynasty and of having been given prosperity and greatness. It is also munificence that redounds upon the stature of the giver. Thus Hrothgar's gestures say, in part, that he shares because glory has been given to him; he shares because he can. Hrothgar's fulfilment of his promise to share and then his distribution of rings and treasure during banquets mark him as the quintessential juridical king in the poem – famous for his war-stature and his liberality. Beowulf will be an even greater king because he has greater prowess physically. This distinction in no way makes Hrothgar's helplessness in the Grendel affair an ironic development at Hrothgar's or the Danes' expense (the usual way of seeing Hrothgar's inactivity in relation to Beowulf's purposefulness).[25]

To call the Danes 'valiant Scyldings' is not ironic because Hrothgar's retainers do try repeatedly and fail bloodily against Grendel. Moreover, comments based on Danish helplessness against Grendel miss the mythological difference between sovereigns – some are more fierce than juridical and some are more juridical than fierce. Consistently in *Beowulf* Hrothgar is highly honoured for being juridical, liberal, and famous for that as well as for his past deeds in battle. At the time of building, Heorot reflects Hrothgar's dual greatness. Grendel brings bloody and unlooked-for reversal of only half that greatness, although the Spear-Danes are powerful and sharp-sighted enough to avoid attacks by neighbouring peoples and to challenge Beowulf upon his arrival. It is as a wise, famous giver of treasure and as formal guardian of his people and of all good customs that Hrothgar is a great king when Beowulf approaches Heorot seeking permission to meet Grendel. Establishing Hrothgar's fame and greatness in terms of hall-life is the poet's main purpose when telling us of Hrothgar's exchange of everything good in the hall.

The instances noted above, however, remain simple when compared to dramatic gift giving. The poet then does more than enumerate gifts or describe general activity. He reports on the particular gifts, describes them and the manner of giving, and reports the words spoken. When all of that happens, we should expect that more is at stake than we had believed before. The heroic scenes of gift giving are not just ethically or socially good or even prestige-enhancing primarily. They contain special acts controlled by special purposes.[26] Moreover, the dramatized scenes of giving are all related. This indicates that special acts of giving can acquire a narrative interest extending over a thousand lines or more – an interest that clearly subsumes the monster fights in the poet's attention to his narrative. That extension, as we shall see, also testifies to the portentousness of Hrothgar's generosity.

The prelude to Hrothgar's giving of magnificent treasures is important for our understanding of what he does. After Wulfgar announces Beowulf's arrival, Hrothgar says he will 'offer,' 'tender,' or give treasures ('madmas beodan') to that good one for his 'modþræce' (l. 385a), for Beowulf's impetuous courage. He will do that because 'halig god,' out of a kindness or favour ('arstafas') requiring reciprocity, has given him cause for hope against Grendel. Hrothgar cannot give gifts to God but he can and must reward the warrior God sends. This comes after mention of gifts ('gifsceattas,' 'gift-treasures,' probably tribute) already moving from Geats to Danes (ll. 378–379a), thus anticipating a fuller mutuality later, should Beowulf's help prevail against Grendel.

Earlier Hrothgar mentions Beowulf's father, Ecgtheow, and speaks of knowing Beowulf, the boy. Mention of the father mainly establishes Beowulf's noble identity and perhaps implies that Beowulf brings a noble courage to the gracious Hrothgar, a courage that Hrothgar can reward if he gets help against Grendel. Presumably he will encourage Beowulf should he announce a willingness to fight Grendel. Hrothgar seems to expand his intentions by expanding the largesse of his promises of reward. The giving he enacts eventually is a 'feohgyft' (l. 1025) – that martial dispensing of treasures which the poet says, in the Exordium, Beow performed. Thus Hrothgar's initial intentions may have been to arrange for martial support only, within a tributary reciprocity – a service, a counter-gift, and that is all. But 'feohgyft' in the Exordium suggests an ongoing reciprocity, while elsewhere, in the Finn episode, it is part of the arrangement binding both parties to each other. Would Hrothgar especially bind Beowulf in some way, especially include him in his *comitatus*? Although initially Hrothgar's promises are vague, it seems he would sound Beowulf's character and intentions before committing himself to particular rewards; eventually he appears to invite Beowulf into his warband as both an honoured retainer and a possible successor.

As indicated by Hrothgar's behaviour in Heorot, he can share almost anything desirable or good, especially if that sharing completes a great act. Building Heorot is one such act; purging it is another – one that will spur Hrothgar to an extraordinary generosity. Does that generosity include an implicit offer of the kingship? Can Hrothgar in effect give the kingdom away by appointing a successor? I think the great banquet scene indicates that Hrothgar can. In what we may read as an attempt to tie Beowulf to himself, Hrothgar first spiritually adopts Beowulf and then seems to offer the right of succession. If this is so, we will see that gift giving can involve quite different intentions when anticipated and when enacted. Intervening events can bring the giver to revise his intentions dramatically.

The great banquet scene is a victory celebration, a feast of song and gift giving. In his narration the poet includes an account of the treasures Hrothgar gives Beowulf and closes with Wealhtheow's speech to Beowulf. Usually readers understand that scene as a complex affair beginning with grand gestures of reward and ending with the poignancy of Wealhtheow's supposedly futile peace weaving. Commentators also stress the uncertain duration of hall-joy among kinsmen, recalled for us through the Finn digression. But such connections overlook the bitterness of 'hall-joy' in the Finn digression to begin with and do not pay sufficient attention to the poet's comments on the unparalleled qualities of the banquet, to the particular gifts given and what they might signify, and to Wealhtheow's concern to address first Hrothgar and then Beowulf, ending with her famous lines about warriors true to each other doing as she commands.[27]

Obviously Hrothgar keeps his promises of reward after Beowulf's great purgation of Heorot. Moreover, he would express his gratitude and honour this superlative warrior. But his purposes have broadened, encompassing more now than he intended initially. Beowulf has become especially dear through his behaviour in Heorot, his victory over Grendel, and his ethical demeanour in general. Therefore Hrothgar would take this best of warriors as a son. He does this before the treasure giving:

Nu ic, Beowulf, þec,
secg betsta, me for sunu wylle
freogan on ferhþe; heald forð tela
niwe sibbe. Ne bið þe [n]ænigre gad
worlde wilna, þe ic geweald hæbbe. (ll. 946b–50)

Now I, Beowulf, thou best of men, unto me desire to love in mind and heart as a son; henceforth hold properly this new kinship. You will lack nothing of the world's desirable things over which I have power.

Hrothgar has pronounced Beowulf's achievement as unparalleled – an achievement he attributes to God's power, and which he admits exceeds any deed the Danes had the skill or wit to perform. He has also said that Beowulf's mother was blest in Beowulf's birth: God the Old Governor or Rules ('ealdmetod') showed favour towards her in her child bearing. The thought of Beowulf's mother may have led Hrothgar to offer himself as a 'father.' If she were blest in the birth of a son become mighty beyond all warriors, Hrothgar must feel blest now in Beowulf's presence. He has given effusive thanks to God for the sight of Grendel's hand, and he has praised God, the Guardian of Glory – may He always work wonder after wonder. In his ecstasy, Hrothgar feels the glory of the moment and of his own incredible good fortune. He is piously thankful and he would (good jural king and protector of his people that he is) appropriate the human agent of it all by extending a spiritual paternity to Beowulf. He would love Beowulf, perhaps feeling as God blest as he imagines Beowulf's mother must have been. But he means this as more than a figure of speech and more than a momentary effusion: 'heald forð tela / niwe sibbe' 'henceforth hold properly this new kinship.'

He hopes this new kinship – 'sibb' in the poem is more like a compact, a tie of peace, friendship, and support – will be mutual. Indeed, he commands its mutuality. In return for holding well this new compact of kinship, Beowulf will lack nothing in Hrothgar's power to give. (That a 'sibb' might not be held well is clear when we look at Beowulf's cowardly retainers, ll. 2600–1, who flee to the woods, putting aside their 'sibb' with Beowulf.) If Beowulf does as Hrothgar hopes, what will follow? Hrothgar says he would not withhold any good thing of the world, anything at all in his power to grant. His verb is 'gewealdan' ('control,' 'wield'), and I think implicitly he differentiates it from the normal purview of reward: 'Ful oft ic for læssan lean teohhode' (l. 951 – 'often I assigned reward for less'). Indeed, simple reward is not enough by all past measures. And when repayment becomes a function attributed to God – 'Alwalda þec / gode forgylde, swa he nu gyt dyde!' (ll. 955b–956) – it is out of Hrothgar's hands entirely (the All-Ruler has rewarded Beowulf's good exercise of strength with victory; may He always do so). No, mere repayment cannot do justice to Beowulf's deed or to Hrothgar's desire.

If 'king' etymologically suggests 'kin-right,' then Hrothgar proceeds properly in making the gesture I think he makes, that is, implicitly offering the right of succession to Beowulf.[28] Through adoption, Hrothgar first raises Beowulf before all the Danes to something like kindred status (son) and then he commands that Beowulf hold well this new compact of peace and support. Beowulf has already demonstrated throne worthiness, evident in God's favour and in his own, noble prowess. In looking to Beowulf, Hrothgar can satisfy the criterion of martial suitability and ethical commitment; having adopted Beowulf in some sense, he can satisfy the demands of kinship. Moreover, youth makes his own sons by Wealhtheow unsuitable. Of course the offer of the succession to Beowulf is not election in itself. Beowulf must first agree and then the 'witan' and the folk must 'choose' him or approve of him in some way – or so it seems.[29]

We do know, from the poem itself, that a direct offer of the kingship can come by way of an offer of the communal hoard and gift-seat or throne; Hygd makes this bold offer to Beowulf when Hygelac dies. Beowulf is a kinsman (Hygelac's sister's son) and a subking himself, having been given vast lands, a gift-seat of his own, and even old king Hrethel's heirloom, the finest sword in the Geat treasury. But what about the possibility of an indirect offer – one that exists if openly acknowledged, but not if ignored? I think the poet calls attention to just such an offer, initially by way of backhanded statements, and finally by revealing the dynastic history of Hrothgar's gifts.

Hrothgar gives Beowulf a splendid battle-standard, a helmet, a corselet, and a renowned sword – all gold-adorned. Gifts of horses and Hrothgar's war-seat follow those kingly gifts. The first four are among the most precious gifts the poet has heard of. Indeed, he has never heard of four, gold-adorned treasures given in a more friendly fashion to a warrior ('freondlicor' and 'for sc[e]onten[d]um'), who need not in any way feel ashamed of them.[30] 'Friendship' in *Beowulf* usually has the connotation of reciprocal support, of a pact or compact between allies (as in Geatish support of the Danes or Beowulf's support of Eadgils against Onela), and of good will between kinsmen. It is with reciprocal kindness and 'ar' that Beowulf counsels ('freondlar') and supports Heardred, rather than accepting the kingship himself, and Beowulf's time in Heorot is still a time of accord among all of the Danes. (l. 1018). Thus friendship is a close tie, a bond that can even have legal implications.

In narrating the initial phase of the banquet, the poet uses two 'I have never heard' constructions. Doubtless he wants to emphasize the unparalleled splendour of the event, its conviviality, and its wealth. One construction concerns the amiable behaviour of the company, and the other concerns Hrothgar's gift giving. Why especially should one note its friendliness? Surely other kings have given equally expensive gifts. In the moment before us, however, the poet emphasizes the worth of the sword and the unsurpassed friendliness of Hrothgar's gestures. More seems meant than a simple notation about good cheer or a conjuring up of past grandeur. The famous prince so generously rewards Beowulf, the poet insists, that no man will ever find fault with Hrothgar's gifts – certainly not anyone who speaks truth according to what is right. These rather broad, if oblique, remarks seem to hint at something. Indeed, why should Beowulf even think that this gift giving might fall short somehow, given Hrothgar's great fame for generosity. Why should we? Shall we say, then, that the poet suggests such magnificence, both in those gifts and in the giver's intentions, that Hrothgar's gesture transcends all possibility of shame or fault and that, just the converse, Hrothgar offers the greatest honour imaginable? The poet remains broadly suggestive only but his backhanded suggestiveness becomes especially notable when we look forward and see that here he withholds identifying information about the treasures. The effect is an accord between Hrothgar's indirection and his – a nice correspondence between the gesture dramatized and his own narrative manner.

Hrothgar gives kingly objects. His treasures are heirlooms but, more than that, they are probably dynastic treasures (see the later reference to Heorogar's corselet in l. 2158, for 'yrfelaf' or 'heirloom' applies in general to gifts given to the Geats). At the least Hrothgar gives items from his personal treasure chest, signifying both his warrior heritage and his past role as kingly war-band leader. By passing on those tokens to Beowulf, Hrothgar invites Beowulf to those roles for the Danes. But because he is a king and the last of a line in his own generation, he implicates the dynastic succession when he gives dynastic gifts. He does not give Beowulf the high-seat because that would require abdication and exceed the act of choosing a successor. And if, as in Anglo-Saxon laws, 'freond' denotes legal responsibility, then Hrothgar also takes full responsibility for his implicit offer. That a king is so friendly is cause for thought.

Having given gifts, Hrothgar commands that Beowulf use them well. Beowulf uses the same injunction when passing on his armour and war-band leadership to Wiglaf. He also uses it when giving Hrothgar's gifts to Hygelac, after indicating the royal, dynastic character of those gifts.[31] The reference in l. 2155a to Heorogar's 'war-dress' includes the sword, helmet, corselet, and banner. Heorogar is the king and brother Hrothgar succeeded. The poet elsewhere associates gold-adorned victory banners exclusively with dead kings. Therefore the command to 'use them well,' given its contexts in *Beowulf*, seems more than a formula accompanying all gift giving – if only because it does *not* appear in all such instances.[32] It may verbally seal Hrothgar's circumspect offer of the succession. That Beowulf uses this command for Hygelac suggests that he understands both the phrase's significance and that of the gifts. He transfers the place of honour thereby conferred to Hygelac. His use of it when speaking to Wiglaf indicates that it is a highly formal phrase accompanying the passing on of roles.

Beowulf in Heorot, however, accepts Hrothgar's gifts without comment. It is as though they signify nothing more than the proper munificence of a ring-lord good to his word and good in his gifts. Beowulf does not even acknowledge their status as part of Hrothgar's royal patrimony. In Heorot he always ignores any suggestion that he has (or will have) anything but a high-minded, favouring relationship with Hrothgar and the Danes. Throughout he insists on his kinship with and retainer relationship to Hygelac. He intends no close connection with the Danes; he came to Heorot simply out of good will and performed a daring deed, with God's assistance. Only twice does he acknowledge Hrothgar's special attentions, once indirectly and once directly: his reply to Hrothgar's adoption speech includes the phrase, 'estum miclum' (l. 958b), a reciprocal term of good will usually associated with kinship (cf. ll. 2149a, 2165b, 2378a); before meeting Grendel's mother he asks that Hrothgar act in a father's place toward him and protect his retainers in the event of Beowulf's death. Beowulf would acknowledge Hrothgar's gestures to that extent and in that extremity only. He never acknowledges a closer tie than that of friendly fosterage regarding Hrothgar and a friendship pact regarding the Danes generally, although in his offer of a continuing alliance he does balance possible future service against the great weight of Hrothgar's gifts. In Heorot during the banquet scene, in both his speech and his silence, Beowulf effectively defends himself by reducing Hrothgar's gesture to the prestige objects themselves, largely acknowledging only those.

But lest we suppose that Beowulf's later account of Heorogar's war-dress is a fortuitous invention, and that the poet means nothing special by his odd remarks or by the particular treasures given, we must consider Wealhtheow's words. Essentially she underlines the significance of Hrothgar's gestures; first she worries about the adoption and Hrothgar's intentions and then she turns graciously to Beowulf with gifts and words. Her gifts given in good will ('est') indicate that she approaches Beowulf approvingly but outside *comitatus* reciprocity – let him be like family, but not designated war-band leader and successor. In her speech, moreover, she would define clearly his best relationship to the Danes generally and to her sons in particular. Her speech to Hrothgar discreetly focuses first on gifts and then on the adoption. Because she would urge Hrothgar not to give Beowulf the kingdom, she avoids reference to the nature of the gifts – as though to undo the invitation. As Irving notes, there is an element of incantation in her speeches. Wealhtheow worries about the here and now, not about a possibly treacherous future supposedly involving Hrothulf.[33]

We can understand Wealhtheow as urging Hrothgar not to give away what, strictly considered, is not his to give as dispenser of treasures and gold-lord of warriors – his patrimony, his kingdom, and rule of his people. To give those away would involve another function, the power to choose a successor.[34] She would not have Heorot now become a meeting place for the choosing of a successor. It should remain simply a bright ring-hall, in which Hrothgar distributes tribute from surrounding peoples.

Wealhtheow turns to Hrothgar and urges him to take the 'ful' she offers. If he drinks to the things she urges, which include being liberal with his gifts and kind in a kinship-like way to the Geats, he will be committed to acting as a noble, friendly distributor of treasure only. So shall a man do! Her deep support of Hrothgar's juridical role in the hall is unqualified so far. But a man has said – and this is stronger than hearsay – that he would have the Geat warrior for a son. This worries her. She strongly disapproves. She notes that Heorot is purged, the ring-hall bright. But instead of giving away 'folc' and kingdom out of his great gratitude and perhaps in an effort to absorb Beowulf into his *comitatus*, Hrothgar should move on. After all, Heorot is now purged. He should use his many rewards, enjoy them, and leave 'folc and rice' to his own kinsmen when the time comes for him to go forth to see the decree of fate. She would radically reinterpret what Hrothgar's response to the purging of Heorot should be.

Wealhtheow is so strong-minded about this that she goes on to offer Hrothulf as a candidate in preference to Beowulf. She knows that her sons by Hrothgar are still young but she asserts that the gracious Hrothulf will hold young warriors in reciprocal honour ('ar'), thus keeping the war-troop intact. She expects (a stressed, imperative 'wene,' l. 1184) Hrothulf to repay her children with Hrothgar all that she and Hrothgar showed in honouring and glorifying him during his childhood – if he is mindful of all that they have done for him. Her tone here is one of command and emphasis, of instruction even; it is not something fragile, like a brave hope or wish. In effect, as a superior voice, at that very moment, she will offer the publicly instructed and prodded Hrothulf as a successor, vigorously reminding him of his reciprocal duties.

She then turns to Beowulf. Apparently Hrothgar has drunk in her words. Now it is Beowulf's turn but words will not be enough. To compete with Hrothgar's gift-laden offer, and thus assert both her status and Beowulf's, she must express herself with gifts. This she does by bringing Beowulf arm-rings, other rings, a corselet, and the greatest necklace the poet has heard of since Hama carried away the Brosing's necklace.[35] Beowulf accepts her 'ful' and listens to her words, which urge him to enjoy his rings, much as she urged Hrothgar to enjoy his many rewards. Moreover, Beowulf should make use of the people's treasure (displacing Hrothgar's dynastic ones) and prosper well. He should declare his strength and craft not by accepting Hrothgar's offer but by being of gentle counsel towards her young boys, between whom Beowulf sits (an odd place for an honoured and mighty warrior). She will reward him for his good counsel, thus establishing a direct relationship outside of the *comitatus* and the lord-retainer hierarchy. She does not ask Beowulf to counsel her boys in terms that invoke *comitatus* reciprocity; instead she uses 'liðe' and 'gedefe,' terms that concern kinship-like feeling, courtesy, and that which is fitting. Thus she does not invite Beowulf to take a superior, protective relationship to boys who are nascent retainers.

Having offered a continuing arrangement, she now urges Beowulf to flourish, wishing him the luck of the gods, 'hæl,' and implying that what he has already accomplished (a feat attracting world-wide praise) should be enough. It is possible for him to behave in a way that would tarnish his fame and glory (and possibly provoke enmity). He should act fittingly and properly towards her son(s) and hold them in joy. Now come her most famous words:

> Her is æghwylc eorl oþrum getrywe,
> modes milde, mandrihtne hol[d],

þegnas syndon geþwære, þeod ealgearo,
druncne dryhtguman doð swa ic bidde. (ll. 1228–31)

Here each warrior is true to the other, generous of mind, loyal to their lord, thanes are united in kindness, the people ever-ready, drink-solemn warbandsmen do as I ask.

Some of the qualities she notes as binding one man to another, and all to Hrothgar their 'mondryhten,' are ethical qualities central to reciprocity within the *comitatus*. D.H. Green, in a strangely neglected work of masterful scholarship, has indicated both the relative antiquity and the vertical reciprocity of terms such as 'milde,' 'hold,' and 'trywe' drawn from that vocabulary. The case for reciprocity is stronger for 'hold' and 'trywe' than for 'milde' ('kind,' 'generous'). However, Green cites this passage in *Beowulf* and sees the relationships proposed as both reciprocal and horizontal on the one hand and vertical on the other: the earls are 'trwye' and 'milde' towards each other and 'hold' towards Hrothgar.[36] That at least is as Wealhtheow would have it. Because 'trwye' and 'milde' often denote a vertical relationship, Wealhtheow's use of them in a horizontal connection indicates a special gesture: she would especially bind each warrior to all others, including Beowulf, in a horizontal reciprocity in which kindness and good favour would be returned in kind. And she would separate everyone from the king, though all are bound to him by a vertical reciprocity. She would have Beowulf remain a much honoured retainer among retainers, in a system of relationships that emphasizes an unusually horizontal reciprocity. She would not have some warriors set above others.

Following her declarative speech, she walks to her seat. No reply is given but everyone begins drinking, which is to say that they agree to what she has pronounced. Her speech does not ask for any response other than drink-serious assent.[37] Had Beowulf responded in speech he would have had to state a new intention or else suspiciously deny thoughts of assuming war-band leadership and right of succession among the Danes. By his silence, and presumably by joining in the renewed drinking, Beowulf remains unimpeachably loyal to Hygelac and nobly in accord with Wealhtheow's arrangements. That he later especially invites Hrethric to visit the Geats, where Hrethric will find only friends, suggests a diplomatic return for the weight of Wealhtheow's prestation, as well as Hrothgar's (the

Geats have been treated well; Hrethric will honour himself by visiting the Geats, who will treat him well ['dugan']). And what Beowulf says in Hygelac's hall confirms that he understands the implications of the gifts Hrothgar has given him. That is clear from the distorted account he gives of banqueting and gift giving in Heorot, an account in which there is more diplomacy than mere recapitulation.

Beowulf arrives home in the glory of his deeds and in the splendour of his plated gold but he emphasizes his utter loyalty to Hygelac. He only went to the West Danes and Hrothgar to settle the feud against Grendel. That he continues to help the Danes, first avenging Grendel's crimes and then avenging Æschere's death, could mean that in some way he has become Hrothgar's man (as his father did before him) or else he has broken off a continuing exchange and created a state of war. Beowulf continually forestalls such thinking, however.[38]

First he speaks of the fierce meeting with Grendel, a well-known meeting, not a secret one, and explains how he avenged the long-lasting misery of the Victory-Scyldings. Everything is in the open and definitive so far. He then stresses the conviviality of great celebration in the hall, especially the numbers of warriors and the liberality of Hrothgar's famous queen. He mentions Freawaru and then digresses into his doubts about the stability of Hrothgar's intended arrangement between Danes and Heathobards (with Freawaru as the peace-bride). This shifts attention away from Beowulf's service in Heorot and suggests his worldly, even juridical grasp of things (he has done nothing naïve or contrary to Hygelac's sense of obligation and good custom) as well as the likelihood that Geats and Danes, unlike Heathobards and Danes, are linked in a firm friendship (cf. 'freondscipe fæstne,' l. 2069a).

Returning to his activities in Heorot, Beowulf tells of Grendel's direct approach, summarizes Grendel's flight, recalls the celebrations and the giving of rewards, and then brings up the mother's attack and her seizure of Æschere so that there was not even a body for the funeral pyre. This was a most bitter ordeal for Hrothgar, who, Beowulf says, sorrowfully implored Beowulf, by Hygelac's life, to seek the mother and perform a heroic deed – for which he promised rewards. Thus Beowulf accounts for the fact of continuing service, deferring it all to Hygelac's name. How, then, when implored in Hygelac's name, could he refuse? The mention of rewards promised is not gratuitous; it suggests a public contract that would end further obligation without foreclosing further relationship. Hrothgar, Beowulf says, was good in his customs (good by his promises) but as far as Beowulf's loyalty goes, everything still depends upon Hygelac's kindness.

In addition, Beowulf transposes details from the two banquet scenes, perhaps to render his relationship to Hrothgar as innocent as possible. Instead of speaking about his seat with Hrothgar's sons as given after the Grendel fight, he speaks of it as given when Hrothgar first learns of Beowulf's purpose. He moves Hrothgar's melancholy moods up to the first victory celebration. He says that by avenging Grendel's crimes, he did honour to Hygelac's people. When Beowulf introduces the treasure, he says that it was given to him after each fight, for his own use at his discretion (his own judgment, 'dom') as though to indicate that none of it ties him to Hrothgar (in effect the gifts are alienated). Also he emphasizes treasure given to him on each occasion almost equally, thus minimizing the first occasion and making it unclear just what was given when.

He culminates his show of good will by bringing all of the magnificent treasure to Hygelac, stating his complete dependence still on Hygelac's kindness. Beowulf's deportment here is the personal, hall-centred complement to the friendship he established between Danes and Geats: dependence makes each relationship an achieved ideal of peace and loyalty, of kindred feeling and trust.

According to his recounting of Hrothgar's gift giving, it is not clear that the four greatest treasures were given at once. Perhaps Beowulf wishes to appear as having selected from his many treasures the very best, the most kingly to give first. But, interestingly, he has them brought in in exactly the same order they were given to him and the poet elaborates upon them in tell-tale ways. Such care would not be necessary if Beowulf were not aware of their purport. They were originally presented to him as follows: the boar-adorned battle standard, suggesting that Beowulf take up the standard as kingly war-band leader; then the high helmet, the corselet, and the sword. Despite his minimizing account of the first giving of treasure in Heorot, Beowulf may still feel the pull of those gifts; he may still be taking care to undo any obligation they might carry – hence the precise order in which he has them presented to Hygelac may be important. Beowulf also says that Hrothgar told him to tell the ancestry of 'this war-gear' (l. 2155); it belonged to Heorogar, who passed it on to Hrothgar, thereby passing over Heoroweard and marking succession in the dynasty. By reporting what did not happen, Beowulf indicates tactfully that he understands the significance of those gifts and that he would pass the honour they pose on to Hygelac. He ends with the phrase, 'use all well.' Essentially he deflects all to Hygelac, having it reflect Hygelac's glory and stature, not his own. He has, finally, behaved well – exactly as befits a kinsman and loyal retainer (the inferior in a relationship). That is what his rhetorically consummate performance and the giving of gifts to Hygelac finally tells us: Beowulf has not compromised his loyalty to Hygelac in helping the Danes and in accepting dynastic gifts. He bestows them all upon Hygelac ('geywan,' 'bestow,' not 'gifan,' 'give') as befits a loyal kinsman and retainer bringing tribute to his lord (only the superior in a relationship can *give* gifts).

The distribution, sharing, and bestowal of these treasures create something we might call a social economy of honour, worth, status, and loyalties. In return for Beowulf's gestures, and doubtless in recognition of the honour he has refused in Hrothgar's hall, Hygelac confers a comparably great honour on Beowulf by raising his status to that of a subking (with a hall and high-seat of his own), further tying Beowulf to the Geats by giving him Hrethel's splendid sword (thus implicating the succession) and giving him seven thousand hides of land (clearly a base for personal and social wealth). Later, after Hygelac's death, Hygd offers the kingdom to Beowulf. As though to underline Beowulf's special, kin-loving probity, the poet tells us that Beowulf chooses instead to champion Hygelac's son. He would not become Heardred's king any more than he would become successor to Hrothgar over Wealhtheow's son(s). Rather he holds Heardred in friendly counsel, kindness with favour ('estum mid are,' l. 2378), as befits an older kinsman and eventual subordinate.

By his various remarks, Beowulf has not so much affirmed his relationship to Hygelac as insisted on its continuing, uncompromised integrity through a series of actions that dramatize the poem's ideal of kinship and retainer loyalty. Beowulf's actions, then, constitute a third instance of unusual gift giving in *Beowulf*. When dramatized, gift giving in the poem carries several intentions at once. A giver may offer a new relationship, counter an impending offer, or clear an established relationship of possible suspicion. According to these scenes in *Beowulf*, aristocratic gift giving is a highly manipulative affair, adaptable in surprising ways to unusual circumstances: to Hrothgar's gratitude and desire, to Wealhtheow's worries and command, to Beowulf's deep probity. Gift giving is not confined to affirmation of relationships within the *comitatus*. Thus *Widsith* and the *Maxims I* and *II* do not give a misleading picture of what is proper and good: kings and queens should be generous, gifts should be returned, and services should be rewarded. But *Beowulf* fills in that picture in surprising and complex ways. In this connection it is fair now to reiterate that *Beowulf*, in part, is a drama of exchange – of violent settlement (a form of repayment) and of gift giving. Once we appreciate this, the formal speeches during hall celebrations suddenly become more than they have seemed. We begin to appreciate the poet for his skill as a subtle delineator of complex gestures, and we may glimpse something of the likely scope actual Anglo-Saxon gift giving had in aristocratic contexts – a scope that includes major differences of opinion as to the securing of future community in Heorot, but no difference between Wealhtheow and Hrothgar as to the community-forming good of reciprocal exchanges, the giving and receiving of gifts on a liberal scale.

CHAPTER FIVE

The Psychological World in *Beowulf*

In this chapter I extend the *psychoanalytical* possibilities of psychological anthropology and suggest the coherence a Freudian reading can draw out of *Beowulf*. This approach is somewhat out of favour in late twentieth-century anthropology, having been displaced by intentionalist studies of relativized cognitive and affective formations that vary greatly with the ways in which individuals in different cultures are partially formed by, interact with, and change the cultural environments into which they grow.[1] To those orientations we can add recent arguments for the total 'imbeddedness' of Freudian thought in Western contexts. Freudianism becomes either just one of several possible responses to a deeper human dilemma or else a misbegotten schema of psychic relationships either totally beside the point or else crudely impositional and reductive when we consider the psychological worlds and the ethnopsychologies (that is, the senses of personhood) of other cultures. These orientations are laudable insofar as they insist on both a context specific, social and cultural engagement with mental and emotional life in given cultures and insofar as they would wrest non-Western peoples out from under some of the patronizingly scientific pretensions fostered by the universalist claims of Freudian analysis. The people subjected to such analyses do have minds, wills, intentions, and moral understandings of considerable subtlety in their particular worlds. While objections arising from such points are reasonable, the accompanying dismissal of Freudian thought or of its relevance in any form is extreme in some cases and self-serving in others. Before looking closely at *Beowulf* in psychoanalytical terms, we should discuss Freudianism in relationship to the anthropological concept of 'personhood,' which has largely displaced an early twentieth-century tradition of psychoanalytic anthropology.[2]

Some discussions of personhood are formed through very generalized understandings of the 'individual' (perhaps a moral person rather than a willing ego) and society, in part affected by Freudian thought or else open to Freudian reflection. Fitz John Porter Poole's (1981) account of a New Guinea Highlands people, the clan-based Bimin-Kuskusmin, discusses a belief whereby semen is thought to transmit to men a 'dual spirit entity *kusem* – manifested as *finiik* and *khaapkhabuurien*' (p. 31). The 'finiik' aspect strengthens and activates agnatic blood, which in turn becomes 'the idiom of lineage identity' and carries the moral and jural aspects of personhood (the social dimensions of personhood); '*khaapkhabuurien,*' in contrast, is a general bodily substance, antithetical to the 'finiik' aspect; it usually represents 'the unpredictable and rather idiosyncratic aspects of individuals,' as it is associated with the disordered, compulsive, and wild aspects of personality. This strongly marked duality has many consequences for Bimin-Kuskusmin gender distinctions and resembles dualities of nature discoverable in the thinking of many peoples, including the Anglo-Saxons and the *Beowulf* poet (consider only the emphases on warriors and warrior-kings awakening from men and the way in which greedy desires contrast with ethical responsibilities). So why not approach these dualities in their cultural contexts psychoanalytically? Why not go deeper rather than consider this dual aspect of semen and blood an irreducible truth for the Bimin-Kuskusmin and for ourselves? Poole does not necessarily stop us from going deeper, but many others practising ethnopsychology today would.

Catherine A. Lutz (1988) disagrees with Milford Spiro's Freudian reading of aggression among the Micronesian Ifaluk. Assuming that Lutz has found weaknesses in Spiro's tools and in his applications of them, what does she gain by emphasizing Ifaluk understandings about their world over a Freudian one? Her point in part is that Spiro's explanations ignore Ifaluk distinctions between anger as an insistence on ideals and 'anger as the emotional correlate of aggression' (p. 195). This point taken, one could then explore Ifaluk ideas and behaviour with more refinement of attention. But more is wanted than subtler attention to local understandings. Those understandings are privileged as Freudianism is itself reduced to a caricature of innate drives and hydraulic operations – a caricature that Spiro's analyses might support, but which is hardly a necessary way to construe Freudian theory in its middle stages. Freud's thinking in his middle period is as much psycho-social as it is biological. He does reach for the universal in his ambitions, for some understanding of our common humanness as a species. As such his theory has potential legitimacy as an analytical tool in any psycho-social, human context, unless somehow we can show the emptiness of its constructs. Can we show that its fantastical character is a reflection of something peculiar in an educated, late Victorian, European, and American culture? But how can that be done without the construction of alternatives? How can one be sure that a given system of psycho-social dynamics is merely fabrication, with no analytical relevance to the social lives of peoples who have not invented similar 'understandings'?

One way is through a pluralism of explanations and understandings drawn from various cultures for such things as emotions and ideas of person, self, and the individual. But inevitably a stabilizing framework will appear at the non-psychological level – in this case, perhaps at a philosophical level above various psychologies or else a cross-cultural level that tries to account for every culture's psychological categories and understandings in social terms for that culture. In other words, the responsibility for coming to terms with Freudian understandings of mind, psycho-sexual dynamics, and psycho-social interactions is escaped entirely. Michelle Rosaldo (1984), as a telling example turns away from an earlier openness to Freudian contributions (1980, pp. 28–9; 268–9) and reminds us of the ways in which our concerns with individuality, emotions, and the inner self may simply be features of our own cultural problems and so of little or no use for understanding the constructs of other peoples in matters of personhood and emotional life because 'the life of feeling is an aspect of the social world in which its terms are found.'

But this conscious and social level of cognition is only one aspect. What else is there and how do we get at it and relate it to social consciousness, morality, and the formation of socially acceptable personhood? Rosaldo's rejection of Freud makes her elaboration of personhood especially important, but there seems to be some bad faith in her eventual presentations of Freudian expectations in relation to the behaviour of a Philippine people, the Ilongots. She becomes unwilling in her later work to accept Freudian thought as anything but narrowly culture-bound and thus hopelessly abstracted from pertinent contexts when focusing on the meanings emotion words have in their users' social interactions (an intensified version of emphases apparent in the 1980 study).

In that move she has much good company. Michael Jackson (1989) sketches Freudian understandings as epistemologically suspect because they can be radically improved upon by other theories of mind

– such as Reich's, Laing's, and Lacan's. This begs the question of epistemology and Western psychological theories generally (pp. 46 – 50). For Jackson, if Freudian theory has any place any more it probably should be left behind as just one of many, equally valid efforts to understand and explain 'our human struggle between yielding to the brute facticity of existence – the sense of being abandoned or thrown into a world made by others at other times – and the necessity of appropriating, addressing, and experiencing that world as something for which we are responsible, something we bring into being, something we choose' (p. 50). This issue arises from human existence itself before humans are awakened to the issue in culture-specific terms.

In a sense analysis influenced by Freudian thought can embrace aspects of this position. Its universality is appealing, as is its reaching for common ground in cross-cultural contexts. The social facts of very different cultures are placed within a universal ontological perspective, one that enables the anthropologist to be a part of another culture while also in some ways detached from it (as is so for our schematic presentations and social analyses of person, emotion, and psychological understandings in any culture). But why move to the ontological and away from theories of the psycho-social? I suspect part of the reason for this move is that otherwise Jackson's ontological perspective in particular would have to be deepened, especially in its weak sense of entanglement and contingency regarding action and responsibility–entanglement about which Freudian theory has much to say. The value of that theory is of course demonstrable only in carefully approached contexts, where analysis draws out coherence rather than imposes. The ambition of this particular chapter is to do this in relationship to the social and cultural world dramatized in *Beowulf*.

A comprehensive analysis of action, form, and style would tax the adequacy of even a book-length approach. However, by suggesting the coherence a Freudian study can draw out of *Beowulf* I think we can probe the 'psyche' of the heroic world dramatized in the poem in a way that relativized studies of different moral structures in different cultures cannot. The moral and the cognitive are inevitably too much a matter of, or too close to, consciousness.

In any culture, moral structures are either implicitly or explicitly clarified perceptions working in a deeper dynamic. For example, the Anglo-Saxon world in *Beowulf* has an ethnopsychology. We can look at depictions of how emotion and thought enter into one and then swell and fill one up. We can consider the several meanings of emotion words, and attend to both the narrating poet's and the characters' accounts of developments of mind, thought, and feeling (as in Hrothgar's prominent account of Heremod's change or the poet's account of Beowulf's uncustomary gloom after the dragon's raid.)[3]

Attention to such matters is important. Both the poet's and Hrothgar's accounts of sorrow and crime, for example, always oppose bad, dark feelings to truth and right social conduct – to happy personhood, in effect. But we cannot at this level of careful observation and respect understand why Heremod turns murderously greedy or why Beowulf, upon seeing the dragon-wrought destruction of his hall, should think that he has somehow provoked God, who seems fiercely offended. Nor can we understand at this level who or what Grendel is or what his intimate links to the good society he ravages may be. We cannot deal with the malicious force of his mother or the horror of the ancient dragon. The poet cannot tell us much directly. Yet perhaps the poem can, even if it is largely an oral composition. However, it will reveal nothing in this regard unless we judiciously explore its many connections and oppositions between such matters as honour, the monstrous, and generosity, looking for ontogenetic possibilities.

The poet's mode of composition cannot in itself preclude a deep psychology – any more than technique does anywhere. The issue, rather, is what counts as verbally meaningful in a text composed of formulaic elements. This question is repeatedly answered of late in ways that contradict strict construings of oral-formula in *Beowulf*, or anywhere else in Old English poetry, thus opening that poetry to aesthetic study at the verbal and even the morphological and phonemic levels.[4] Psychoanalytical reflection is a part of aesthetics in that it responds to the articulations and emotional qualities of the object, especially to portentous, vivid moments presented within the drama (whether in conflicts between individuals, between individuals and the community, or between communities). But caution is needed here in supposing a personal voice or an especially introspective poet. The psychological venture I propose here requires no such voice, although the obtrusive narrator responds directly to aspects of the story he tells.[5]

I propose a psychoanalysis of heroic action rather than of the poet or the characters. The former is impossible; the latter is forever problematic because the characters are mainly functions or roles with names. One can probe the dynamics of those roles, the contrasts and oppositions, reaching for an understanding of whatever produces the terrible instability many readers have found in the heroic world of the poem. An instability informs that world's central institutions, including the institution of feud. Nevertheless feud finds some stability in battle as jural settlement and in settlement by wergeld; a peace in the latter case that may have been much more common in Anglo-Saxon communities than the heroic literature would make it seem.[6] Such a probe will show the poet's investment in the attitudes and postures of his noble characters (who invariably show some identification with fathers or predecessors, whereas the Heremods of this world forget both God and their ancestry). It will also enhance our understanding of the unifying nexus of exchange for the poem's foreground of monster fights and its background of feud relations between neighbouring peoples. To the extent that a psychological study can unify our sense of the poem's foreground and background; to the extent that it lives with the poem's terms; to the extent that it interrelates elements that most critics only with difficulty harmonize together – just so far would such a study command attention, respect, and possibly assent.[7]

Much of the poem's foreground of monster fights and 'background' of feud relations between peoples has a socio-economic context – the context of 'exchange,' of services and gifts given and received. The outlaw Grendel refuses to exchange with the Danes or to pay for his murders. Grendel, to be sure, is an unusual, serial murderer, perhaps a zombie. But the heroic world produces mundanely human versions of Grendel, along with lesser Beowulfs. Beowulf is the super-ego nemesis (sanctioned by God, behind Whom is Tiu) of all that is Odinesque, of monster cannibals, gallows-mindedness, lawless feud, and hoarding, treachery, and kin-murder in the mead-hall. Potentially, each warrior, each woman, and each king can turn away from proper exchange, proper service, and proper settlements towards terror, strife and treachery – essentially towards the monstrous; and the potentially monstrous can turn towards proper exchange, proper service, and proper settlement. Overall, my sketch for a psychological study of the poem will claim the thorough-going appropriateness of foreground and background, as presented through the centralities of exchange and feud; I will then suggest causes for the heroic world's instability – an instability Tolkien made famous, and one which still haunts readers who sadly trace Beowulf's death.

Those same readers often characterize the poem's conflicts in psychologically laden but unanalysed terms. They see motifs of light versus an inevitable darkness, of ethical good versus monstrous evil, of order versus a threatening chaos, of peace-weaving versus envy and greed, of heroism versus helplessness or cowardice, and so on. Most of these oppositions can apply to any polarized conflict; thus they reveal little that is unique about *Beowulf* and they do not take us far in understanding the poem's deeper coherence or explaining why the combination of feud stories, hero tales, and monster folk-lore is brilliantly intuitive, even from different aesthetic points of view, and not an artistic mistake or a simple, story-telling datum. Looking directly at the poem from a psychoanalytical viewpoint can illuminate rather than merely characterize the poem's action and its material.

The reciprocities of exchange, especially of gift giving and of 'loaned' gifts, is crucial for any reading of the poem. They become absolutely central for any psychological reading that wants to understand the violence in *Beowulf* and the presence of monsters. As it were, exchange forms the social face of energies underlying heroic life. It is the central clue to a Beowulfian psychology that ties the actions of monsters to the lives of men so deeply that in the monsters we have human impulses become externalized and given a creaturely life of their own. This kind of projection occurs in many cultures. For example, the dead female's ghostly *khaapkhabuurien* among the Highland New Guinea Bimin-Kuskusmin is a wandering, predatory ghost (Poole, 1981, p. 133) most likely to attack male in-laws.

Psychologically, in its economy of gift exchange, especially in the expectation of warrior service for rings and martial gifts, the heroic world in *Beowulf* is at an early stage of the dissolution of the Oedipus complex. Among other things, this forbidding characterization involves an unsure (because highly idealized) development of conscience in the heroic figures, a weak ego, and strong desires strongly suppressed (if not repressed).[8] This model accounts for the array of figures, attitudes and behaviours the poet creates; it also seems appropriate, even predictive, for the networks of loyalty, and for the outbreaks of treachery, ambush, and lawless feud that in part characterize the heroic world seen historically – beyond particular settlements and friendly relations.

Our word 'loan' derives from 'lean,' 'reward' or 'gift.' Insofar as a king's or a lord's gifts require service in return, they are loans. Thus, materially, obligatory prestation shapes the institutions of exchange and feud, with both creating the war-band arrangements Tacitus made famous, the *comitatus*. This is so completely the case that early in the poem, and outside of his own war-band, Hrothgar thinks in terms of gifts and service. After Wulfgar announces Beowulf's arrival, Hrothgar says he will 'offer,' 'tender,' or give treasures ('madmas beodan') to that good one for his 'modþræce' (l. 385), for Beowulf's courage. When we further consider that 'services in return' means combat when war comes – 'þonne wig cume' (l. 23b) – as it inevitably does, then a psychological shaping also occurs. The retainer must prepare himself for violent acts on his lord's behalf; that is why his lord gives him rings that, in effect, materialize a relationship in the first place and bespeak the giver's continuing personal and social presence (thus they are not simply given away).[9] This readiness to do violence, of course, finds expression in the passing on of weapons – both in the kinship line (through feud one may owe a service to one's kin, especially if a slayer is not of one's people or kindred) and in the retainer's relationship to his lord. This passing on of objects may or may not be accompanied by speeches. Psychologically the rings, armour, and swords carry their own, harsh law quite independent of any particular attitude one's father or one's lord might express. Consider the mutely compelling, legalistic use of the sword in the Finn episode; consider the sword Wiglaf has from his father, booty from the settlement of a feud at Eanmund's expense, which becomes instrumental in Wiglaf's assistance to Beowulf against the dragon.

The ties of loyalty and legalistic violence make one a man; reciprocity and kinship identification place one in the world and characterize one's ethical life. Without these ties and identifications one is a boy, perhaps, or worse, an outlaw. Readers have not considered this bond of violence very much in analysing the world created here. Usually we note that violence is a steady feature of Beowulf's world, often best seen as a circle of responses, while we indiscriminately jumble lawless feud and jural settlement together in our rush to condemn the heart of revenge. We do this on behalf of a poet we like to distance from the world he labours into being, a world in which readiness for violence on behalf of one's friend, lord, or kinsman (sometimes the same person) involves taking on others' needs as one's own, internalizing them. So shall a man do, the poet might say, when he at battle thinks to gain enduring fame (ll. 1534b–1536a).

More than anything else, this taking on of the war-lord's needs indicates a psychologically precarious point. Energy is borrowed, so to speak, from the father – borrowed for the repression of Oedipal and pre-Oedipal wishes. Out of that borrowing, so Freud would have it, an aggressive super-ego forms – aggressive because something like the harsh, punishing father-ideal has been internalized.[10] Generally Freud would have the super-ego form out of the decline of infantile Oedipal wishes, when the child transforms his emotional ambivalence towards his parents into an identification with them. The son internalizes the father as a prohibitor, but this process may occur or begin, at least, before the Oedipus complex disappears. As Melanie Klein has articulated this, a pre-Oedipal super-ego would be less resilient and could be harsher than the agency that succeeds the Oedipus complex, presumably because the child is still in a partially sadistic, oral stage and (given frustration and rage at being denied the breast) may see the world as composed of 'split' objects, either ideally good (the nurturing and desired breast) or overwhelmingly persecuting (the 'bad' mother or breast, projected from the infant's feelings of anger and of desire to bite and devout, born of frustration).[11]

In this connection it is significant that Grendel is understood (by the poet) as living in a wasteland, a heath(en) place, somatically hurt by the conviviality of men insofar as each day he suffers or endures the hearing of their hall-joys; so, balefully afflicted by the sounds of human joy, he goes to the hall and slaughters all the retainers he finds there, exulting in his carrion booty ('huðe hremig,' l. 120a) as he returns to his home. Exultation, presented as a self-sufficient state in *Beowulf*, always has ties to objects given or taken (e.g. treasure given, weapons taken). But Grendel's treasure, his booty, is the corpses of slain retainers, who are thus bad bodies projected and sundered at the same time (although at another level Grendel himself, as a hating hallthane, is a projection also, split from idealizations of the good object).[12] His exultation, unlike Beowulf's later in treasures received, is an anti-social, cannibalistic triumph. To understand the nature of that triumph we need to develop his relationship to heroic society in the hall and its likely tensions. Doing so requires a return to the formation of the super-ego.

A harshly aggressive super-ego precludes a strong ego, establishing a psychological dynamic reinforced by each loan requiring aggressive repayment. Thus in a sense the economy of exchange – of gifts for services and services for gifts, as well as of lawful vengeance for crimes suffered – continually reenacts loans from the father, keeping the ego weak (although not in a paranoid state because to some extent the reciprocity here presumes a successful integration into the ego of positive images of the father, along with values associated with the father). The critical outcome is that emotional affect is not completely withdrawn from monstrous (id) impulses, such as the desire to tear the loved object into pieces (one side of separation anxiety and ambivalence). The super-ego's demands for renunciation are in force, however, and therefore destructive id-wishes become suppressed, perhaps completely out of all consciousness. Yet they remain suppressed (or later repressed only) rather than finding expression in a deflected or sublimated form that might lessen their strength and lead to a more independent, better integrated ego.

Of course the poet states nothing like this; he does seem to intuit it in the close proximity of the monstrous and the good, of malicious feud and righteous revenge, and the general instability to which even Beowulf contributes. By avenging his lords' deaths (on Frisians and Franks for Hygelac and on Swedes for Heardred) he establishes the peace of the strong hand but not the continuing exchange he establishes between Danes and Geats. Beowulf, however, remains an ideal warrior-hero and people's king to the end, the jural warrior-king, the rightful nemesis of all that is monstrous. On behalf of the Geats, Beowulf has internalized a punitive super-ego so that he hunts down whatever gigantic sea-creatures have afflicted the Geats, avenging Geatish suffering: 'þær ic fife geband, / yððe eotena cyn, ond on yðum slog / niceras nihtes, nearoþearfe dreah, / wræc Wedera nið' 'There I bound five, / destroyed a race of giants and in the waves slew / monsters at night, suffered privations, / avenged the affliction of the Geats' (ll 420–423a). If a vestigial impulse makes him momentarily the monster's familiar, he turns that strength against the creature, as when he wrathfully grinds up a group of giants ('forgrand gramum,' l. 424a). His vengefulness is something like that of Grendel's mother, although he is mindful and she, perhaps, expresses something from Beowulf's past, when he was a slothful youth not yet initiated into a manhood of powerful readiness on behalf of his uncle and his uncle's people, the Geats.[13] Finally, in his delight in treasure, he shares something vaguely with the dragon – that creature who chanced upon the unguarded 'hoard-joy' – although in conscience and in action he is ever the harsh chastiser who, so he tells Hrothgar, avenged his people's affliction. The dragon, of course, illegally possesses the hoard it discovers, ruling over it to no avail.

Socially, monstrousness for the *Beowulf* poet takes the form of two crimes: fratricidal destruction and treachery within the hall, and lawless, evil feud between peoples. Associated with Cain, the first is primal, the worst of crimes (although literal fratricide may be accidental and is legally not avengable in any case); the second is one of the more persistent of worldly conditions and invites lawful settlement in war whenever possible – settlement that in turn may or may not invite eventual reprisal. Monsters figure in both crimes in one way or another. Through the numerous parallels between monster fights and the world of feud between men we can glimpse the poet's intuitions as well as his melancholy stake in this world he has written large.

A series of ironic puns that connect the reciprocal economy of gift giving and service to affairs of feud and requital establishes the poem's centre. The monsters become a dark apotheosis of those affairs turned to extremes, even unhinged. Those puns, ironic 'reward' or 'requital' for services rendered, when the services are ambushes, indicate the difference between true reward and revenge. The words 'forgyldan' and 'gyldan' express it succinctly: the former, with its intensifying prefix, signifies a deadly paying back; the latter means a return gesture, gifts for services or services for gifts in an ongoing exchange. Reciprocity, which equals continuity in this world, is missing from 'forgyldan' because the repayment here is extreme: a definitive attempt to settle usually hostile relationships. God in that sense pays giants for their services; Beowulf pays Grendel for hateful crimes; a Swedish king, Ongentheow, repays a violent blow; and the dragon would repay men for the loss of a cup. Late in the poem, the poet says that Beowulf pays with his life for a portion of treasure previously guarded by the dragon. Thus intense repayment is inevitably deadly.

When Grendel warred against the Danes, he refused to settle the feud by payment ('fea þingian, l. 156b). The same phrase applies to a feud Hrothgar settled for Beowulf's father (l. 470b). After the first monster fight, the mother comes to avenge Grendel. In doing so she slays a Danish warrior, making it necessary for Beowulf to seek her out and, as Hrothgar says, 'feo leanige' (l. 1380b), earn payment as a reward. The verb 'leanian' means 'reward' or 'recompense' rather than lawful settlement ('þingian'). It can include a reciprocal relationship, evident in the various contexts that have 'lean' – a word related to modern English 'loan.' Thus revenge merges with gift giving, which is always something loaned (as we saw in the preceding chapter, gifts invite a return and a continuing relationship).

Exchange in this world, then, is either continuing reciprocity or deadly paying back (in lawless feud or an attempt at settlement by the sword). The consequences can be pernicious in the latter case, with regrettable suffering and death. Even in the Finn episode, where a bitter settlement is full due, the poet calls the final phase a grief-meeting, conveying a regret that even shadows Grendel a little as the outlaw creature flees, life-sick, knowing surely that his life is at an end, the number of his days limited. Even for a dreadful creature this must be a terrible knowledge, although the poet withholds any further sympathy.

How is it that exchange can come to have unhappy connotations, even monstrous ones? The key lies in the idea of reciprocity itself. In any reciprocal relationship, each party can make demands on the other, while one party is less dependent than the other. Dependency, a source of strength between parties in a vertical relationship, can be a source of aggravation when the parties are connected horizontally; the latter connection leaves room for envy, greed, jealousy, or the beginning of grudges as some retainers will simply be more powerful, or promising, or privileged than others. In this regard Hunferth initially finds Beowulf's counsel in Heorot aggravating. The poet tells us that Beowulf's arrival and offer of help was to Hunferth a great vexation (as though vexation comes into one) because he did not grant that anyone should have more glory than himself. This is a case repeatedly expressed in the poem. Hostile feelings come into one, especially before action, or in response to something, or in lieu of action. These feelings can lead to grudges and to rising ambivalence, much as the relationship with one's lord may be ambivalent. Reciprocity may break down and lead, in the worst cases, to regicide or patricide and to the murder of one's fellow 'hall-kin,' the 'kinsmen band' – a form of fratricide.

Something like this can also occur for the lord: the soul-slayer, Greed, can act within his mind also. Why should he be generous, tying himself to his retainers as he ties them to himself? He may begin to feel invulnerable in his war strength and forget that his reciprocity toward dependent retainers mirrors his dependency upon the Granter of Victories (something Hrothgar never forgets). He may become niggardly and hostile, regressing from the noble posture of kindness and sharing. More commonly, because of intense injunctions to behave well in reciprocal relationships, he may engage in lawless attacks on neighbours and poisonous strife between tenuously accommodated in-laws (when neither close kinship nor clear dependency has had time to develop one does not internalize the other's needs as one's own). The poet alludes to several such 'breakdowns': in-laws will cause strife in Heorot; following Hrethel's death Ongentheow's offspring wage lawless war against Geats; Heremod maliciously slaughters his own retainers; and tyrannously Modthryth has peaceful retainers bound and slain (presumably for the crime of gazing at her). However, in Modthryth's case she eventually marries the best of kings and becomes vice transformed. Modthryth lives in 'high love' with Offa. This suggests that transformation can occur, either as a regression to dark wishes – to crime and the status of predatory wolf (cf. Grendel's mother's merewolf status) – or as a rise to super-ego mastery through some kind of dependency – a taking on of the 'father,' as arranged by one's actual father, one's taming prohibitor and protector.[14]

In the heroic world men must be ready to do violence in return for violent wrongs suffered – for monstrous behaviour in men and for the behaviour of monsters toward men. In this connection, as perpetrators of crimes, the connection of the Grendel family with Cain is not merely accidental or associative. In *Maxims I* (ll. 192–8) Cain's fratricide is given as the origin of strife and the beginning of the need for battle-readiness. In *Beowulf* the link is largely topographical rather than lineal (or, if lineal, it is associatively lineal, giving Grendel a history that goes back four generations – a typical kin-line depth for Danes, Geats, and Swedes as well). Grendel lives in a border place that once was home for monsters and giants long since condemned as Cain's kindred. His association with Cain comes mainly through the catalogue of misbegotten creatures that descended from Cain, whose fratricidal spirit lives on in all acts of dark violence, not just Grendel's. Grendel's wasteland is of this world; so is his violence. The real relationship with Cain then is not spiritual, but creaturely. Cain was the first man to commit murder but Grendel has priority in the psychic life. The topographical link is most important here because those wastelands predate Cain. They come of original sin – psychologically the fall from bliss to rage at being denied pleasure (whether it be the mother's breast or hall-joy).[15]

The story of Cain is one of fraternal rivals for the Father's favour – the ideal, not the actual father. This is a harsh Father and so psychologically the Cain story suggests violent unwillingness to accept the Father's law and abide his distribution of favours. Monstrous fratricide (as distinct from literal brother-slaying among men) involves permanent regression. Cain is permanently exiled, as are Grendel and his mother, although Grendel differs notably; he is more devilish in the associations given him while his mother is more like nature's dark creature (see Irving, 1984, p. 13). However, the more essential difference between Grendel and his mother is that the mere is her home but his grievance. This finally is the spirit of Cain: murderous grievance over the Father's law or a denied blessing. That Grendel in a sense has no creaturely father – or none known to the Danes in the poem – suggests the pre-Oedipal desire to possess the mother even before the father comes into the picture. But that is not the Cain principle as finally enacted. By killing the brother one would attack the father, rival him, and thus take his place. The father is very much to be contended with here, perhaps especially in his moment of high glory and munificence (from the Cain point of view a grievously unfair munificence).

The poet intuitively plots something like this in his introduction to Grendel's rage. Hrothgar commands the building of a great hall, which he names and in which he rules munificently and honourably. We are told that the wide-gabled hall towered high; it awaited destruction. The namer's hall, if not the namer himself, will be attacked by the sword-hate of in-laws (part of the meditation on how one can establish and nurture order). But this will not happen yet. What awakens now is 'se ellengæst,' he who awaited in darkness, suffering much when each day he hears the joys of men, song in the hall. The poet alludes to a later time but then describes an earlier one. Intuitively he understands the two in terms of each other: the Grendel in us is what awakens when sword-hate occurs. The hall, whose identity includes awaiting hateful fire, also (or really) awaits the bold-demon from the dark. This creature would avenge itself for having suffered the Father-inspired joys of others. The impulses that inhabit Grendel have a continuity all their own despite God's punishment of Cain and His requital for the 'services' the giants gave Him. Grendel's habitat predates Cain and the kind of greediness we see in Grendel has obviously survived God's destruction (in the flood) of the giants.

It is now time to suggest just how the poet plumbs the depths of those desires and their crossings in the monsters, while firmly establishing Beowulf and retainers like him as super-ego heroes.[16] The poet's primary realization is of the persistence of those desires. They recur again and again. Indeed, his poem is about recurrence as much as about anything else, including transcience.

In *Beowulf* no matter how successfully overcome or transformed those desires are, and no matter how noble the kings, queens, and warriors are those dark impulses will recur. That recognition, more than anything else, produces the poem's melancholy. We tend to ascribe this melancholy to the poet; it makes him understand the impermanence of any great people sadly but not in contempt of this world and its affairs. His is an attenuated melancholy, an inability to accept the world as lost although everything in it has its day and no more. What we love, the poem seems to say, we care for and are anxious about – much as Hrothgar will become loving and anxious about Beowulf – even though we know that everything will eventually come to an end and die or decay. But the values we have in this world, our joys, loves, and happy reversals are splendid all the same. It is good to nurture warriors, to give bright gifts, to avenge crime, to weave nets of peace, and to love noble retainers. The poet and his characters are attached to this world. We can appreciate this more fully by comparing the mood of *The Wanderer* with that of the last survivor in *Beowulf*. In *Beowulf* a kind of empiricism informs the elegiac and the elegiac is something we experience, not a pretext for dismissing all the lovely things recalled to mind (implicitly caressed) only to be consigned, as in *The Wanderer*, to a world that will itself eventually crumble and fall idle. True, the so-called last survivor laments the death of his people, the decay and lifelessness of their goods and armour, and even the general end of celebration and of human and animal life in the hall. This is sad, but it is not rhetorically posed in the service of a higher or deeper point of view, as in *The Wanderer*. Indeed, death and the verbal and physical consignment of once actively used treasures in the *Beowulf* passage are seen as either sad or evil. But the poet does not consign the world as a whole and everything in it to decay and death.[17] Even the hoard, useless to men when buried, is subject to reopening, to reevaluation should men bring it out and distribute it – as the last survivor's people once did and as Beowulf hopes to do, seeing the hoard as wergeld for his people for his death.[18] Consistently in the poem, and notably in its tonally dark final third, treasure is valued as good, as joy-arousing. Only *buried* treasure elicits a sense of uselessness, although even a buried hoard can arouse pleasure in the most loyal of hearts.

Death can be evil only because life is good and so are things of this life when valued in connection with hall-joys and with defence of the hall. Of course violence continues in both its dark and justified aspects. To explore the psychological roots of that violence, we can focus on how the monsters operate in the poem, beginning with Grendel. His fratricidal cannibalism expresses the essentially oral-sadistic impulses animating him. His attacks are fratricidal in the sense that he is linked associatively to Cain; he is also a hall-thane of sorts, slaying those who are in the kinship band.

Typically, Freud thinks of sadism as a compound of aggression and sexuality. However, he and others, including Melanie Klein, sometimes separate the two elements. Sadism has come to mean aggression mainly, especially for the orally dependent but frustrated or denied infant. Aroused to hostility, but fearful of reprisal, the infant might here form the germ of later images – images of the devouring mother. Similar ambivalence and splitting occur in relation to the father and to siblings when they are seen as rivals, later, for the mother. Grendel takes a dark pleasure in his special work; he only devours retainers. Essentially, then, Grendel is seen as both a bad brother and a bad comrade figure, a fantasied, negative hall-thane (healðegnes hete,' l. 142b) who takes up all the bad residue of both sibling and comradely rivalry and hostility towards the father or king. Not only does he ambush young and old retainers alike ('duguþe ond geogoþe,' l. 160b) but he rules Heorot by night, rendering Hrothgar instantaneously old, even impotent. In Hrothgar's deep sorrow over the attacks of Grendel, whom Hrothgar at one point calls 'my invader' ('ingenga min,' l. 1776b), Grendel in a sense gains entrance into both Hrothgar's hall and his body; Hrothgar is in a borderland of dread although he never loses sight of God's (long unexercised) ability to stop Grendel if He chooses to. Beowulf's arrival and progress towards Hrothgar's permission shift Hrothgar into a reparative mode, into hope against dread, and finally into caring and love after experiencing the great joy of Grendel's defeat. Uncannily this reenacts the dynamic Melanie Klein posits for very young infants – down to the splitting now of the woman-queen-mother in the advent of Grendel's mother.

But to return, Grendel is associated with Cain's brood, and occupies the same wasteland. This helps us to understand his otherwise mysterious presence – Beowulf says Grendel is a 'sceaðona ic nat hwylc,' l. 274b – in a way that makes social and cultural sense and acquires a mythological clarity.[19] He becomes a fratricidal ghoul, part of the Cain-engendered violence in the world, against which men must arm themselves and stand prepared (though he soon overwhelms Hrothgar's hopes of defence). Unknown to all, his body is charmed against swords (a power attributed to Odin according to Toller and Campbell, *Supplement*). His is a virulence against which armed strength is useless. Only a naked, bodily encounter will subdue him.[20] Meanwhile, Grendel's attacks decimate Hrothgar's war-band as he strives against right, one against all, accepting no peace or settlement. The poet associates Grendel with Cain and shares that knowledge only with his audience and not with characters in the poem (Osborn, 1978, p. 976). He keeps Grendel's movements and activities murky enough: Grendel is a 'dark death-shadow,' of whose comings and goings men cannot know (ll. 160–3). His lawless acts further define his presence in the hall, but their savage roots go deep. They go deeper than early Oedipal hostility toward siblings, working into an earlier psychological stage of anger: oral aggression organized out of the primal rage that follows the first loss (the breast).[21]

In his dark joys Grendel is damnably fiendish and orally rapacious. As the poet narrates his deeds, a vocabulary of loathing intensifies. Grendel becomes an 'unhælo' creature (l. 120b) for what he intends. 'Grim ond grædig, gearo sona wæs, / reoc ond reþe' (ll. 121–122a). The tracks from the hall to Grendel's lair are those of an accursed spirit. The poet upholds the good of hall-joy and retainership as well as of gift giving in exchange for vows of service. In Grendel, then, the poet presents a deeply malignant anti-retainer, an unholy creature driven mainly by oral rage. Thus he seems to intuit the oral and generally bodily hostility underlying internecine slaughter among ill-accommodated hall-thanes, a bodily hostility, however, that surfaces more conspicuously in analogues than in *Beowulf* itself.[22]

The hero comes to the Danes as the greatest of mankind in strength, noble and huge. Giant-like, his hand-strength is that of thirty men (balancing Grendel's feasting on thirty Danes). Beowulf is no lawless giant, however. Crucially, he has undergone severe tests of his strength and of his avenging courage against monsters, on his people's behalf. He has been well initiated into warrior manhood and now he appears among the Danes out of heroic philanthropy, offering to settle this thing against Grendel. He is vague about what sort of creature Grendel is, but not about his own determination. This suggests a great gap in Beowulf's psyche between his conscious and his unconscious, a gap he may be said to maintain by volunteering for purgative monster fights. On behalf of Geats he cleared the sea-lanes of monsters and for the Danes he purges (or in a sense sacrally purifies ['fælsian']) Heorot and the mere.

What we see of the fights may reflect a late survival of the shaman-assisted initiation rituals Germanic warriors apparently undertook – rituals in which they did psychic battle against beasts and animals, perhaps for a time becoming the beast they confronted before emerging again into the consciousness of warrior and man. The figure of the dancing warrior between two beasts (or shamans dressed in bear or wolf furs) offers a tantalizing clue to these initiations.[23] Stories about shape-changing warriors, such as Sigmundr and Sinfjotli in *Volsunga Saga*, provide further indications of struggle, metamorphosis, and return. The two, as marauding outlaws, change into wolves and then back again into men before taking revenge on Sigmundr's brother-in-law. Research on the origin of 'warg' or 'wer'-wolf adds other clues, contributing to a picture of the Germanic warrior as a purposeful figure who has undergone a transformation of some kind, involving animal energies, before taking on his adult roles.[24] As a warrior he was apparently a defender of the folk and a purger of pestilence, as well as a guardian of fertility. These offices were fulfilled by slaying enemies, settling matters with outlaws, and arranging for the continuing defence of the people. Grendel is variously an outlaw, a borderland ghoul, and bloody pestilence – all of which Beowulf overcomes in the course of purging Heorot.[25]

In facing Grendel, Beowulf reenacts the initiation ordeal suggested above in shadow only, and then he does so only in part. Beowulf and his monstrous adversaries receive the same identifications when joined in combat: he and Grendel are 'angry hall-guards' ('reþe renweardas,' l. 770a) and each is hateful to the other. But their opposing roles envelop them, keeping the narrative dramatically bipolar. In their anger and hatred, as energies, the adversaries are indistinguishable. Thus 'aglæca' can apply to either or to both collectively: in *Beowulf* the same term can have contrary denotations, as do 'payment,' 'settlement,' and 'aglæca.' Beowulf is called an 'aglæca' when fighting in wasteland places; perhaps sympathetically, he is seen as a wretch or an outcast in his hazardous ordeals.[26] But in how they are marked, the dedications inscribed deeply upon them (mythologically expressing Odin or Tiu) – that is how the poet keeps absolute control of both the narrative and Beowulf's status as super-ego hero.

Severely disarranged during the fight against God's adversary, Heorot receives a general refurbishing and Hrothgar holds a great banquet.[27] During the festivities he rewards Beowulf and various bards recite tales of Danish victories in other feuds. Here the poet relates the Finn episode, with its scenerio of sudden, lawless attack and terrible death among in-laws – including the cameo of the mourning queen, Hildeburh, placing her brother and son side by side on the swallowing pyre. This is one of those stunning moments, perfectly expressing the poet's verbal, descriptive, and psychological genius: 'Lig ealle forswealg, / gæsta gifrost, þara ðe þær guð fornam / bega folces'' Flame swallows everything / the most greedy of spirits, those whom there battle snatched / of both peoples' (ll. 1122b–1124a). This is a greedy fire-spirit, as is Grendel's mother ('gifre ond galgmod,' l. 1277a): it swallows, much as Grendel swallows Hondscio ('synsnædum swealh,' l. 743). Linked by diction to the life and activity of the Grendel creatures, this elemental engulfing both parallels Grendel's and anticipates the mother's, thus deeply integrating the evil character of lawless human feuds (the initial state of conflict between Frisians and Danes) with that of monsters.[28] Other details enrich the integration: Grendel's attack comes suddenly, as does initial slaughter between Hengest and Finn; Hrothgar endures twelve, bitter years before help arrives – a long winter of sorrow; and Hengest endures a bitter winter before the arrival of spring and an opportunity to settle the feud.

With a grim, psychological beauty, the Finn story resonantly ties the monster fight narrative to the material of feud between peoples. As it were, the poet brings human feud forward onto the same physical and psychological plane as the monster fights. Feuds between peoples no longer rest in an allusive background.[29] Others have seen something of this, but the connection achieved here suggests the organizing value of a psychological study and something about the psychology of feud. Given Grendel's impulses and deeds, his dark desires and his oral hostility, we can suppose those to reach the roots of feud, especially of malicious feuds (as in the initial stage of the Finn story). These feuds are nearly always between in-laws and hence fratricidal in character (even Swedes and Geats may be connected in some way through Beowulf's Wægmunding side). Of course some marriages in the heroic world are arranged as hope against feuds, as settlements. This notwithstanding, we can posit a process as follows: lawless, baleful, sudden attack springs from a deep-seated, fratricidal hostility directed away from the immediate group. The hostility is directed away from the group because the reciprocal bonds holding warrior to warrior and all to their lord are likely to be strong (or are strong in the poem's idealization of them, though they can weaken). When they are weak or when they somehow dissolve, then direct, internecine feuds can occur. Beowulf and Wiglaf remain exemplary, however, both in their loyalty and in the righteousness of their battles; Beowulf is given the poem's most striking lines on unavengeable fratricide, first in his charge against Hunferth (ll. 588b–589a), then in his gloominess prior to engaging the dragon (he considers the accidental killing of brother by brother a 'feohleas gefeoht,' l. 2442a), and finally in his comment that the Ruler of men need not blame him for the murder of kinsmen (ll. 2741b–2742a). Beowulf is resolute against the dark and fratricidal.

He focuses on what is right and on compensation. He has no deep awareness of the oral base to fratricidal feud and lawless violence, although he is quite aware of feasting as a hostile metaphor, telling Hunferth that he once fought sea-creatures who thought to dine on him.[30] Here 'þicgan' connects the sea-creatures with Grendel (l. 736a) and with eating and mead-drinking among men. Beowulf's sword is his reply to the water-monsters, much as his hand is when he dismembers Grendel and crushes Dæghrefn. Against Grendel's mother he arms himself with the righteousness of revenge, along with an outfit of remarkable chain-mail and a wondrously ornamented sword (although man-made and insufficient in the event). Grendel's mother apparently eats Æschere's body but Beowulf pays no attention to that. His focus is on avenging the death of a friend – a motive not much removed from her own gallows-mindedness in one sense but levels apart in another.

We can add the monster mother's motive, then, to the analysis of feud. In a sense, she is a cut above her degenerate spawn: she wants revenge for the death of a kinsman – a desire that carries the inevitability of an ancient fate ('geosceaft,' l. 1266a). Yet this desire is tainted by her state of mind. Odinesque, greedy and gallows-minded she undertakes a sorrowful journey of revenge (ll. 1277–8). Her slaughter and her dark joy ('atol æse wlanc eftsiðas teah, / fylle gefægnod,' ll. 1332–1333b) make her infamous, tying her deeply to Grendel and allowing us to see inchoate revenge as preceding oral hostility but as subordinated in prominence. The poet's psychology of revenge turns around and around on these two affairs: orally hostile, all retainers want revenge (originally on the denying mother) but here revenge emerges through the mother on behalf of the dead son, who was killed by the father's righteousness. Apparently the poem poses this intuition: the mother-son bond is deep enough to overcome ambivalence and, in the most dire of cases, to deflect that ambivalence towards the father (with mother and son in league). Even the poem's strikingly lethal 'mother,' Modthryth, is really the bad princess (a father's daughter) who needs transformation if she is to function as the father's good queen and wife. Otherwise mothers, with Wealhtheow as the paragon, are either deeply involved on behalf of their sons against the father or worry about recruiting protection for them. (Wealhtheow opposes what she sees as Hrothgar's move toward Beowulf; Hildeburh through terrible disaster ends up in bitter opposition to her son's father; Hygd prefers Beowulf's protection over her son's right to the kingship.) In a sense, Grendel's mother, 'Grendles modor, / ides aglæcwif' (ll. 1258b–1259a), is wife, queen, lady, and mother all in one for the son. No father is known. It is the father's world, the father's loans that civilize one away from this incestuous possessiveness. Once one is in the father's world, the only good mothers are the fathers' queens. Such queens are honoured but they are not what the deep self really wants. Even Beowulf notes something of this when he foresees the likely outbreak of feud in the Ingeld and Freawaru story, no matter how good the bride (ll. 2029b–2031). What is wanted, apparently, in malignant feuds is dark joy with the mother at the expense of all rivals when the loaned energies from the father weaken, dependency ends, and regression begins.[31]

The retainer or king slain by greed and then forgetful of God and heedless of duty cannot of course actually repossess the mother. The best he can do is repossess a sword or else hoard everything considered good: the hall, treasures, weapons, and even the lives and lands he takes from others. Jural revenge opposes this deep wrong, this greediness that turns everything into useless booty (hoarded treasure becomes useless, armour decays, life ceases). There is another, brilliant intuition in the poem's sense of these affairs. Of Grendel's raids the poet says: 'þanon eft gewat / huðe hremig to ham faran, / mid þære wælfylle wica neosan' (ll. 123b–125). Rejoicing in his booty, Grendel seeks his home where, now we know, his mother also lived. If the poem's arrangements of these matters reflect a deep human intuition in this world, then in it original ambivalence towards the mother (the infant's frustration when denied the breast) needs to be understood as something overcome in a possessiveness of the mother and in oral hostility directed accordingly at all rivals (whether the father or siblings). Favour and honour from the father, then, can be seen as compensation within the father's reciprocal world of loaned energies for loss of the mother, who is, in a sense, 'erased' in that act of compensation. She is subject to recovery only in idealized ways within the father-world's terms (infused by Beowulf's victory over Grendel, Hrothgar pronounces Beowulf's unnamed mother as God-blest or favoured [giving within the kindred] in her child bearing).[32] Perhaps we can in this connection even understand the creature Grendel as beginning his life in the poem on the borderland of the father's values; excluded from hall-joys, he grieves until he begins his twelve-year gathering of retainers. Then he rejoices, in a sense having actualized his true self and shed the misery of exile.

Perhaps, also, this orientation toward the mother accounts for the extraordinary difficulty of the fight in the mere. By seeking her Beowulf becomes the aggressor and his motives, although high-minded, are something like hers. Revenge, no matter how well formulated or how clearly on God's side, is never absolutely severed from the taint of the mere, that uncanny place, whose more deeply abiding genius is Grendel's mother. Even Beowulf is monstrous in action, savage and grim ('hreoh ond heorogrim,' l. 1564a) when cutting through the monster mother's body with the sword of giants – a psychic overcoming in that he turns the welded strength of giants against a giantlike creature (called a sea-wolf when she first grasps Beowulf). After Beowulf beheads Grendel's corpse with the same sword, the blade melts, suggesting that the impulses that animated Grendel are still corrosive. Beowulf seeks a super-ego revenge here of head against dark body in an economical exchange: by taking Æschere's body and leaving the (counsellor's) head, the monster mother enacts a repossession of the body; by splitting the mother's body and recovering Grendel's head, Beowulf enacts the reassertion of the head and its righteous, juridical values. But what he cannot do is end monstrousness, no matter how deeply he dives into the world's weird depths and now matter how many monsters' lives he takes. Indeed, he almost fails in the realistic world of the poem. He can never succeed in its psychic one if by success we mean the end of dark energies.

Paradoxically, Beowulf needs monstrous creatures or monstrous energies to realize himself as super-ego, as dark energies drawn up into the father's service. Metaphorically, he needs a periodic dive, armoured and righteous, into the sea of beasts, whether ocean or mere – a sea never too far from the hall (Hrothgar says,'Nis þæt feor heonan — þæt se mere standeð,' ll. 1361b–1362). As Hrothgar speaks of Grendel's mother, he moves between two ways of thinking about her: as an object of revenge, she is criminal only; as the spirit of place, she is foul, weird, and mysterious. Beowulf can engage the criminal and punish her mortally; he can even purge the mere of its monstrous creatures; but he cannot overcome Grendel's mother as weird spirit in her sudden coming and going. Pride, for example, always appears suddenly and shoots a bitter arrow, something Hrothgar calls a perverse command. Pride is a 'wergan gastes,' an 'accursed spirit' with impeccable, Grendelian credentials in the appellation (cf. ll. 102, 133, 1274, 1351, 1357). The Grendel creatures are not allegorical or abstract whereas Hrothgar's account of the Grendelian in life becomes so.

The 'great man perverted' parable – the poem's most extensive passage of 'ethnopsychological' explanation – follows upon mention of Heremod as a singular, historical contrast in the Danish-Scylding past to Hrothgar's expansive sense of Beowulf's accomplished renown and worldly honour, which Beowulf governs in strength and wisdom of mind. The poet here reveals a moral psychology that rests above the Freudian and seeks an understanding of greed. By attending to Hrothgar's articulations we gain oblique confirmation of our Freudian analysis of the Grendelian in Hrothgar's world.

Hrothgar begins by urging his beloved Beowulf to guard against the inner perniciousness that overtook an unwary Heremod. He should do so because no moment is guaranteed to last – not without human effort. Beowulf should choose the better for as long as he can: eventually everyone's glory comes to an end through one means or another (ll. 1758–68).

Hrothgar is both loving and worried. He now says that clearly Beowulf was born the better man (he said this earlier about his brother). Here Hrothgar's modesty is quite sincere as he speaks in the role of 'se wise,' the wise one, who furthers truth and right among the people, stating clearly what is so. (Hrothgar furthers, Beowulf accomplishes – both are ethically mindful.) He has been almost priestly in pronouncing the upsurge of Beowulf's glory: 'Blæd is aræred / geond widwegas, wine min Beowulf' (ll. 1703b-1704). Hrothgar publicly acknowledges Beowulf's super-ego dedication to all that is right and good. Beowulf is a legislator-warrior, unsurpassed for ferocity but not a malicious berserker, not an unhinged, Woden-like figure. That fate is Heremod's who raged in the hall and cut down his hearth-companions, despite his great, God-given gifts. On the surface Heremod's fate is inexplicable. Initially he reigns as God-blest in that mighty God raised him up in the joy of strength over all men; nevertheless in spirit he grew bloody-minded. Hrothgar says all of this and more, not because he thinks Beowulf will succumb to Heremodian bloody-mindedness, but because he loves Beowulf and worries over his well-being.

He would have Beowulf learn by Heremod's example and perceive what is manly, virtuous, and generous. He worries about this so much that he moves on to a parable-like passage explaining what happened in Heremod's case. It is a wonder, he begins, how mighty God dispenses wisdom, land, and lordship to men. Sometimes in His love he lets the intellect of an aristocratic man move about (achieve its aims) and gives him earthly joy, prosperity, and power over others so that the man himself, in his wisdom, is not able to think of his end. Now experience of health, peace of mind, and lack of external threat only confirm such a man in his sense that the whole world turns as he wills. One day pride grows and flourishes while the soul's guardian sleeps. A slayer lurks – evil, niggardly thoughts like bitter, sharp arrows shoot into one's heart from within. These arrows are thought of as the crooked, perverse, strange, or mysterious commands of an accursed, Grendelian sort ('wom wundorbebodum wergan gastes,' l. 1747, the last phrase applying also to Grendel's first, bloody trail in and out of Heorot).

This lord in the parable no longer gives gold rings in the hall and he is unmindful of his destiny, the shaping forth of his life. Eventually he dies and all of his hoarded gold falls into another's hands, who distributes it, ending what had been a reign of terror. Thus honour, power, and prosperity require mindfulness of the future and attention to reciprocity. Otherwise one will succumb to perverse, niggardly, essentially Grendelian thoughts and end badly.

As many have noted, Hrothgar's parable has Christian, homiletic overtones but it also reflects strongly communal values in gift-giving cultures. Other ethnopsychologies emphasize similar oppositions and ideas. Marilyn Strathern (1988, 1990) speaks of the Hagen, a New Guinea Highlands people, and their insistence that mind and will become visible when 'a child shows feeling for those related to it and comes to appreciate the interdependence or reciprocity that characterizes social relationships' (p. 90). Something of this mind and will is what Hrothgar would have Beowulf keep to protect him against all persecutors, particularly against those that come from within the psyche, even to God-blest men. The thought of possible loss here for such perfection is especially sad for Hrothgar, whose life reflects a reparative and caring stage still acutely conscious of persecutory possibilities (in his case coming from without, as he once sat joyless, enduring a strong sorrow for his thanes slaughtered by Grendel).[33] Hrothgar would have Beowulf guard himself, through mindfulness of the future and by mindful reciprocity, against dark perversity – against all but the inevitable, those losses of strength, youth, and life that can come through fire, water, the sword or spear, or just hateful old age. In their parting scene, when Hrothgar embraces Beowulf and kisses him, we have a contrast of two worlds within the embrace of the same values: the young man's in which the loss of dear ones is relatively unknown; and the old man's in which loss is a part of one's lot on this middle earth. But Hrothgar's is, perhaps quintessentially, the consciousness of the superlative, juridical king, a consciousness aware of but not darkened or impaired by the furor of the terrible sovereigns who, like Heremod, bring grim disaster to their people or, like Hrothgar's father, do better and become battle-fierce in the poet's estimation ('guðreouw,' l. 58), but still do not become battle-famous ('guðrof,' l. 608) like Hrothgar himself.

At this point, almost two-thirds of the way into the poem, Beowulf returns home and we have the great giving of gifts in Hygelac's hall. The poet rapidly moves on from that exemplary and socially complex scene to Beowulf's last day alive. The ideal warrior-retainer has proved himself in every way possible, in combat and in the hall. Indeed Beowulf remains beyond even the suspicion of putting himself ahead of others when offered the Geatish kingship by Hygelac's wife, an offer he could easily and honourably accept. Instead he refuses and supports his cousin, Hygelac's son. To what, if anything in this violent world, is he vulnerable? And just how will this great battle-king, this most victory-blest of men die? Both questions are addressed on Beowulf's last day alive by means of the dragon fight and the lure of treasure – a deeply psychic lure that no one can escape, not even the generous warrior-king fully involved in defending his people and avenging his losses and theirs.

Beowulf's dragon is the only such creature known to wound the Germanic hero mortally. The dragon as unlawful hoard-guardian is a good king's nightmare, a greedy and vindictive avenger, who would destroy everything and everyone. Superficially, we might place the dragon psychologically by stressing its anality and its phallic shape. But this would be misleading – the result of easy associations for the modern reader rather than of close consideration. Although possessive in his pride ('maðumæhta wlonc,' l. 2833b) and therefore anal in ordinary life, the 'wyrm' is oral in his rage, a fire-breathing destroyer. This 'ligdraca' differs from all others in not being a phallic terror, a bad father-figure, set for the Oedipal hero in a libidinal drama (the role of huge serpents in Germanic folklore). Beowulf faces here an energy like his own: the dragon would pulverize everything ('forgrunden' links the two as in ll. 424, 2335). As Beowulf once dealt with monsters on behalf of the Geats, so now the dragon would deal with the Geats themselves. Opposed here are grim and savage energies; these opponents are absolute in their dedications – the dragon to consuming destruction, Beowulf to absolute revenge. Although ethically Beowulf is everything the dragon is not, the matching of extreme energy here, and Beowulf's susceptibility to the dragon's bite, suggest a secret kinship between the great king and the terrible hoarder.

Whether Beowulf tragically errs in this last fight (and to what extent) has been a tiresome issue in reader reaction to the poem. After Beowulf's death, Wiglaf, his loyal retainer, moralistically says that now Geats will suffer because of one man's boldness. Is this deep criticism or merely sober observation?[34] Is Beowulf's last day, then, a vainglorious and lustful one, unmindful of God? Putting the question that way, I think, misframes it and would provoke even the poet's denial. The poet works hard in this last third of the poem to show that Beowulf is a good king, functioning as a king should: Beowulf has always repaid his kings in vigorous, violent service, and so he would now repay (himself) and implicitly still honour Hygelac in seeking the dragon; moreover, he seeks the dragon alone because that is his mode and because he would protect his retainers; finally, Beowulf is thankful that he has won the treasure for his people, not himself. Indeed, he has little choice but to seek the dragon, despite Wiglaf's counsel. Enraged, the dragon has already scorched hall and lands; he will attack again once night falls, exhaling death for everyone and everything within reach. Far from quiescent after his fire-spewing raid, the dragon waits in his barrow, breathing such fire that no one can enter (ll. 2548–9).

But much is made of the treasure and later we hear of a curse once laid upon it. Beowulf does exult in rich rewards, even though he passes Hrothgar's great gifts on to Hygelac. He does not closely question the exile who brings an attractive cup into the kingdom (from the dragon's hoard, as it turns out). Rather, he magnanimously accepts the gift and extends his friendship. When he learns of the dragon's rage and the utter destruction of his mead-hall, he immediately supposes that he has offended the Lord over some ancient law and he sinks into gloom – a right-thinking dismay that is legalistic to the core as he wrestles with dark, uncustomary thoughts.

Here the poet presents Beowulf's emotional personhood, so to speak, in a dark moment before he turns to a means of revenge. We are told that there was rue and regret in his heart, the greatest of sorrows. What could cause such sorrow? What for Beowulf would be the greatest of sorrows? Not loss of lord or kinsman, but something worse. His breast surges and boils with dark, gloomy thoughts. This was not *of custom* for this good, wise, public king whose values are constituted socially and whose particular emotions (sorrow, love, and joy, for example, as distinguished from those dark surgings) have been ideally channelled in their expression.

Beyond projected grief and lament we are not told exactly what dark thoughts occurred to Beowulf. They must have involved self-doubt and feelings of betrayal and hopelessness (like those Hrothgar felt after Grendel's raid); they may have included grim and murderous impulses (perhaps to seize and crush the slave who brought the cup). In any case, nothing comes to consciousness except fearless determination to avenge himself and his people, and to do so without raising an army because, we are told, Beowulf thinks of himself finally as blest with victory; he is the warrior who purged Heorot, who dismembered Grendel's loathsome kind, and who repaid Hygelac's love and generosity by literally crushing Dæghrefn and annihilating Dæghrefn's war-band. This is the fierce law of the avenging super-ego.

Nevertheless, the poet has Beowulf focus on the dragon's gold eventually. We are told that this is Beowulf's inevitable day of death and the dragon's also, and that Beowulf himself senses his own, impending mortality (although he does not have sure knowledge of his impending death). Moving past those moods, Beowulf tells his retainers that he will fight for the hoard or battle, the deadly bale of life, will take him. Does gold then have a mind-darkening hold on Beowulf? Or does he estimate the gold in some way that we miss by thinking of his focus as inevitably a gold-lust of some sort? What might the gold signify to Beowulf as super-ego hero, keeping in mind that he may have a regal right to the accidentally discovered hoard (see Anderson [1977])?

Before descending into the mere, Beowulf stated a similar resolve: he would fight with Hrunting or else death would take him (and before meeting Grendel he said he would do the will of the Danes or else die in the mead-hall). Hrunting is instrumental, as is Beowulf's acceptance of Hrothgar's and the Danes' needs as his own. Could the treasure hoard, then, be similarly instrumental? In his mind Beowulf seems to associate the dragon's gold with its life and therefore with victory for himself and his people, as well as payment for a terrible battle.

Treasure does matter to this paragon because reward for services and services for reward are just exchanges in the father-lord's world. In a sense, rewards are necessary because they are compensations for primal overcoming – compensations that tie one in a reciprocal dependency to the battle-king and his values, just as giving ties the battle-king to public virtue, to the anti-terrorist world of generosity. Without reward, services cannot be demanded, for that would make one a slave and negate the deep sacrifice involved in that primal overcoming (ritually achieved or reenacted through the warrior initiation, and refreshed, as it were, with every violent service in repayment for gifts and honours given). As Beowulf says, he repaid in battle the treasure Hygelac had given him. Only rage could follow such a negation. But within what reciprocity and dependency does Beowulf now live? Who will reward him for his service? He is now his own battle-lord and ring-giver, his own king; he must avenge losses to his kingdom on his own behalf (and his people's). The dragon's hoard becomes a means of found reward as well as an exchange for the dragon's life. To act properly is to seek just reward and avenge unlawful injury and crime. Perhaps this is the core of Beowulf's uncustomary gloom at first: the king's dependency is upon God as giver of success and glory in war. How can one repay that in liberality and protection shown to one's retainers if God has abandoned one, unleashing terror upon one? But, if he has it, that dismaying thought passes and Beowulf prepares fearlessly for an engagement about which he has forebodings but about which he does not know the outcome.

The dismaying underside, then, of heroic life within the dependencies and reciprocities of gift giving and the institution of feud is this: a terrible feeling that one has been utterly abandoned and rendered a slave to terror or else the awful threat that one might turn into the monsters one is committed to oppose. This latter threat buoys up all gifts for services, all reciprocities in the heroic world, and leads to Beowulf's stipulative consciousness concerning proper exchange and worthy behaviour among kinsmen and in the hall. The link between Beowulf and the dragon should be understood as entirely ghostly, something deeply repressed but never quite erased, as Beowulf fulfils his proper roles and prepares himself for heroic combat, alone – the only warrior role he knows, whether against creatures or men (in Hygelac's service he was always walking ahead of the troop, 'ana on orde,' l. 2498a). Indeed, as against the Grendel creatures, Beowulf needs powerful adversaries to realize himself (he regrets that he cannot close with the dragon hand-to-hand). This is why he consequentially scorns an army, although he cannot undo his death-day: not fearing combat or the dragon's great strength, Beowulf responds to his obligations as a king should but to his task as a warrior.[35]

Beowulf, as already indicated, meets the dragon with a comparable energy, on the field of rage. The narrative of the fight, of course, indicates the dynamic opposition here as the poet modulates his names for the dragon, deepening their horrible character as the fight progresses. Before the fight, we have mainly a 'wyrm,' a hoard-guardian, a people-harmer (l. 2278). When the dragon attacks, it becomes a shocking force, called a 'strange terror' (l. 2560), a 'glittering horror' (l. 2576), a 'savage spewer of fire' (ll. 2581–2). Qualifying adjectives intensify the horror. When Wiglaf joins Beowulf and thereby forms a war-band, the dragon becomes 'atol inwitgæst' (l. 2670a) and harmer of people, a terrible fire-dragon (ll. 2688–9).[36] Against the nuclear *comitatus* – unlike the cowards, Wiglaf rightly remembers the weapons and gifts Beowulf repeatedly gave him – the dragon assumes a Grendelian character, becoming a 'gæst,' a weird harmer of people. Beowulf's loans to Wiglaf were not thrown away, even though Wiglaf knows that Beowulf planned the fight as a singular encounter. Wiglaf essentially has internalized Beowulf's needs as his own, no matter what the terror they both now face, with Wiglaf urging Beowulf on (dependency within reciprocity). Super-ego mastery triumphs here, even though Wiglaf is a lesser figure and is potentially capable of criticizing his lord (whether his comments literally do or not). His address to the cowards is the voice of the super-ego, and his later edict against the cowards (ll. 2884–91) does not include himself; he focuses on the cowards themselves and on how they and their kinsmen will fare now that the receiving of treasure and giving of swords must end, along with the joys of home and their land-right (held on the lord's behalf).

After the battle, with the dragon dead and Beowulf dying, we hear about the gold again. It is very hard to win the gold; Wiglaf reacts in awe when he enters the mound, as though the splendour shakes even his loyal heart (momentarily). Furthermore, we hear eventually that the gold long ago had a curse wound around it. This is mentioned in a passage that moves from the dead dragon to the treasure and on to Beowulf's death (ll. 3045–75). Super-ego assurance aside, this business of the gold refuses to go away. The poet works here, I think, with the treasure as a fatal lure, but not for Beowulf or even Wiglaf. Intuitively the poet understands a regression – formed on the dragon's scathing beastiality – that dwarfs the human, becoming huge, ancient, awful, and elemental. Heremod, Hrothgar's vision of the terrible king, is puny in comparison. Monstrous possessiveness and the death of all rivals – wishes never completely erased – surface here and take to the air. The dragon's hoard is not the father's loan (although that is exactly how Beowulf tries to resignify it and why he thanks 'Wuldercyning, ece Drihten' for sight of the treasure before he dies). The earthly lord in the case of the treasure has died and would, by wrapping a curse around it, keep the treasure rather than pass it on as loaned energy for a future people (unless the person who received it had the owner's kinship-like favour, 'est'): the treasure remains the honour and favour of the race who possessed it when alive. God of course can unwind the curse, for he is the True King of Victories (l. 3055a). He can open the hoard – presumably has done so for Beowulf – and release the treasure to men who can use it then in their exchanges. This could happen and it does in part. But Beowulf dies and so a kind of curse on the artful treasure continues. The treasure deepens in valence, becoming a symbol of everything wrongly hidden away, possessed in darkness, spell-bound by evil thought so that the possessor's favour is turned into a curse, not a gift, for those who disturb the treasure-place (a way of understanding 'agendes est,' l. 3075a).[37] This connotation, however, does not cling to the treasure as Beowulf's hoard, honouring him, although the poet says that in the ground the treasure is as useless now to men as it was before.

As something other than material for loans, as a decaying heap in the dragon's burial mound, the cursed treasure takes us deeper than we were with the Grendel creatures, deeper than fratricidal rivalry or inchoate revenge or oral hostility. There is no 'father' and his happy favourites here (in relation to the ancient treasure, that world has died and therefore cannot compensate anyone for any primal overcoming or renunciation). Someone has taken the father's place, someone who has no intention of sharing anything. The dynamic here goes far beyond a weakening of super-ego mastery: we have collapsed psychic life entirely into pure possessiveness with no opposition and no resistance. This is a claim of evil omnipotence; any loss provokes pure rage. In the dragon we have the primal infant's first, purest, and most uncomprehending, unrelenting rage. Such a rage precedes even those fateful impulses manifested in Grendel's mother – the inchoate need for revenge that already is channelled and aware of weakness (she flees Heorot when challenged by swords). Beowulf survived his struggle with that source of the grim and greedy, but he cannot survive his struggle with primal rage, with a deep logic apparent only in a psychological perspective – at least not insofar as he quenches the shockingly huge and criminally opposed source of that rage (a connotation possible in 'wiðerræhtes,' in how the dragon lay dead opposite Beowulf).

Thus the three monster fights have drawn successively upon elementally deeper and older levels in the psyche. They correspond closely to the increasingly monstrous or less recognizably human character of the creatures (Grendel is a hall-thane, his mother a sea-wolf, the dragon a terrible horror) and to an increasingly ancient perspective attached to the creatures (the mother comes to Heorot as an ancient fate might ['geosceaft'] and the dragon, three hundred years old, guards a treasure that has lain still for a dark millennium). The dragon's rage is omnipotent rage unhinged, brooking no cessation except in the utter destruction of its object. The human parallel to the dragon is Ravenswood (hence the prominence of that story in the messenger's expectations of future strife).

The enraged guardian at Ravenswood is Ongentheow, an ancient and terrible warlord ('eald ond egesfull' links him to the dragon, 'egeslic eorðdraca,' l. 2825a, and to Grendel's terrible head, l.1649a). Apparently a war-band of Geats has raided his kingdom, in response to lawless feud on the part of his offspring, Onela and Ohtere (as king, Onela becomes great and laud-worthy). The Geats have carried off his wife and some gold. He pursues them, recaptures his wife, kills many Geats, and surrounds the rest in Ravenswood where they endure a night of fierce, Odinesque threats as Ongentheow rages. Come morning, he says, the Geats will die – some by the sword and others by hanging, and they will become sport for birds. Death, dishonour, fierce revilement, and mutilation await them and their bodies. They suffer the prospect miserably, but a rescue party arrives, routs Ongentheow, and chases him to a hill-fort, where one Eofer eventually slays him in single combat. Hygelac then gives great treasure to the victorious warriors (two brothers struck at Ongentheow – Wulf and Eofer, names that signify battle-ferocity, wolf and boar). The analogue is partial but telling. Beleaguered Geats are saved by their king's thanes from an enraged guardian (Ongentheow is called a 'folces hyrde,' l. 2981, as he falls dead).[38] An old sword of giants, as in the Grendel's mother episode, does him in – presumably because Ongentheow would have survived, as terror might, the blow of a lesser sword.

Great treasure comes to the victors yet enmity lives on in a complicated setting. Framed as a settlement, the ending is definitive but as with the Danes and the Grendel family, a renewal of strife does occur. The messenger who tells the story fears a renewal of feud after news of Beowulf's death reaches the Swedes, who are still in a mixed state of unsettled 'kinship' called peace (without dependency and exchange with the Geats). Beowulf has had good and bad relations with various Swedish princes and he may in fact be related, or at least connected through his father's service, on his Wægmunding side to the Swedish house; a Geat herald thinks feud is in the offing, nevertheless, especially when Onela's kindred learn of Beowulf's death.

Both Ongentheow and the dragon have their day of rage and neither one prevails for long in the moments allotted to him. But Ongentheow's rage may have its way yet – a rage that is somehow part of historical enmity and war between the two peoples, involving, as between Franks and Geats, no reciprocity and dependency between the peoples and thus no taking on of the other's needs as one's own (the best lord-retainer relationship is a model for the best cross-group relationships). We can link the dragon, then, to the deepest of psychic levels and to the broadest of feud relations between neighbouring peoples. Despite its form, Beowulf's dragon is not a symbolic penis (comically gigantic) in a boy's Oedipal quest for treasures and princess. The *Beowulf* poet has deepened the beast-father into a glittering horror, a possessor of everything, who refuses to share; his possessions are not loaned; indeed, they are spell-bound against appropriation; he would rather destroy than establish reciprocities. As guardian of his people and as battle-king, Beowulf resolutely arrays himself against such a bestial king. But who can be wholly immune to the dragon's gold, to the primal possessiveness that gold signifies, even though no one can ever actually return to the first moments of such wishes? No man alive, not even the greatest of men in those days, let alone any of today's men.

Ravenswood has brought the dragon into human feuds across time. But both Wiglaf and the messenger recall more. Their dire speeches realistically incorporate the mood of lament set earlier in the speech of the last survivor (who buried the hoard in the first place). I think the poet here would emphasize the potential for violence in Beowulf's world on Beowulf's last day alive, his first day dead. The poet seems to recognize that super-ego mastery, which would prevent grudge feuds or lawless grievances, is not general in the world. When achieved its dimensions are heroic but it does not last. Eventually its examplars die and where war has not been transmuted into dependency and exchange we can expect the encouragement of feuds and the outbreak of dark impulses.

The poet's melancholy may reflect that awareness: super-ego mastery is rare, impermanent, and (even in its exemplars) necessarily rests upon, and draws from, ghostly susceptibilities to impulses otherwise fully suppressed or else repressed in the service of super-ego mastery. Only in heaven, perhaps, can super-ego values be permanent, can requital for crimes be final. Yet the poet does not dismiss Beowulf's world: good kings may appear again and Wiglaf shows many of Beowulf's virtues, forming a noble and battle-brave war-band around himself. The poet, while speaking of God as the glorious ruler of all, is nevertheless tied to the world he writes large in a reciprocity and dependency of belonging and regret – a world he does not transcend. Indeed, with so much connected to everything else in this world, God becomes the guarantor of requital and punishment, the ultimate resting place for values no one questions.

In the course of the poem, the poet has dramatized a composite ideal of retainer and king. The force of that idealization is complete: Beowulf has no actual taint, no culpable weakness. Kings are praised, even idealized (Heremod excepted). Fathers are always good, although they may suffer tragic losses. This idealization of king and father suggests that Oedipal and pre-Oedipal conflicts are not completely resolved. Perhaps this is because the Oedipal crisis is fixed at a fairly early point in the deep dynamic of the heroic world dramatized in this poem, a dynamic where harsh super-egos are formed along with repressed but active ids. Weak egos are caught between them. That effectively would prevent a realistic appraisal of fathers and kings.

The warrior initiation seems to leave a weak ego and a very strong super-ego, which remains in intimate touch with unconscious impulses. Because few warriors or kings achieve the mastery Beowulf does, regression apparently occurs often, in one guise or another. The strength of super-ego dictates may not wane altogether; indeed, they may remain strong enough in many cases to deflect aggression away from one's own group. Perhaps intuitively realizing this, the poet's moods of regret and loss express his recognition that the desired super-ego is not easily achieved, and that achieving a super-ego is usually a precarious business. Yet, like the world he depicts, the poet is caught up in both a material and psychological economy of loaned goods, loaned energies, and dependency. The poet affects us, as readers, in the last third of the poem only if we have some stake in Beowulf's super-ego mastery, in his superlative generosity, his harmony-inducing favours, protector-kindness to his people, and eagerness for renown (central, kinship-like virtues framed by two drawn from the *comitatus* – 'milts' and the desire for good repute). The battles with monsters may in themselves not move us, but if Beowulf's death does, that happens because we too are children of the super-ego – albeit to different extents and in our own, reflective orientations.

Conclusion

Beowulf's perception of his situation regarding the dragon has been discussed in terms of his dismayed turmoil of mind – the basically right-minded but momentarily dark and tumultuous supposings of an ethical battle-king. When his people say of him that he was of world-kings the most generous (rather than 'mildest') of men, the most given to tying men together in kindred harmony, to his people the most kind and most eager for good repute, they speak of him in superlatives drawn from both *comitatus* reciprocity (the generosity of the lord as expressed in 'milde') and cohesion-oriented social values within both kinship relations and the egalitarian group of retainers (expressed by 'milde' also, then doubly reinforced by 'monðwære' and 'liðe').[1] These values are of the sort Wealhtheow insists upon when, after Hrothgar's adoption attempt in Heorot, she would have Beowulf assume a less than lord-like relationship toward her sons and the Danish warriors assembled in the hall – all of whom are to favour and support each other, while standing in a vertical relationship of reciprocal honouring ('hold') toward Hrothgar.

Thus Beowulf's people do not eulogize him primarily as their superior in a reciprocal, *comitatus* relationship. They do something of the sort, of course, insofar as 'milde' can apply to the superior person and also to inferiors who reciprocate with gratitude, say, for the lord's generosity of spirit. But more than that they emphasize Beowulf's socially cohesive behaviours, the way in which he, while clearly awesome in his prowess, would *not* insist upon superiority involving loaned energies – although he accepts gifts, and gives gifts either in return or in expectation of having them used on his behalf. Their praise suggests their view of his unaided approach to the dragon (he did not think it 'fitting' – 'gemet,' suggesting judgment when said of God – that anyone other than himself should undertake that journey, thus freeing his retainers of their immediate obligation). Those left behind must feel gratitude for his efforts on their behalf: Beowulf died in the course of winning that treasure for his people. But contrary to the lamenting messenger's grim suggestion that they burn the treasures on his funeral pyre, they instead bury a good part of it in the grave-mound they carefully build over a ten-day period. Then they ride around the mound and sorrowfully speak about him and praise him. He was not proud nor did he tyrannically demand their energies on his behalf; instead he befriended them and took immense risks upon himself (the tenor of which we miss when we evaluate his heroism as selfish in some way or interpret his focus on the gold as betraying greed). The fame he sought is the renown of those who think and act rightly.

Thus the Geats, in their sorrow, idealize Beowulf's harmony-making social qualities, expressing kinship and group values they no doubt hold dear in their diminished and threatened status (as the poet probably does in his world). Yet their values conform with Beowulf's last thoughts when he thanks the eternal lord, the King of the World, for the treasures upon which he gazes and which he signifies as something for his people; Beowulf adds that now because he is dying, Wiglaf must attend to the people's needs. He then commands that a barrow be built, high on the cliff, as a memory for his people and as a navigation point in his name for seafarers (here returning, in a sense, to his earliest tasks on behalf of the Geats, that of clearing the sea-lanes of monsters). He then hands on a kind of leadership in material form – neck-ring, helmet, and corselet – before his soul seeks the judgment of those firm in truth.

This is truly a kinship-fostering king concerned for the harmonious maintenance of his people, who, despite his apparent wishes, inter the treasure he won for them in his burial mound, honouring him. The extent to which Beowulf values kinship (and support in kinship terms) has been little noted in the critical literature because of his obvious prominence as a terrifying force when in battle. However, we need to consider the overwhelming themes of his brooding discourse before rising to challenge the dragon. He speaks of the dispiriting event in which one of his uncles slayed another. It was an accident and thus without compensation; it could not be avenged because of the kindred relationship. This tragedy brings their father, King Hrethel, to think less well of the slayer. Beowulf likens King Hrethel to the figure of a mourning father who must endure the execution of his condemned son without taking revenge and who then becomes a lonely and pathetic formula, the elegiac figure for whom the world is now empty. Prior to these scenes Beowulf speaks of the love and honour he received from King Hrethel when he became foster son among the Geats, no less dear to Hrethel than either of the two sons involved in the accidental slaying or Beowulf's own, dear uncle, Hygelac (the third son). These thoughts precede his turn to stories and memories of feud settlement and thus his shift to a state of physical resolve regarding the dragon. So Beowulf expresses vulnerability in terms of intimate losses (father's losses of sons) and intimate cherishing (Hrethel of him and he of Hygelac). Thus it is no wonder that his first words after suffering the dragon's mortal bite are of kindred – his regret that he has no son to whom he can leave his battle gear. He notes that he ruled his people for fifty years in such a way that no one dared attack the Geats or threaten them and he never sought battle or swore oaths falsely. Then he emphasizes that, although in great pain and dying, he can take comfort in his knowledge that the Ruler of Men cannot accuse him of the killing of kinsmen (or even of displacing cousins, given that he refused the kingdom after Hygelac's death).

As noted in the preceding chapter, Beowulf is clearly the super-ego nemesis of all that is Odinesque. He becomes this nemesis through the calling up of monstrous energies in the father's service. As such a hero, metaphorically, he needs periodic chances to overcome the monstrous – whether it be creatures beyond the human or the monstrous things humans do. Psychologically this monstrousness includes the oral rapacity of the hating hall-thane, Grendel; the gallows-mindedness of the monster mother's partly dissociated feelings of revenge; and the incredibly niggardly, omnipotent rage of the dragon-like. As a warrior of Tiu Beowulf would oppose all of this, mythologically reasserting and periodically reconfirming the priority of right and settlement in matters of hall reciprocity. Here the dragon's rage is definitive for in its monstrous possessiveness is the death of all rivals: there is no father and his happy favourites here, no community for the hating Cain or the vengeful mother, but simply niggardly, omnipotent rage unhinged. The particular social forms this three-level monstrousness takes include hoarding, fratricide and treachery within the hall, and malicious feud between neighbouring peoples. The lingering underside of heroic life in these reversions, for the super-ego hero, is the terrible feeling that one has been abandoned by one's lord or by God; for some others of great achievement, like Heremod, that underside is the threat of turning into a monster oneself. This threat, in effect, buoys up all gifts for services, all reciprocities in the heroic world, and leads to Beowulf's stipulative sense of proper exchange and worthy behaviour among kinsmen and in the hall. That right sense, of course, means that exchange is both continuing reciprocity in the hall or else deadly, definitive paying back in an attempt at settlement.

As nemesis Beowulf forms himself first through ties of loyalty and then through legalistic violence. These are what make him a man. Retainership, reciprocity, and kinship identity further place him in the heroic world and characterize his ethical life, keeping it on course, so to speak, and continually compensating for any renunciations of dark desire, reenacting loans from the father or lord. Here we can detect a ghostly, deeply suppressed link between Beowulf and the dragon – delight in treasures. Treasure *are* important, in some sense absolutely so, but primarily because without reward one would seem a slave, one's deep sacrifices negated. Thus treasures matter; they are things in which to exult because they are, as rewards for services, compensations for a primal overcoming, compensations tying one in a reciprocal dependency to the battle-lord and his values and needs (or else to God as Lord, where one is one's own king).

Given these considerations, it is especially fitting that the surviving nobility among the Geats praise this most generous of kings in the way in which they do. He is idealized not as a fierce battle-king like Scyld Scefing nor primarily the legislator but as the superlative upholder of kinship-like generosity and amity. This, I think, is an unusual portrait of a secular king: he exemplifies not simply munificence, wisdom, and battle prowess; not Christ-like mildness and mercy;[2] and not something in-between. Rather than conceptualize the overlay of lordship upon kinship ties in the person of a childless Beowulf, the poet has merged the two with an emphasis on kinship values and feeling. That merger in effect makes the most of kinship as a template for every relationship outside of marriage, bringing together the familial and the social within the kinship of the hall.

We need to enter this world of values and perceive it in the way Beowulf, Wiglaf, and other Geats do before we pass judgment on it. We also need to see how deeply committed the poet is to the world he has written large for us in *Beowulf* and how important his sense of impermanence is. When psychological mastery is achieved, its dimensions are heroic; when its exemplars die and war has not been transmuted into dependency and exchange we can expect the encouragement of feuds, whether in the form of malicious attacks, suspended settlements, or opportunistic raiding.

The burden of this book has been to reanimate that world and its values, to see it as Beowulf, Hrothgar, and others do and to reposition the poet in relation to the heroic past he labours into being. The poet's double-perspective on the world of his noble characters might have led him to a Christian distancing from his material. Instead, I have argued, he everywhere underwrites the essential values of that world, which he owns as well, and which he sanctions by every means available to him. If the poet's theistic Christianity has done anything for him in his view of the heroic past it has extended ultimate truth to the rightly oriented perceptions of his noble characters. Thus Grendel is not simply an evil-minded, misbegotten creature; he is of the lineage of Cain by association, of devils in some way, and thus of mankind's enemy in some cosmic sense. These ideas are not given to the poet's characters but are obviously shared, as Marijane Osborn has shown, with his Anglo-Saxon audience. But the world goes on in its changeable and violent ways: there is no clear view in the poem that times have got better since those days. Beowulf is both an unsurpassable battle-king and an ideal social king for all times; his death and the subsequent plight of his Geats are poignant aspects of life, not part of a doomed past from which Christians have miraculously escaped through Christ's intervention.

The poet, in effect, asserts his temporal, social, and cultural ties with the heroic past he projects for us in *Beowulf*. At the social level he deals repeatedly with facts of relationship or construction – consanguineous kinship, constructed kinship, lord-retainer relations and kinship-like amity, in-law hopes and tensions, the modes of customary settlement as distinct from baleful feud, the terms of reciprocal honouring and giving, and the morally framed construction of personhood. At the level of culture he focuses on a wide array of legends and on mythologically inflected deity either as ways of defining values or as carriers of them.[3]

The nomenclature for kinship in Old English is fairly sparse with very few relationships singled out beyond those within the immediate and extended family, to the third generation. Vocabulary for in-laws is especially lean, perhaps reflecting the relative unimportance of such ties or oath-like bonds. Of course, in the poem in-law relationships are notably fraught, as in the case of Hildeburh and Finn and that outbreak of violence when her brother visits, or in Beowulf's view of prospects for the marriage of Freawaru to Ingeld as an abortive attempt to settle a bloody feud. But *Beowulf*, and Anglo-Saxon society in general, shows us a bilateral (cognatic) kinship structure in which any given person has ties to both father's and mother's families and can inherit from either equally (although in *Beowulf* we only hear of kings and fathers leaving inheritances to their sons). The uncle-nephew, that is, brother's-sister's-son bond is a prominent one in *Beowulf*, as it seems to be for Anglo-Saxon societies and Germanic ones generally. When Anglo-Saxon societies come into focus historically for us they are clearly hierarchical and often involve armies and war-bands where reciprocal loyalty and trust exist between the war-band leader and his retainers first; then, the war-band leader has a relationship to a greater lord or king. As it were, Byrthnoth in *The Battle of Maldon*, as entered in the *Anglo-Saxon Chronicles* for 991, is Æthelræd's thane but his men are *his* thanes: they fight and die for him, not for his king.

Tacitus reports that Germanic war-bands were kinsmen bands, an observation, if we credit it, that holds ambiguities. Were they bands of natural or constructed kinsmen or both? In *Beowulf* we see bands of mixed peoples in the cases of Danes and Geats. But the important point here is that the band in the hall is a 'sibbegedriht,' a kinsman band, however disparate consanguineously. We err in thinking of the lord-retainer relationship as imposed upon and even eventually superseding unnecessarily idealized kinship ties. In *Beowulf* the strongest and best relationships are reciprocally martial and honouring, agnatically biased in aristocratic contexts, consanguineous, and partially constructed – that is, formed and resignified over time in various circumstances given the exigencies of violence, requital, need, victory, and defeat. Here we need to reconsider Beowulf's intensified relationship with Wiglaf – a kinsman generally but not as close as a son or a near relative; yet he is someone who becomes especially dear by what he does, voluntarily coming to Beowulf's aid against the dragon. Wiglaf does not act automatically in some fixed melodrama of illustrative loyalty, any more than Beowulf's exemplary love of and loyalty toward Hygelac is mechanical.

As for revenge and feud, *Beowulf* scholarship reflects a nearly settled view that the poem implicitly undermines the ethic of revenge by showing how vicious, interminable, and destructive it becomes – all kingdoms suffer through hard times or simply come to grief. Yet Beowulf himself announces the good of revenge, Hrothgar rejoices in the prospect of it, and God effectually underwrites it as an honourable action – note the revenge He takes upon giants and Grendel and his favour on Beowulf's behalf. Even Hildeburh, one might say, gains a mixed measure of revenge, after bitter sorrow, when reinvigorated Danes lethally punish Finn and his remaining hall-troops (a band of Frisians who are called giants). So it goes: we are not to say that revenge is awful but rather we are asked to consider the vicissitudes of a violent world. Thus, while considering the fragility of Hrothgar's peace efforts in the prospective wedding of his daughter to the Heathobard king, Ingeld, Beowulf knows that some righteous, old warrior will harbour bitter thoughts when he sees the bride's escort wearing a sword taken from slain Heathobards. The violence Beowulf expects is awful but the issue of revenge is in itself unexceptionable: the question seems to be, rather, just how is one to achieve a peaceful settlement between previously warring people? This is a pressing question in that it applies within a temporal scheme that incorporates past and present rather than separating a more violent past from a somehow less fraught present.

Since Tolkien's time an enormously influential and variously fruitful line of criticism has seen this issue of feuds and time differently. The poet has been separated in his Christian sense of time and value from the noble but doomed world of characters in the poem. A review of time schemes in the poem, however, along with a consideration of the past as social and cultural myth, has shown that *Beowulf* is a repository for values and arrangements that reinforce those existing (or desired) in the present. Thus we are led in another direction entirely – to seeing the poet's (and our) relationship to the poem's world as though to an ancestral one understood as past but not deeply so and not alienated. Indeed, this is a past brought up to the near present – one world incorporated.

This can be seen in the poet's statements concerning good and splendid behaviour and events, in the ways he has God underline heroic events by his favour, and in the shared areas of theism the poet gives over to his noble characters – a sharing that is nearly complete. The poet emphasizes great sameness with only some differences, rather than great difference finally with some sameness. We can understand the poet's temporal sense of this ancestral world as reflecting not clock time but genealogy, not a darkened past but descent, not separation but continuity from the perspective of the near or actual present. We thus move away from a curiously doubled reduction – the poet's ostensible reduction of his pagan forbears, however noble, as marked by doom, failure, and darkness; and our reduction of the poet to a cultural past in some sense deracinated of values other than the desperately compensatory ones of transcendental Christianity.

To reenter the poem's world then means to try and see it as its characters do and as one can suppose the poet does, unless he says otherwise (as in his denunciation of heathen idol invocations). This reseeing certainly takes us into the great scenes involving Beowulf's approach to Heorot and the subsequent scenes of gift giving. Much *Beowulf* commentary, when it notices these scenes especially, is satisfied with general evocations of colour, heroic world grandeur, poetical convention, and the protocol of the stereotypically diplomatic, when not obsessed with Hunferth's character or the somnambulence of Beowulf's retainers before Grendel comes. But if protocol and diplomatic aspects of those scenes are stereotypical, just how is that so and according to what known models?

If we look closely we can see the social drama involved in Beowulf's approach to Heorot, within Heorot itself, in the great scene of post-Grendelian gift giving, and in Wealhtheow's counter giving. All is not tapestry as much as a world riven with danger, defensiveness, requirements of honour, customary law, and evolving intentions. Wealhtheow, as I have argued, is not slated arbitrarily to make either nice or worried speeches. She speaks in contexts, in response to developing situations, as does Hrothgar himself and several Danish warriors – from the coastguard to Hunferth – who successively challenge Beowulf in different environments and in different relationships to his equally changing and amplified statements of purpose.

In brief, Beowulf's approach to Heorot is not a negotiation between two powerful, warring parties involving the voices of aggrieved clients and the mediating influence of wise counsellors. Nor is his thought of helping Hrothgar the result of any kind of fosterage or prior bond whereby Hrothgar has extended a reciprocal friendship (as Raymond Firth, 1967, tells us might have obtained for nineteenth-century Tikopians). Indeed, it is something of a puzzle ethnographically why Beowulf in fact comes, although the outcome eventually involves an alliance between Danes and Geats. We could think of this affair as something like a medial alliance such as the bilateral Taurigs (a Filipino people) make with each other in particular circumstances. Their medial alliances, however, are changeable and unstable – Taurig groups may be allies one month and foes the next. Certainly Grendel is Hrothgar's 'trouble' case but he has not called upon Beowulf, who comes unsummoned, out of generous impulses perhaps elicited by his memory of Hrothgar's good lordship vis-à-vis Beowulf's father. His coming is less obligatory than magnanimous, but it is a carefully advanced gift (in character for Beowulf, whether young or old). So while there is a social context for Beowulf's arrival and a plausible motive, his appearance in the poem is larger than life, serving cultural as well as social purposes.

Beowulf, I think, has come as a warrior of Tiu – if we believe Georges Dumézil's account of Tiu as the war-god of law, the first father of the heavens, who is associated with light, rightful settlement, and the drawing of boundaries. But in his own consciousness he comes out of good will and favour, to honour Hrothgar and ask a boon of him – that he and his retainers might gain stewardship of the hall against Grendel. This purpose and the commitment behind it become fully apparent only through successive statements and encounters, until finally Hrothgar out of his special need does grant Beowulf a special office ('sundernytt' – not just defence against Grendel, something many Danes have already tried and bloodily lost). Heorot is entrusted for the night to Beowulf to have, to hold, and to defend against the awesome, lawless, and finally unknowable Grendel.

The scenes of gift giving in Heorot and, later, in Hygelac's hall, have elicited considerable commentary in *Beowulf* studies. Perhaps no practice in the poem has been so fully remarked upon in study after study of the war-band and the relationship between lord and retainer. This aspect of the poem's social world then is the best known and yet, paradoxically, the one most often misunderstood, after that of revenge.

The causes for this seem two-fold: first there is a tendency to see gifts as mainly contractual and matter-of-fact, as due rewards for services and services for rewards, tying lord and retainer to each other as part of ongoing relationships, which are reaffirmed simply with each subsequent act of reciprocity; then there is disquiet with gift exchange as something that reflects an undercurrent, potentially, of unseemly delight in riches, competition between retainers, and greed – or even reciprocity collapsed into murderous niggardliness. None of this is wrong on the face of it; it is simply not right and dynamic enough to account for the scenes of gift giving, for what is said and done in various contexts.

There is, of course, a competitive mode – of honour especially – that involves several principles: only those with honour can confer it; only those like Hrothgar and King Beowulf, with freedom to give, can modify prior intentions or commitments and resignify promised giving after the fact of notable developments; and only those who are famous in the world can remedy breaches by giving great gifts for which some return or at least restoration is implicitly looked for (consider Hunferth's loan of the sword Hrunting and Beowulf's eventual return and praise of the sword, even though Hrunting could not dent Grendel's mother). Others can enter into a scene of gift giving for their own purposes, giving gifts they signify in their own way. I think of Wealhtheow here especially; she has no obligation to give great gifts, unless we see her earlier exultation over Beowulf's boasts as an implicit commitment to reward him should he happily confront Grendel on behalf of the Danes. And one can even speculate plausibly here about Hygelac's bereaved queen, Hygd. Once honoured by Beowulf when he returned from the Danes, she strongly, even commandingly ('gebeodan'), offers him the kingdom, the treasure store, rings, and the throne after Hygelac's death, doing so in preference to her own son both because of his youth and because she would greatly honour and tie this powerful warrior-nephew-in-law to herself and her family.

Gifts in *Beowulf* are alienable, becoming the recipient's to do with as he or she chooses; but often something of the giver's gesture attaches itself to the gift. Thus gifts are not mute objects so to speak: they bespeak their givers' hopes, wishes, longings, suggestions, doubts, invitations, and assertions.

My anthropological methodology has been analogical, comparative, and cross-temporal. Direct ethnographical comparisons of the world of *Beowulf* with some anthropologically witnessed worlds similar to Beowulf's where face-to-face, non-centralized people still live, escape us. The best we can do, I think, is look at relevant institutions and customs among peoples organized in ways that illuminate salient aspects of Beowulf's social and cultural world. This involves societies where the kinship structure is bilateral; where constructed kinship is apparent for groups acting together in common need or purpose; where gift giving is central and gifts alienable; where revenge and feud are forms of customary redress and settlement, involving the recruitment of support groups from among kinsmen and interested neighbours; where there is social hierarchy tending toward monarchy, involving chiefs and warriors; where there are myths and stories that incorporate into the present the values and enactments of either legendary or actual ancestors and figures from the past.

One might, of course, attempt a meta-ethnology, working towards models of bilateral kinship systems generally, towards gift-exchange principles in relationship, say, to commodity markets and the societies organized through and around them (Marilyn Strathearn, 1988), towards theories of feuding that account for the ways in which groups define and relate to each other and to themselves, and towards the normative ways in which myths and legends function culturally, giving rise to suggestive arrays, variants, and types of manipulable stories. But I do not attempt such overviews with *Beowulf*. Rather, these subjects when focused on through point-to-point inspections open up perspectives on the world of *Beowulf* in many and often surprising ways, much as they begin to suggest why some of the features of face-to-face bilateral worlds are as they are.

For instance we might ask how a bilateral, agnatically inflected, aristocratic social organization shapes feuding patterns and resources, giving to aggrieved parties a need to recruit widely in some cases because local ties of kinship may not provide sufficient support. Kinship groups can disperse, yet 'kinship' is a powerful concept and in fact seems to become an idea for tying consanguineously unrelated people together, through affinity, adoption, and reciprocal service into common groups or for common cause. Marriage practice seems to move mainly toward alliance and then, through fosterage, to possible coalescence of inheritances and common cause in the next generation (as is the case, eventually, regarding Geat and Wægmunding holdings when Wiglaf notes that Beowulf honoured him by giving him ancestral lands). Again bilateral kinship groups tend to disperse, mitigating against establishing stable marriage patterns between (stable, corporate) groups. The brother's-sister's-son bond may also be a way in which the sister is not given away (her precious offspring returns).

Gift-giving practices operate within these exigencies and are highly manipulable given the ties one wants to form or reinforce. Even customary ideas of right and of good and proper behaviour are affected by the centrifugal tendencies of dispersal. Local variations cannot be enshrined for long; ancestor cults, and corporate rights and territories do not exist, and so they cannot reinforce local custom. What is right and good becomes formulable (and no doubt variable) within broad terms, approaching the gnomic (as in Beowulf's pronouncements and the poet's statements of 'so should a man do'). A region's myths, legends, and ancient genealogies may be given meaning in the ways they are used idiosyncratically. They are not local, corporate possessions; they can be owned and appropriated by those who need to construct (incorporating) justifications for their emerging or achieved power. West Saxon kings seem to do this and so does Hrothgar in a sense when he commands the building of a hall he *names*, the only named hall in the poem and so a kind of myth in itself, where the Danish dynasty lives and where Hrothgar practises an ideal munificence. Halls in general are perhaps the most dynamic and comprehensive of places and ideas in that they merge thane and kin concepts into the kinship band idea of retainers, thus establishing dual ties between retainers and each other and retainers and their lord.

When we step back to consider these things as they appear in *Beowulf*, the poem becomes multi-dimensional in its social reality, gaining a social coherence, I suggest, that is not apparent if we do not see the poem's actions and details as part of a world that works socially and culturally – a world far removed from our own, boasting values and customs we have left behind or else seriously modified. We have, in brief, misinterpreted many things in *Beowulf* because we have not sufficiently appreciated the social world within which the poet works – at least at the level of the values that bring him to project an heroic world of theistically overseen strife, right, reciprocity, loyalty, and honour that floats above Anglo-Saxon, historical concreteness.

When seen for the social milieu dramatized within it, *Beowulf* becomes very different, open still to all the aesthetic analyses we can manage, given the plentitude of special interests concerning gender roles, patriarchy, psychodynamics, reception theory, literary history, social history, ideology, religion, and the various formalisms that underlie all empirical efforts at analysis. As a projection from the considerable past of a heroic world, *Beowulf* is clearly other than any projection we would comfortably make from within our own worlds. But it is not inaccessible nor need we necessarily flatten it out given our own interests, although we will never escape our own subjectivities. We can entertain, I submit, the great 'as if' of looking hard and imagining ethnologically just how a foreign world might and perhaps indeed does work – in this case the world framed by Scyld Scefing's glorious deeds and those kinship-like, social superlatives with which Beowulf's Geats fittingly honour him while they encircle his funeral mound.

Notes

Introduction

1 See Adam Kuper (1988), Rodney Needham (1971), Roger Keesing (1968, 1970), W.H. Goodenough (1962).
2 See David Dumville (1977), Jack Goody (1983, repr 1988), and William I. Miller (1990).
3 This is H.R. Loyn's quite proper complaint (1962, p. 289).
4 T.A. Shippey (1978, pp. 8–22). Many of his interpretations, however, still reflect thematic assumptions that need social winnowing, so to speak.
5 For the ethical vocabulary of the *comitatus*, see D.H. Green (1965); for boast and drink, especially the presenting of the 'ful,' see Helen Damico (1984); for the social cohesion fostered by drinking in the hall, see Hugh Magennis (1985); for gift giving and exchange, see John M. Hill (1982); for the uncle-nephew relationship, see Rolf H. Bremmer, Jr. (1980); for legalistic diction, see E.G. Stanley (1979); and for a general sense of archaic social structure and the different valuation that puts on worthy objects, weapons, and so on, see T.A. Shippey (1978). The feud and revenge as situations and motifs are discussed in too many places to list, although very few scholars have focused on the feud as a social and even legal institution (aside from noting the wergeld apportionings stipulated in various Anglo-Saxon law codes).
6 W.W. Lawrence (1930, pp. 53–8) is still a serviceable example of this: he notes two areas under 'social organization' – fealty to a liege lord and allegiance to kin. Conflicts of loyalty and obligation can arise in both areas, creating dramas of divided loyalties (say between lord and kin or between a lord back home and a temporary lord to whom one is bound by necessity – as Hengest is with Finn for a miserable winter). Lawrence's generalizations are no longer valid; indeed there were studies contradicting

such claims as revenge duty falling upon the whole kindred even before Lawrence wrote – see, for example, Bertha Phillpotts (1913, repr. 1974), in which she finds no evidence in Anglo-Saxon England for the kindred cohesion needed to support Lawrence's statement, although the cohesion of the kindred apparently did survive the migration period in areas of Denmark and Holland and among the South Germans. Nor was wergeld in Anglo-Saxon law paid out to an extended kindred; and it seems that neither revenge nor wergeld was exacted within the near kindred (thus mitigating some conflicts between kinship and lordship). The point here is not that W.W. Lawrence mistook something, but that similarly erroneous generalizations are still current in much *Beowulf* criticism.

7 Indeed, even the poem's elegiac tones near the end and the messenger's foreboding of attack from hostile Franks and Swedes may well reflect the kinds of feelings that inhabitants of powerful, successful Anglo-Saxon kingdoms might have when formidable kings die. Consider the prospects West Saxons must have posed for themselves when King Athelstan dies, succeeded by a young Edmund not much tried in extended campaigns of defence or the subduing of hostile armies. In the event, West-Saxon England is attacked successfully by Irish vikings, its northern tributary kingdoms cut off and then ceded in a peace settlement.

8 Frances Gies and Joseph Gies (1987, pp. 100–3). Their account blends information from different Anglo-Saxon periods and thus needs to be taken as a general description only, perhaps especially so in the cases of wills and inheritance. The comment on royal succession generalizes unfortunately from an Alfredian arrangement. Most Anglo-Saxon kingdoms have a history of difficult, contested successions, sometimes involving close kin, sometimes distant collaterals (Yorke 1990).

9 Lorraine Lancaster (1958, p. 232).

10 Alexander C. Murray (1983, p. 3).

11 Ibid., p. 5.

12 See, for example, J.D. Freeman (1961), Rodney Needham (1971), Thomas M. Kiefer (1972), and Adam Kuper (1988). H.R. Loyn (1962) wants to separate kindred from family (p. 289), but perhaps should merge the two concepts given bilateral kinship as sketched above. He also eventually notes 'the steadying influence of community over kindreds' (p. 294), thus reminding us of the complexities involved. No doubt communities were made up of interested kindreds because of local ties, responsibilities, and mutual vulnerabilities. A neighbour's interest could become acute in cases of impending blood feud and could stand for non-violent settlement (but see Kiefer, whose bilateral, non-aristocratic Tausug usually require violence, along with munificence, as a mark of manliness and a de-

fence against shame). From among such groups might also come a surrogate kindred, based on interest and proximity, for the person who has no consanguineous kin – perhaps the 'gegildan' referred to in Alfred's law-code (Loyn, 1962, p. 297).

13 N.H. Goodenough (1962, pp. 5–8).

14 In these matters the poet may well have his eye on dynastic strife in Anglo-Saxon kingdoms, such as the internecine warfare between distinct but perhaps linked families (kin groups) that weakened both Northumbria and Mercia in the eight and ninth centuries, and which even touched Wessex shortly after Alfred's death, given Æthelwold's violent refusal to accept his cousin, Alfred's son, Edward. For Mercia, Patrick Wormald (1982, p. 138) speculates that Cenwulf's brother Ceolwulf gives way to Beornwulf, 'whose name suggests the possibility of a link with Beornred, Offa's rival in 757. To judge from their names, neither Ludeca, who replace Beornwulf in 826, nor Wiglaf (827–40) were related to their predecessors. In 840, the "B" dynasty returned in Berhtwulf (840–52) and Burgred.' But a Ceolwulf II (874) succeeds Burgred.

15 Milton McC. Gatch (1971, p. 54) thinks Tacitus exaggerated Germanic virtues to censure Roman degeneracy by contrast. Many others have noted this and some scholars even doubt the ethnological integrity of customs and behaviour attributed to Tacitus' Germans, seeing close parallels in reports of other peoples. Probably these issues cannot be resolved or untangled fully; barbarian peoples in Tacitus' world may share customs or be seen as similar in their customs. Tacitus remains a point of reference, and credibly so, if we can see circumstantial confirmations in the historical record.

16 William Holdsworth (1903, p. 88).

17 That there can be no feud within the near kindred is a point that Frederick Klaeber finds hard to accept; yet it is claimed by Seebohm and others and it has ethnological parallels. Thus Hunferth's fratricide, whether deliberate or accidental, would have been settled without a blood feud; the accidental death of Hrethel's son is unavengable; and Onela does not avenge his nephew's death at Weohstan's hands.

18 Patrick Wormald (1977) differs from the conclusions of nineteenth-century scholarship, which focused on arguments concerning the development of judicial institutions and centralized government, and distinguished between law and administrative regulations, especially as represented by H. Brunner in *Deutsche Rechtsgeschichte* (1887–92). Wormald surveys a wide variety of Germanic law codes and, in Alfred's case at least, suggests that a primary motive was 'to set out the relationship between Divine Law and the laws of the Anglo-Saxons, who were thus in-

vited to fuse as a new holy people. Indeed, it may be that we should explain the association between the *dombuc* and the Anglo-Saxon chronicle in two early manuscripts ... as an attempt ... to present a sort of West Saxon counterpart to the book of Exodus, in which an account of the people's wanderings is followed by a record of its law' (p. 132). The promulgation not of laws but of a written code would then mark a new organization of society. The king does not in this context make law; the society's customs, fused with new law and embracing the church, make the (now almost theocratic) king. For comments similar to Wormald's, although less visionary, see J.M. Wallace-Hadrill (1971, p. 149); see also H.R. Loyn (1984, p. 44) for lawbook-giving as bringing a Christian *ministerium* to the kingship. William A. Chaney (1970, p. 185) would link the giving of law codes back to the sacral character of the Germanic king, especially in laws relating to the church. However, one should note that sacral luck and customary law are separate domains, even when they intersect in victorious, lawful warfare. Hiroshi Hayashi (1981) thinks of the law codes as aiming for *Rechtssicherheit* primarily and a control of the blood feud.

19 William Ian Miller (1990, pp. 77–9, 93–4) discusses some of the distinctions involved.

20 Compare R.W. Chambers (1959, p. 2) and John McNamara (1976, p. 61). McNamara suggests that the fictional Beowulf's noble presence on the Frisian expedition in effect redeems that historical moment. However, Geats and Frisians may well have a respectable, raiding relationship: something short of open warfare, something more turbulent than a tribute relationship, yet hardly something disreputable, even if not amicable.

21 However, the poem has an early 'feel': no mention of bookland, administrative units, stone forts, emporia, coinage, or trade. Also the ethical vocabulary reflects reciprocity more than rule from the top and centralization. I owe the points about names, bookland, administrative grids, and stone fortifications to discussions with my Naval Academy colleague Richard P. Abels. Regarding trade, it seems that mints mean trade and emporia, but just what coins mean can be highly problematic. The Sutton Hoo grave goods include coins as part of the aristocratic treasure stock, but perhaps something the poet would not notice in relation to such prestige items as decorated helmets, swords, shields, and large neck-rings.

22 Kenneth Sisam (1965, pp. 26–7) says this in response to Klaeber's concern.

23 Dorothy Whitelock (1951, pp. 13–19) has long offered us a salutary reminder of the positive valuation given to feud in Anglo-Saxon England. But her comments on attempts to curb the blood-feud, drawing especially upon King Edmund's code (tenth century), do not sufficiently no-

tice that this is an imposition of royal authority upon customary arrangements concerning kindreds. In some African tribes there is no central authority but there is the institution of the feud (an institution of settlements) – indeed, what Max Gluckman calls the peace in the feud, a point of view endorsed by J.M. Wallace-Hadrill (1971, p. 42). Moreover, Whitelock's use of Beowulf's remarks concerning the spear not remaining bowed for long after the fall of men neglects that remark's social referent: an attempted settlement through marriage between *hostile* groups, between whom there is no continuing exchange or dependency (see chapter 4). Intrinsically, this is one of the most unstable arrangements in a non-centralized world.

24 For an elegant review of such studies, see George E. Marcus and Michael M.J. Fischer (1986, especially chapters 2 and 3). Also a remarkable study of leadership in face-to-face groups by Waud H. Kracke (1978) suggests the fruitfulness possible when an anthropologist's psychoanalytical awareness informs a deft approach to marriage rules and social obligations.

25 All citations are from Fr. Klaeber, *Beowulf and the Fight at Finnsburg* (1950). Translations are mine. The collocation of 'healdan' and 'tela' is telling: it differs in formality and social status from appearances of 'tela' (with implied reciprocity) in Wealhtheow's counter-speech to Beowulf, as she urges him to prosper and says that she will reward him well. Thus it means something more than being well rewarded and well attended to in a mutual relationship. It concerns official rule, as when Beowulf ruled well for fifty years. Note also that the collocation occurs in Alfred's *Boethius*, chapter 41, section 3: God gives freedom to men,who should hold it well; in exchange God will give men eternal power or rule. But misuse will bring lethal punishment. If Beowulf holds well this new kinship, Hrothgar will reciprocate by giving Beowulf *everything* over which he has power (which clearly includes, as Wealhtheow fears, his kingdom). He means exactly what he says in the lines 'Ne bið þe [n]ænigre gad / worolde wilna, þe ic geweald hæbbe' (ll. 949b–950). When 'læst' replaces 'heoldan,' 'tela' itself suggests absolute commitment (in extremity) as when Wiglaf urges Beowulf to perform well before the dragon. In exchange Wiglaf will support Beowulf. 'Tela' then implies reciprocity whenever it appears in *Beowulf* within a context of urged behaviour. 'Tela' itself has a formulaic regularity placed at the end in the b half-line, and, in six out of seven cases, it is in a type c line.

26 Few readers have noted that Beowulf could choose here. Andrew Galloway (1990, p. 203) is an exception, arguing that Beowulf's adventure with the Danes 'gains him a position in which anything he does is a matter of choice.' But Galloway does not see choice here or anywhere else

as socially conditioned or entailed. His explanations are opaque, ad hoc.

27 Kemp Malone (1959, p. 113) suggests that both Wealhtheow and Ecgtheow are of the Wulfingas.

28 H. Munro Chadwick (1926, p. 345–6).

Chapter 1 Feud Settlements in *Beowulf*

1 See James A. Brundage (1987, pp. 128–9).

2 See Jack Goody (1983, pp. 246–8) for a review of these matters covering various early Germanic societies.

3 George Clark (1990, p. 80) perceptively notes Hildeburh's directives here, supposing that her burial action is also a peace move, correlated with Finn's. This is ethnologically possible, given that her lament-song can have socially healing power for all the saddened Frisians and Danes. Such a lament is formal speech, perhaps even ritual wailing here and at poem's end (when a Geatish woman, her hair bound up, presumably sings a lament). Stephen Feld (1990, p. 257) thinks of ritual wailing, at least among the Kaluli of New Guinea, who live in long-house communities, 'as a "pulling together" of affect rather than its "falling apart" signaled by dispersal of [negative and] emotional by-products. Ritual wailing for Kaluli serves much more to centrally display and focus the aesthetics of emotionality, and to positively value these social articulations as organized, thoughtful expressions of personal and social identities as deeply felt.' Hildeburh does not express her feelings, but the immediately graphic bursting of heads and bodies in the pyre's devouring flames suggests, through the poet, considerable bitterness on Hildeburh's and Hengest's parts, which in turn shifts the psychology of 'mourning' toward anger and derision (possible in 'bemearn'). That her son's body should rise up and burn in flames curling up to the skies may suggest his innocence and his noble virtue (much as does the heaven-received smoke of Beowulf's pyre); the focus shifts quickly from that to a potentially hostile view of heads melting and blood springing out of hateful body bites, as the fire swallows up those of both peoples whom war took. A lament tone ends the scene as the poet notes that for the dead their glory was departed.

4 Moreover, even the idea of peace-weaving ('freoðuwebbe,' applied to Modthryth in contradistinction to murderous terror) is an equivocal one if linked to ideas of settlement or else, as in Wealhtheow's case, to her argument for priority on her sons' behalf. We can also see that blood-taking may be peace-making, a settling of scores and personal turmoil.

5 Lorraine Lancaster (1958, p. 248).

6 See Levi-Strauss (1988) and especially Roxana Waterson (1990, pp. 163–6). There she discusses Levi-Strauss's concept of 'house societies,' which seems to fit the arrangement of the bilateral Toraja (in the mountains of west Indonesia). In such societies houses function as centres of kin organization; houses have names and elaborately decorated facades; they are the sites for important ceremonies; they have groups divided by ancestors who founded the houses and may involve an alternation of generations, 'with a belief in the reincarnation of grandparents in their grandchildren' (p. 139). Typically such societies use 'house' imagery to express aspects of kinship and marriage. Where rank and inheritance matter greatly, marriage usually is either with close relatives or is quite distant. Some of these features appear in *Beowulf*: a group centralized by the hall, in which a king sits and a queen circulates, also called a house (although the tendency is to call it by some term for a hall – 'heal,' sele,' 'reced' – in connection with ceremony). Heorot has a name, although the hall given to Hengest does not; Heorot is a dynastic centre for several generations of agnates, who alternate generationally in producing either fierce or famous kings, and it is a centre for ceremonies, as seems the case with all halls mentioned in the poem. Moreover, could he adopt Beowulf, Hrothgar would reincarnate his grandfather's name in this new son. The halls are intricately ornamented and decorated on the inside (and probably on the outside as well, over doorways at least) and exterior roof-gable treatment is possible. Words for kinship in *Beowulf* have no relation to 'house' or any word for 'hall,' but the body is called a 'bone house' (protecting the vital spirit) and the armour that protects it is analogous to the strong timbers that protect the community of close kin and kin-like ('sibbegedriht') retainers gathered around the lord in the hall. In Heorot's case, the building of the hall is communal, involving many people from far and wide; it is Hrothgar's effort to confirm and perpetuate the fame and wide dominion of a noble and powerful family of agnates; presumably it contains dynastic treasures and is the stage for a theistic hymn of creation. Thus, as the centre of kinship, amity, and cosmology, it may reflect sacral and magical functions as well as the deeply serious, drink-confirmed reciprocities of the lord to retainer relationship. Wealhtheow and Freawaru, indeed Beowulfian queens in general, preside as 'peace-weavers' and offer the 'ful' (a sacramental cup possibly), thus having quasi-priestess functions within the hall; and even if the hall is eventually destroyed it is certainly remembered.

7 Alan Bliss (1983, Appendix C).

8 William I. Miller (1990, pp. 211–13) gives a subtle and penetrating discussion of this, among many other relevant issues.

9 This is to say that the Danes subliminally would taunt the Heathobards;

to wit: we give you Freawaru to penetrate, but we come as your conquerors, sporting trophies of your emasculation (the sword). For a general treatment of this kind of possibility, at too far a remove from particular social practices, but interesting still, see Devereux (1978, pp. 185–215). At psychological levels, a similar hostility may underlie the Finnsburg episode as well, although here, if the episode were clearer, we would consider the psychology of the taker of a woman who is given but not given away. In relation to these episodes (the one remembered, the other projected), Beowulf's model alliance with the Danes interestingly involves no exchange of women, but only traffic back and forth and the promise of martial aid. Of course other queens in the poem (such as Wealhtheow and Hygd) have come from their own people, with whom no apparent strife occurs; indeed, in Modthryth's case marriage sublimes her, turning her from a terror-princess, who has gazers upon her (would-be rapists?) killed, to a queen who lives in high love with Offa of the Angles. So if there is universal hostility underlying these exchanges, that hostility can be consciously suppressed. Thus the alliance can have binding functions.

10 Jenny Wormald (1986, pp. 191–2) reminds us of this in a sixteenth-century Scottish context.

11 Anglo-Saxon 'friendship' can imply legal responsibility, as I note especially in chapter 5. But here Beowulf seems to state, given his maxim-like formulation, a moral good, similar to that embraced by the bilateral Tausug (Kiefer, 1972, p. 60), who form friendships for mutual support (potentially the case between Danes and Geats). Thus they establish a kinship-like relationship between two men, who would then exchange gifts, but in a competition of increasing values. Supporting a friend is a moral need although friendships can change, even drastically, so that today's friend is tomorrow's enemy. Such a change will in turn alter the already shifting compositions of allied groups for feud purposes, given that ties exist between individuals (who may bring along armed collaterals and clients), not between groups, and that different 'cases' or grievances will involve different individuals and their networks. However, in Beowulf's world of war-bands, kings, and defended territories, we do not see anything as fluid as the situations Kiefer describes for the Tausug, among whom warfare rarely concerns territory or conquest, and for whom ultimate political power rests with the Sultan.

12 Alexander C. Murray (1983, pp. 145–7) cites part of Salic law, in its earliest redaction, especially section 58, 'De Chrenecruda,' ll. 20ff: 'Et si eum in conpositione nullus ad fidem tullerint, hoc est ut redimant de quod non persoluit, tunc de sua vita conponant' 'And if no one stands in

surety for him, to redeem his unpaid debt, then his life be the reconciliation.' That, dear reader, is to the point.

13 Max Gluckman (1955, pp. 80–1). See also Fred L. Cheyette (1978, p. 161) who notes that early medieval settlements did not consider the parties as abstract categories or apply rules to cases. Rather there was a search 'for a resolution in which the status and self-esteem of both parties would be saved and a continuing social relationship created or renewed.'

14 See Eleanor Searle (1989, pp. 165–75).

15 See Christopher Boehm (1989) for an account of ambivalence in blood feud relations.

16 William Ian Miller (1990, p. 275).

17 See Jacob Black-Michaud (1975, especially pp. 63–85) and Christopher Boehm (1987, especially pp. 191–207). Schlegel (1970, pp. 27–57) does not anticipate this dispute perhaps because his work with the bilateral Tiruray in the Western Cotabato mountains of the Philippines did not put him in the middle of competing groups (if they existed) or perhaps because the Tiruray have evolved a system of customary law and morality that could effectively bring even 'bad' blood feud to some kind of peaceful settlement.

18 Perhaps Geats and Franks are even in an incipient state of warfare in the Hobbesian sense: that is, there is a known disposition, even in the absence of actual fighting. David Turton (1979) notes just such a relationship between the Mursi and Hamar of Ethiopia.

19 Catherine Carsley (1992) interestingly points to the invented, genealogical unity of the Scyld Scefing prologue – as a kind of cultural memory – and analyses the poem as a meditation on that memory. The key points concern kinship, heroic action, and fratricidal feud. The episodes involving Finn and Ingeld are held up as emblems, finally, of kinship filled in with a pessimistic combination of heroism and fratricide. The Swedish-Geatish wars are seen as more than raiding practices and rather as a matrix for embroiled allegiances. This fascinating essay, however, misses the jural focus involved in much of this and overreads some of the entanglements: Beowulf owes nothing to Hrothgar and the Danes by poem's end; nor does Wiglaf compromise himself in relation to his father's service on behalf of Swedes, despite wielding the famous sword with which his father slew a Swedish prince befriended by Beowulf's king (Heardred).

20 L. Pospisil (1971, pp. 395–431). See also Bohannan (1963, p. 290) who thinks of feud as self-help getting out of hand.

Chapter 2 The Temporal World in *Beowulf*

1 Bronislaw Malinowski (1961, pp. 327–9). Schlegel (1970, pp. 23–4, 42, 46–7) confirms Malinowski's insight – the tie between myth and custom – but approaches it as a projection of custom into the worlds of spirit and myth.
2 Bronislaw Malinowski (1961, pp. 328–9).
3 Jack Goody (1991, p. 83).
4 Kenneth Sisam (1965, p. 51; and 1953, pp. 322–6).
5 Lorraine Lancaster (1958, pp. 366–7) notes this in a passage from the *Northleoda laga*, referring this and other charter citations concerning status to Dorothy Whitelock (1955, pp. 562, 431, and following).
6 Audrey L. Meany (1989) has plausibly argued that the Scyld Scefing prologue to *Beowulf* 'has one clear source which provides one clear *terminus post quem*: the genealogy of Æthelwulf from the pre-ae *Chronicle* translated by Æthelweard, which *could* not have been fabricated before 858, and probably was not before Alfred's reign' (p. 37; Meany's emphasis). She suggests an Anglo-Danish audience, supporting John Niles's championing of an early tenth-century date for the arrangement of the poem as we know it. If so, the Scyld Scefing genealogy for the Danes would then be part of a post-Alfredian incorporation of the pan-Germanic past into an illustrious, West-Saxon hegemony.
7 While the society he discusses is not organized like the ones in *Beowulf*, Max Gluckman's (1965) review of these concepts, drawn from E.E. Evans-Pritchard's work with the turbulent Nuer of the southern Sudan (1940, pp. 276–7), is a good place to begin defining them. For the Nuer, a unilineal, clan-based society, time is expressed in terms of social relationships and social relationships are understood in terms of family and tribal cycles (repeating lineage depths for the Nuer; but three to four generation kin-lines, attached to agnatically coloured king-lists that ascend to mythical and biblical strings for the West Saxons). The depth involved appears in hierarchical, bilateral societies as well, even in cases of fantastically elaborated, great genealogies – to which a more immediate, ten or eleven generation, chiefly genealogy might be attached (see Marshall Sahlins, 1987, p. 20n18).
8 If anything like this happened in accounts known to the *Beowulf* poet, we might have an anthropological answer for the seeming riddle of Hrothulf's nobility and fame in later, Scandinavian accounts: by assuming Hrothgar's position in the family tree, Hrothulf (Hrolfr) may have taken on the young Hrothgar's characteristics, with the issue of treachery (if there ever were such an issue) shunted to the side in the form of in-laws.

But see Kenneth Sisam (1965, 1971, pp. 80–2) for a plausible resolution of the 'þa gyt' ('then still') phrase applied to Hrothgar and Hrothulf and often translated in context to suggest that uncle and nephew would not always live together in amity or else that Hrothulf will not support Hrothgar's sons. Sisam would have the phrase express time only – a habit among various peoples today when they say that something happened after, say, their schooling but before they married. Hrothulf's future treachery may be entirely a literary invention, serving the tragic ironist in us. That a Latin account has Rolfo born of incest (mother's father) could reflect his original rise in genealogical position, becoming 'son' to his grandfather. In *Widsith*, of course, we are told that Hrothgar and Hrothulf kept peace together the longest (for the longest time?) after they routed the Vikings and destroyed the Heathobards at Heorot. They are famous, it seems, not for the treachery of one to another but for their long-lasting amity. Perhaps that fame is especially notable given that Hrothulf is not a sister's son to Hrothgar (who then is not Hrothulf's 'eam,' uncle though he is).

9 Lorraine Lancaster (1958, pp. 235–9) has done Old English kinship studies an inestimable service by organizing these and other kinship terms into a model, genealogical tree. These speculations regarding cyclical movement within the generational triad are entirely my own, encouraged by such comprehensive terms as 'fæder'(a) used to mark different places in the tree. Helen Spolsky (1977, pp. 234–5) sees 'suhtergefæderan' as cross-generational, covering Hrothgar and Hrothulf from Hrothgar's perspective as well as his sons.'

10 The importance of the 'sister's-son' and sister's brother relationship among Germanic peoples is as well attested as any kinship fact can be for an historically remote people. In *Beowulf*, of course, the uncle-nephew relationship generally, whether sister's son or not, is important in both Heorot and Hygelac's hall; in both halls, within and surrounding the present action of the Grendel fights, it is a relationship of great amity and peace (between Hrothulf and Hrothgar and Beowulf and Hygelac, respectively). Max Gluckman (1963, p. 63) briefly sweeps across many patrilineal peoples in saying that the sister's son 'is tied to his paternal kin by strong interests in property held in common [as Beowulf would be to the Wægmundings] ... He begins to build up his own personal estate from small stock given to him by his mother's brother [although not very small stock, note the corselet Hygelac gives Beowulf]. And the sanctions in this line of descent are moral and ritual, rather than legal.' This is reflected in *Beowulf* but does not hold for Anglo-Saxon, bilateral descent. Indeed, Beowulf's relationship with Hygelac is both one of great,

mutual favouring and dependency and one of inheritance right as Hygelac bestows ancestral lands upon Beowulf (an indirect inheritance from the mother's father's side).

11 Perhaps, then, Ohtere more than Onela led the lawless feuds the two waged against Hygelac's Geats, for which settlement occurred at Ravenswood. This pairing of a figure of terror and a figure of magnanimity (a 'legislator') is part of a deep pattern in Germanic kingship, a central issue discussed in chapter 3.

12 See Max Gluckman (1965, pp. 268–75) for an excellent overview of time in the histories of various African peoples. For remarks about diffusion in bilateral systems, see Lorraine Lancaster (1958, p. 376); for an account of countervailing influences, see J.D. Freeman (1961) and Meyer Fortes (1969, pp. 122–37). Among the African Iban, organizing into family longhouse communities with a titular head and with a keeper of the group's customs helps; a preference for marriage between cousins is another centripetal factor, as is the ability to call upon affiliation through either one's father or one's mother, although not both at once. These latter strategies would be especially attractive in bilateral societies, where dispersal of kin and assets is all too likely (on cousins, compare the Anglo-Saxon church's outrage at close cousin marriages – in 874 Pope John VIII complained to the Mercian king, Burgred, that men fornicate widely and presume to marry within their own kindred [Dorothy Whitelock, 1955, p. 810]). As for primogeniture, having a son not move away but stay to inherit a significant part of the family's estate also helps. In times of feud or other legal or economic difficulty, an ad hoc kinship group of locally available 'kin,' whether cognatic or affinal, or neighbours, clients, and friends, could be mobilized by calling on kinship amity and moral obligations – as seems the case in Anglo-Saxon England (and which Beowulf extends even to Æschere, Hrothgar's boon counsellor, slain by Grendel's mother). These ad hoc groups have a temporary solidarity of focus and purpose; their existence presupposes either a prior kinship structure or 'kindred' feeling as a template. But they are not the reflex of kindred solidarity (which does not exist in Anglo-Saxon England). Moreover, the presence of the war-band organization and the increasingly sacralized and Christianized kingship can greatly alter the social functioning of cognatic kinship in England, although in the final praise we hear of Beowulf, kinship-like amity toward his people is what he is most famous for.

13 Frederic Seebohm (1911, p. 60).

14 See Max Gluckman (1965, pp. 274–5) and E.E. Evans-Pritchard (1940, p. 288).

15 I take the genealogies from Charles Plummer's compilations (1965, p. 6) and note here that both West Saxon and Northumbrian lines roughly accord with the eleven or twelve generation rule – at a time when these kingdoms are no longer unlettered.

16 Kenneth Sisam (1953).

17 John Niles (1983) and Roberta Frank (1982) illuminate such possibilities in the tenth century, stressing continuity between the heroic past depicted in the poem and the poet's Anglo-Saxon present. See also Robert T. Farrell (1982) for an informative overview of culturally friendly relationships between Anglo-Saxons and Scandinavians. He observes, moreover, that alliance and continuity are possible between people who at other times might have been at war, especially in relation to the (mistaken) view that Swedes eventually exterminate the Geats.

18 John Niles (1983, p. 116). He does not, of course, rule out an earlier date.

19 In Charles Plummer we find a Chronicle entry under 921 in the Parker manuscript detailing the submission of a Danish force in East Anglia to Eadward. They swore an agreement to wish for whatever he wished for, protect whatever he would protect, and have him as their lord and 'bearer to hand' or guardian. The ethic of this is good and traditional, however unstable this or any other similar arrangement might prove. A common feature, if we look to genealogical adjustments above the 'working' level of actual social and political arrangements, is that additions – placed below Woden and above the founder king – are of absorbed and perhaps 'minor' kin-lines, indicating a political assertion: 'my kindred embraces yours, but I do not in any powerful way descend from you.'

20 Depending upon how we count strings of names, we can see instances of or even aggregations of nine generations, with Woden the ninth name, in several Anglo-Saxon genealogies. Thomas D. Hill (1988, especially pp. 165–8) surveys these lists and notes that nine is a magic number in Germanic cultures. The important place of Woden as the 'ninth father' in some of the segments may be an ultimate signature of nobility for whomever the genealogy is compiled.

21 Dorothy Whitelock (1981, pp. 70–1).

22 Kenneth Sisam (1953, pp. 326–9), concerned mainly with the clerical character of Anglo-Saxon genealogical records, suggests that the various genealogies were consistently adjusted to reflect a common number (14) for the lines of descent. Sisam also sees little evidence anywhere to suggest an oral history of genealogical descent for the various kingdoms – a point of view convincingly disputed by Herman Moisl (1981). Moisl finds strong, albeit inductive, support for the claim that Germanic peoples had oral, dynastic histories, and that these histories continued in song and

poem down to at least the English eighth and ninth centuries. What differentiates an oral tradition from a literate record is both the structure of the list and its function. The clerical genealogies can go on forever; as they become indefinitely extended, they mainly record claimed or actual lines of descent (although they also assert something social and political for the ecclesiastical community that constructs them). The oral model is less a record than an argumentative structure of relationships and identifications, a structure that asserts a continuity and sameness of values and kinship arrangements that justify political power, rights, and obligations. It is something constructed to live within – the people's social and political house as oriented by the ruling family. That this is so, ethnologically, could explain why various Anglo-Saxon lists were merged in the post-conversion period and why Woden emerges at the head of all but one of them: shifting political relationships between the kingdoms were adjusted genealogically. See David N. Dumville (1977, p. 79). Also Sisam (1953, pp. 301–5), this time for the observation that the West Saxon line between Woden and Cerdic is Bernician.

23 Roberta Frank (1982, p. 62). Many critics have observed Beowulf similarly. For a relatively recent comparison between Beowulf and the Volsungs, to Beowulf's noble credit, see Thomas D. Hill (1982).

24 Roberta Frank (1982, p. 63).

25 J.R.R. Tolkien (1936).

26 Fred C. Robinson (1987). For a few examples of the dismissive, see H.L. Rogers (1955); Margaret E. Goldsmith (1968); and Alvin A. Lee (1972). Less dismissive, but still arguing for a clear separation of poet from the world depicted in the poem is Robert W. Hanning (1974). These and other readings like them ignore the poet's time schemes and his extension of value into the past, relying instead, circularly, on assumptions about the poet's faith – that it is necessarily a faith like Bede's, for example – and proceeding by asserting that what is like a particular Christian conception is identical with it. But for counter arguments drawing from the poet's statements of approval and his applications of God's governance, see Stanley B. Greenfield (1976).

27 Bronislaw Malinowski (1926, p. 58).

28 Fred C. Robinson (1987, p. 12).

29 Kirsten Hastrup (1990) should be noted for a parallel point regarding the 'utilegumenn' of Iceland, men and occasionally women who 'had left the social and, so to speak, gone wild ... Because law and society were one, the outlaws merged with the wild' (pp. 255–6). Grendel is also something of an ogre or troll and, as nightwalker, a kind of living dead. A wasteland creature in a human shape, he intrudes upon human habitation – thus

making him heathen in that his is a terrible and unlawful otherness. Similarly, the resort by some Danes to idol worship as Grendel's attacks continue is vigorously condemned as wrong. It is 'heathen hope' – a compound for the idol worshippers of deep ignorance and blinding custom. They did not know the right law, the Ruler, the Judge of Deeds.

30 Beowulf tells us that Hrethel did well to leave his kingdom to his offspring when he chose God's light. Choosing God's light can mean that Hrethel chose the right rather than that he only grieved and perhaps thought to harm Hæthcyn.

31 Edward Irving (1968, p. 201).

32 No one in the last thousand lines or so actually reflects on his past, looking there for meaning. Beowulf is uncustomarily gloomy after the dragon's fierce raid and talks his way out of dark, uncertain thoughts into heroic resolve; the lament of the last survivor is a lament, not a search for meaning; Wiglaf mentions past feud to admonish the cowards; the messenger brings up the likelihood of future strife by recalling histories of past feuds 'settled' only temporarily, by Beowulf's war-might, which then blessed the Geats with fifty years of a peace that can only have been a truce (in the absence of either a tributary or a continuing exchange relationship).

33 See D.H. Green (1965). In *Beowulf*, 'ar' appears in compounds and in simplex form. As the latter it marks the holding of reciprocal honouring or oaths (ll. 296a, 1099a) and it indicates Wealhtheow's later expectation that Hrothulf will honour others for honour given (ll. 1182a, 1187b). The word in relation to God and Beowulf (l. 1272, 'ond him to Anwaldan are gelyfde') implies a reciprocity: because God gave Beowulf that great strength, Beowulf counted on God's support (that He would honour him). 'Ar' is used quite differently in other poetry (e.g., *The Phoenix*, l. 663; *The Seafarer*, l. 107; *Christ and Satan*, l. 208; *The Wanderer*, l. 114) where it indicates a mainly non-reciprocal state of favour, grace, or blessedness (although faith and blessedness tend to come, in Old English poetry, to those who deserve it, because of their orientation toward God).

34 Robert B. Burlin (1975) focuses on the way in which this and other passages draw the poet's audience into the narrative, while also asserting the ties that hold a society together.

35 Contrary to Alvin A.Lee (1972, p. 223), *Beowulf* is not a dramatization of the destruction of heroic energy. Heroic energy continues through time, as does this mutable world, as do these days of strife (we might say).

36 Fred C. Robinson (1987, p. 49) would have the poet use words like 'metodsceaft' to remind his audience of pre-Christian meanings, of a fate that can only be malicious. Robinson quotes E.G. Stanley (1975, p. 121)

on what this dark 'wyrd' would mean to the heathen mind: 'a subject for gloomiest speculation and darkest fear; Christians, and among them the Old English poets, recognize in *wyrd* the exclusive aspect of an ultimately beneficient power.' This issue, however, begs two points: that we know the poet's Christian commitments outside the poem; and that the poet is intent on re-creating heathen meanings or heathen mentalities. In Beowulf's case especially this does not seem so: Beowulf has a strong sense of himself as a just king in the very passage in which he uses 'metodsceaft' – the Ruler of Men need not charge him with the slaughter of kinsmen. Following Beowulf's remark that fate has swept away all of his kinsmen except for Wiglaf, the poet tells us that his soul went to seek the judgment of the truly firm. I presume it is in that state of mind that Beowulf dies, rather than in heathenish fear. Moreover, we simply cannot assume that the poet sees 'wyrd' in its sense as 'fate' within a providential scheme. In relation to Scyld Scefing's funeral, he says that men, whether hall counsellors or warriors under the heavens, simply do not know who or what received Scyld's funeral ship. This is a mystery for all men. He shares his characters' sense of the shape of life, not betraying any clear sense of Augustinian providence, nor denying the Father's embrace to dead ancestors (aside from the nameless ones who succumb to devil worship).

37 Marie P. Hamilton (1946) eloquently reads providence in *Beowulf* as God's governance through time, viewed in the light of eternity, and expressed in language of God's favour (such as 'ar') as a sign of grace. This language, however, needs to be evaluated carefully in the light of D.H. Green's work on the ethical vocabulary of the *comitatus*. Hamilton, moreover, presents concepts of providence and grace in impoverished form; we hear nothing about states of grace or divine sanctity, no mention of providence as a scheme of redemption extending into eternity, and no references to divine omniscience or to a divine present. Grace becomes, then, little more than an adjectival accompaniment to instances of God's favour. Mary C. Wilson Tietjen (1975) similarly works with a loose conflation of 'favour' and 'grace.' If we have to impoverish notions of providence before we can read them in the poem, perhaps simplicity of assumption is better: the poet's notions do not reach the rightly providential, any more than the poem gives us Christian allusions for which we have sure Latin sources or even precise scriptural sources, as John Niles (1983) has well observed. Moreover, the poet simply does not 'clue-in' exegetical ways of understanding his material; this has given rise to a proliferation of neo-patristic readings by those minded to construct them.

38 Fred C. Robinson (1987, pp. 52–3).

39 This is a nice observation, especially when Fred Robinson shows that 'sylf,' 'soth,' and so on were used in other contexts to distinguish between false gods and the Christian God, citing *Maxims I* where Woden working woe is contrasted with the Ruler of the Heavens, the Self-same Truth-King, the Savior of Souls (ll. 132–4). But I do not see the *Beowulf* poet working in this way at all. In effect, he shares a wide centre of theistic truth with his noble characters, who do not utter the names of false gods, nor do they ever imply belief in a pantheon. He does, however, extend that range of theistic truth beyond anything his characters say, but not far and mainly in explicit assertions of God's power in relation to heathen prayer or to a war-lord's chant-curse on the hoard (which God Himself, the True King of Victories, can implicitly unwind by opening the hoard to whomever He would). One of the functions of the 'legislator' god of war (see chapter 3) is to unbind even 'hell-bonds' of terror, just as he unbinds the icicles of winter, implicitly likened to the 'slaughter-ropes' of the melting, pattern-welded blade in Grendel's den. Far from setting heathenism loose through his noble characters, the poet strongly indicts it in the two passages where he refers to distinctly heathen events.

40 Thus it would be a mistake to assume as Leonard Tennenhouse (1971) does that even similar kinds of events are offered by the poet as interchangeable examples of something. Even if we look for latent psychological material, we must first look at each event for whatever it reveals in itself about the world.

41 Lester Little (1978, p. 7) follows Georges Duby (1974) in observing that the burial of treasure with the dead in Germanic Europe more or less ended in the eighth century. The poet's attitude towards useless *buried* treasure in the case of the hoard might indicate a late eighth-century date at least. But his apparently approving narration of Scyld's funeral – complete with a 'ne hyrde ic' phrase, which always marks a splendid moment – could indicate either an earlier date or a more than tolerant attitude towards the honorific practices of the past. Wade Tarzia (1989, p. 115) thinks Wiglaf may superstitiously rebury the disturbed hoard as soon as possible.

42 For eloquent arguments to the contrary, see George Clark (1965), but also note a much different, more embracing view in Clark (1990): the final words of the poem underline the hero's fame, and confirm the value of a heroic life. In temporal perspective, Clark now imagines the poem's Anglo-Saxon audience as perhaps seeing the world of the poem and the hints of future events as a 'whirligig of time and revenges,' a whirligig

that forms an endless cycle 'of men, generations, dynasties, and nations,' a cycle of disasters and glories rather than a Christian dynamic of good and evil (p. 91). See Kathryn Hume (1975, p. 25) for the idea that the poet's sadness 'seems directed at the impossibility of realizing the ideal pattern of heroic society indefinitely, not at the limitations of this ideal from a Christian point of view or at life in general.'

43 Such a curse would not be more powerful than God, who can easily loosen the binding curse, something Christian magic depended upon (see Flint, 1991, p. 231). The Anglo-Saxon charms combine Christian and pagan invocation as well as incantation, in effect resting ultimate magic power with God, who can only be repaid through one's thankfulness for the efficacy, say, of the charm against cattle theft. The weaver of this charm thinks of St Helena and of Christ hanging on the cross (behind which in this context may lie an image of Odin hanging upside down). For this compare Marshall Sahlins (1972, pp. 164–5) on the exchange between master and sorcerer's apprentice: the successful charm repays the master. But there is danger also for the charmer or maker of curses if he becomes too powerful or overbearing, especially in the case of chiefs, who can become their own victims. In that Beowulf and God opened the hoard, one can say that the curse-maker has been defeated, killed twice in that the binding or terror curse is the near-dead's weapon against rifled honour. Recently Raymond P. Tripp (1985) proposed a fascinating retranslation and repunctuation of the lines about the curse wound around the gold (ll. 3051–2), offering Wiglaf and the Geats as the pronouncers of the curse. But this is troublesome for an already troublesome passage full of indefinite 'thens' or 'moreovers' and 'swas.' 'Þonne' in l. 3051 could mean 'therefore' and then could apply to the dragon, who possessed the gold illicitly and whose measure has been justly taken. Possessing the hoard did him no good and God did not open it to him. The next mention of the 'deep, oath-like declaration' apparently is a parallel response to Beowulf's death, to the idea that he did not know through what means his worldly departure would happen, or that he should unknowingly come across a cursed hoard, even though the old and good king was favoured enough to slay the dragon and open the hoard. On this fatal day, the 'victory-blest' man's death, not his life, is the great misfortune.

44 Notable epithets reserved for the poet are that God is the Life-Lord, the Helm of Heaven, the True King of Victories. Perhaps, because he shares these epithets with his audience, he insists for our benefit that Hrothgar's God and ours is certainly the same 'Drihten,' the Helm of the Heavens.

Chapter 3 The Jural World in *Beowulf*

1 Bellman (1985) is an exception. He notes that Beowulf will in fact enforce the law. He also points out that Hrothgar's entrusting the welfare of his hall to a relative stranger is no small matter (pp. 53, 69), even though Hrothgar knew Beowulf as a boy and some kind of kinship connection might exist here.

2 Morton W. Bloomfield (1959). Bloomfield knows that evidence for what Henry Charles Lea (1892) calls the 'wager of battle' in England postdates the Anglo-Saxon period. See also A.S. Diamond (1971, p. 311) for the observation that only after the Norman conquest was the ordeal by battle 'foisted upon a reluctant, small and insular England.' Nevertheless, Bloomfield is right in seeing something deeply legalistic in Beowulf's combat against Grendel. For the oath-demanding function of Wealhtheow's 'ful' see Helen Damico (1984, pp. 54–6). This is the fullest treatment I know of for the social significance of drinking in *Beowulf* and in related analogues. But also see Hugh Magennis (1985) and Michael J. Enright (1988) for comments on the cohesion-making significance of cup-bearing queens in *Beowulf*.

3 Morton W. Bloomfield (1962) reads 'ealde riht' as natural law. Margaret Pepperdene (1966) charts the protocol of Beowulf's encounters with the coastguard, with Wulfgar, and finally with Hrothgar. But more than appropriate diplomacy and speech is involved in Beowulf's movement from uninvited stranger to unusually entrusted guardian of Heorot. Malcolm Brennan (1985) is one of the few readers who sees this as he emphasizes the political tensions in Beowulf's approach to Heorot.

4 Here the mythological pair of Woden and Tiu, as sovereigns, is equated with terror (or reigns of terror) and rightful settlement respectively. A legislator warrior or king may act ferociously on the battlefield, gaining victory through the Wodinesque or even through invocations of Wodin – see Russom (1978) – but only in the service of settlement, and not of terror or crime. Cults of Woden may have absorbed some of Tiu's original functions, especially in Sweden, but both deities were honoured in Anglo-Saxon kingdoms – the rune for Tiu appears on cremation urns; see Owen (1981, pp. 28–31) – and Tiu was honoured especially in Denmark.

5 Woden, known for his deadly trickery, may blend with Tiu when Tiu practises trickery. However, Tiu's trickery is legislative. It seeks an end to terror. In *Gylfagynning*, Snorri tells us, Tiu places his hand as a pledge in the mouth of the frightening and quickly growing wolf, Fenrir, who in that way is tricked into allowing the gods to bind him a third and suc-

cessful time. George Dumézil (1988) comments on this action: 'Tyr's action is precisely of the kind appropriate to a jurist-god. An entrapping pact must be concluded with the enemy, one that entails a pledge forfeit in advance, and Tyr, alone among all the Ases, offers that pledge.' In losing his hand, Tyr 'not only procures the salvation of the gods but also regularizes it: he renders legal that which, without him, would have been pure fraud' (p. 142). The association of law and divinity becomes apparent in the historical record if we link Tyr or Tiu with Mars and Woden with Mercury. Then perhaps we can accept a British, Romano-Frisian altar dedicated to 'Mars-Thingso' as indicating Tiu's juridical function (Turville-Petre, 1964, p. 181). This assumes that 'thingso' does not mean 'warrior' in some sense – see Helen Damico (1984, p. 203n27) and Davidson (1972, p. 2). That divinity and law go together in Germanic societies is apparent even in the anomalous context of Iceland, where the 'goðar,' from O.N. 'goð,' were chieftains with judicial functions.

6 Georges Dumézil (1973, p. 46). William A. Chaney (1970, pp. 13–14) notes the basic distinction here between two kinds of kingship, and refers it back to Jan de Vries, thinking of it as 'ingenious' but not improbable, although not inscribed in the historical record.

7 That Tiu's original functions were partly absorbed by cults devoted to Odin and to Thor seems clear enough given some gross, mythological facts: at the destruction of the gods, Odin, not Tiu, will be slain by Fenrir; Tiu will be slain by the previously bound hound of hell; and Thor will be slain by the cosmic serpent's poisonous bite. But Tiu was worshipped in Anglo-Saxon England; thus we might infer that his jural sanctions as the war-god of victory were kept separate from Woden worship and from Thor's functions. Thor perhaps is most often invoked in agricultural contexts, in relation to weather, and by seafarers, rather than by warrior elites in their roles as defenders of hall and folk (although in their fertility functions and as defenders of or purgers of the land, perhaps Thor would matter). A kind of syncretism is possible here as different actions reflect the sanctions of different gods: thus Beowulf's combat with the dragon can suggest Thor's cosmic battle, although Beowulf's role is explicitly juridical. He avenges his ruined hall, his injured people, and his scorched land. Craig Davis, in private correspondence, suggested this idea of pagan syncretism.

8 Jan De Vries (I, 1935) has given a succinct, landmark account of Tyr or Tiu (*tiwaz) as the god of lawful war (pp. 173–4). Tyr's most famous act is the giving of his hand as a pledge in the gods' third and successful attempt at binding the cosmic wolf, Fenrir. Associated with the law court or

Thing, Tyr is also connected with the sword as a means of settlement (cf. 'schwerting,' O.N. 'vapndomr,' and a sword named 'tyrfing,' although its settlements are in moments of heat and death-dealing). Even when subordinated in later legends to Odin or Thor, Tyr is a voice of truth and good counsel, as in *Hymisqvida*, v.4, ll. 5–6a, ed. Hans Kuhn (1962): 'unz af trygdom Tyr Hlorriða / astrað mikit' 'Until out of truth Tyr formed a loving counsel for Hlorritha.' Tyr's praise of Freyr in *Locasenna*, however, is even more revealing: 'Freyr er beztr allra ballriða asa gorðom i;/ mey hann ne grœtir ne mannz kono,/oc leysir or hoptom hvern' 'Freyr is the best of all heroes among the divine/maiden harms he not nor man's wives but unties those who are bound' (v. 37 in Kuhn). The best of warriors does not molest women or wives; moreover, he loosens the bound from their fetters. Of this Tiu deeply approves.

9 See Fred C. Robinson (1987, pp. 10–11), who shows how the poet reminds his audience of *Beowulf*'s pagan setting while suppressing anything unacceptably heathen (such as blood sacrifices and the names of the gods). Dorothy Whitelock (1951) has said approximately the same thing, and T.A. Shippey (1978) comments similarly when he sees the poet creating an image of 'heathenness,' especially in the monsters, from which Beowulf and Wealhtheow, for example, were separate (pp. 43–4).

10 See Audrey I. Richards (1940, pp. 115–16) for the ways in which the African Bemba tribe fits Christian missions and authorities into their traditional structures of loyalty and dependence.

11 For evidence of Tiu worship in Anglo-Saxon place-names, see Frank Stenton (1970, pp. 292–3). For further speculations on Tiu's original All-Father and Sky-Father status, see Brian Branston (1957, pp. 74–5). Stenton thinks that Tiu may have been associated with a red horse cut into the side of a hill above the foot of a 'great escarpment which borders the plain of south Warwickshire' (p. 292). Gale R. Owen (1981, p. 29) notes that the runic mark for Tiu (ᛏ) 'was traditionally carved on weapons to ensure victory.' Perhaps this then is a 'victory rune' as well as being the most common runic mark found on Anglo-Saxon cremation urns, either drawn freehand or stamped (Arnold, 1988, p. 124). The Essex royal genealogy traces descent back to Seaxnet, perhaps a name for Tiu, which is given as the name of one of Woden's sons (probably after the cult of Woden usurped some of Tiu's functions as well as his place). For the identification see William A. Chaney (1970, p. 29). G. Turville-Petre (1964, p. 100) associates Seaxnet with Frey, for which there is also a link to Tiu. For a superb sketch of Anglo-Saxon testimony to a history of resurgent paganism and insecure conversions within various kingdoms, see

Karl P. Wentersdorf (1981). He supplements Bede's few but often cited remarks by tracing a history of denunciations and worries that seems to reflect a reality exacerbated by the Danish invasions.

12 F.G. Cassidy (1970, p. 31) has noticed something of this in linking light with victory as part of a symbolic word-group.

13 D.H. Green (1965, pp. 302–6). William Whallon (1965, p. 22) has shown that the pagan-heroic denotations of poetic vocabulary long survived that vocabulary's gradual absorption into a Christian universe.

14 Thomas D. Hill (1981, p. 412) discusses how the poet of *Christ and Satan* emphasizes the concepts of measure and measuring to parody Satan's effort to usurp the place of Metod, the measurer of all creation. Clearly this sense of 'measure' is not that of a baleful fate; in *Beowulf* it is reflected, perhaps, in the measure taken of the dead dragon – as a judgment, as a definitive setting of limits to terror.

15 That background is perhaps reflected in *Hymiskviða*: Tyr helps Thor find the way to Tyr's father's house as he searches for a cup that will hold the sea and thus quench the thirst of the gods (obliquely reflecting the link between drinking and vows?). This adventure suggests a link between Tyr and conviviality in the hall, a conviviality cleverly won from the terror-father. Tyr's father is the frost giant (which suggests that the power of unbinding the fetters of winter is part of Tyr's power as the jural god).

16 'Ginfæste gife' (l. 2182a) is something directly from God for those who are to be blest with victories. In *Genesis A* an angel speaks to Abraham and stays the hand that would slay his own son (reversal), saying that Abraham would receive an ample gift, a true gift of victory from heaven's king (ll. 2919–20). In *Juliana* her radiant beauty is called an ample gift by her prospective husband, who also calls her his sweetest splendour of the sun (ll. 166–8), before asking that she honour his gods.

17 See Ursula Dronke (1969, p. 65), who follows Dumézil in this observation.

18 Earl R. Anderson (1977) has set the dragon's hoard, as treasure trove, within a legal context that 'affirms the Germanic principle of treasure-regality (the ruler's right to all treasure trove), which in turn encourages the belief that Beowulf has a right to the treasure' (p. 142); the dragon who unjustly keeps treasure hidden under the walls (ll. 3059-60) has no right. But see Wade Tarzia (1989) on the cursed aura a Germanic treasure hoard could have. In this connection the dragon is the curse come alive. Both legality and curse could coexist.

19 This language, as a cluster of associated ideas, is so powerful that Cynewulf seems to draw upon it, almost gratuitously, when establishing his

narratives of Christian martyrdom and heroics. Both *Andreas* and *Fates of the Apostles* identify the disciples as glorious heroes, as 'tireadige hæleð' and as 'torhte and tireadige' respectively. In *Andreas* their glory does not fail in battle ('campræden'). The root, 'ræd,' suggests the intimate relation between counsel and battle. For a collocation of Moses' literally definitive binding of the enemy and God's gift of the lives of kinsmen and of territory, given significantly enough by the Ruler of Victory ('sigora Waldend,' ll. 15–23), see *Exodus*. This difficult and much discussed passage, with its emphasis on words for kinsmen and for folk-right or authority (e.g. one 'folcriht' overcome and another implicitly established) seems to combine mythological and exegetical motifs. Victory by the King of Glory, the unbinding of peoples, and the binding of demonic enemies form a motif that recurs as a consequence of various harrowings of hell (cf. *Christ*, ll. 561–70) – something to which Biblical parallels no doubt contribute, especially the temporary binding of the old serpent in *Revelations* 20:1–3. But the emphasis on definitive binding of devils and of evil and the releasing of mankind into victory and light fits uncannily into the Germanic context sketched above, a context into which *Judith* clearly falls when she calls upon 'torhtmod tires Brytta' (l. 93a and noted above) for victorious vengeance. That is precisely what the (Tiu-like) highest Judge awards and which leads both to the beheading of Holofernes and the agony-producing fettering of his spirit.

20 See Levin L. Schücking (1929) for an early and well-articulated view of ideal kingship in *Beowulf*. M.R. Gerstein (1974) convincingly sets out these 'sacral' functions for the Germanic warrior.

21 T.A. Shippey (1978), while quite aware that 'social signs in *Beowulf* function systematically' in systems the poet does not invent, nevertheless slights Beowulf's exchanges with the coastguard and Wulfgar as redundant to the story as a whole, but as reflections of the audience's interest in displays of oral skill and good manners (p. 14). The way to official permission for an uninvited stranger is not simple in this or any other social world; direct as well as indirect speech in *Beowulf* is never window-dressing.

22 George Clark (1990, especially pp. 64–8) discusses the social context of Beowulf's arrival and progress, emphasizing how his appearance turns the story into a drama of human relationships 'between characters whose inner lives and motives are not explicitly disclosed' (p. 54). However, he does not focus on the language and deeds of reciprocity that inform the exchanges with the coastguard and others.

23 D.H. Green (1965, pp. 142–62).

24 Green (p. 142n6) cites *The Anglo-Saxon Chronicle* (ed. C. Plummer) for 1085:

'ond ealle hi ... weron his menn ond him hold aðas sworon þæt hi woldon ongean ealle oðre menn him holde beon' 'and they all were his men and to him swore oaths of loyalty that they would against others be reciprocally loyal to him.'

25 Felix Liebermann, ed. (vol. 1, 1903, p. 396).

26 Stanley B. Greenfield (1974), following up on a suggestion by Arthur Brodeur (1959), would have the person approaching the gift seat be Hrothgar, who cannot then approach his gift-seat at night (pp. 110–11). But I think the idea of permission supports Klaeber's (pp. 134-5) parenthetical sense of the lines and thus keeps them applied to Grendel.

27 Stanley B. Greenfield (1982, pp. 49–50) suggests that the coastguard refers here to Beowulf's perceptive sense of the advice he would offer Hrothgar and possible outcomes should that advice become action. But Beowulf has said nothing to give the coastguard a sense of this. For other worries over this gnome, see M. Pepperdine (1966), Howell D. Chickering (1977), and T.A. Shippey (1978).

28 See E.G. Stanley (1979, especially pp. 76–82) for an account of 'ðing gehegan' 'to hold a meeting' and its legal purview in Old English poetry, along with nearly synonymous constructions in legal texts, such as 'sace seman' (to settle strife). Stanley would interpret the phrase, following Klaeber, in a figurative rather than a literal sense: we do not have here 'lawyer's terms,' a phrase used by Edward B. Irving (1968, p. 63) as part of his sense of irony between the violence of battle and the way in which it is spoken of. But there is no irony if battle is the 'thing' or jural settlement itself; nor is there anything figurative about 'ðing gehegan' when seen as the 'law' of war arrived at through rightful council. The collocation nearly reappears in *Maxims I*, as Stanley points out, although here it is used simply in its sense of council, stemming from God-given customs ('Metod' also called 'ælmihtig god'), during which the wise shall meet with the wise and settle strife ('sace semaþ'), teaching peace (ll. 16–20). Stanley also cites *Andreas*, where Beowulf's phrase meaning 'to hold a council' means a monthly council of blood-thirsty, greedy cannibals (ll. 157–158a).

29 I agree with Brodeur (1943, pp. 301–21) in establishing the common meaning of 'refuse' (permission) for 'wyrnan,' 'forwyrnan,' and 'wearn' (l. 366 where Wulfgar urges Hrothgar not to refuse Beowulf's request for an exchange of words). In the heroic poetry these words appear within the context of rightful, efficacious battle: in *Maldon* Eadweard 'swenges ne wyrnde / þæt him æt fotum feoll fæge cempa' 'blows refused not / such that at his feet the fated (Viking) warrior fell dead' (ll. 118b–119), for which Byrthnoth thanks him; and in *Brunanburh* the Mer-

cians 'ne wyrndon' hard handplay with those who cast their lot with Anlaf.

30 Many readers (Arthur Brodeur [1943] for example) have eloquently appreciated the Finn episode either as a conflict of loyalties or as a scene of deep pathos and unaccountable horror, focusing in the latter case on Hildeburh's sorrow as both her son and her brother are burned on the brother's funeral pyre. Hengest, after a winter of truce and oath-given peace between him and Finn, whose 'giants' may have begun the slaughter (see Tolkien, 1983, for the suggestion that these are Jutes), takes revenge in the spring and annihilates what is left of Finn's hall-troop, including Finn himself. The story is recited as a Danish victory and seems suitable for that moment in the general revelry after Beowulf's great victory on the Danes' behalf. Grendel's depredations were a bitter and long-lasting sorrow, as was Hengest's winter ordeal. Beowulf's settlement, his avenging of crimes the Danes have suffered, is exactly parallel to Hengest's juridical settlement when he accepts the sword placed in his lap and takes revenge upon Finn (and thus, Tiu-like, upon 'giants'), bringing back much treasure and reinstating Hildeburh among her people (where she is not erased – contrary to Overing, 1990, p. 86) where her primary jural and kinship identity has always rested (a social fact that must inform any postmodern, Lacanian view of her).

31 This suggests a prior social arrangement that makes Beowulf's voyage to the Danes socially thinkable; indeed, some connections between Beowulf's family and the Danes may have preceded Ecgtheow's arrival and thus justify Hrothgar's unusual act, that of *settling* a feud on behalf of the Wægmunding, Ectheow.

32 See D.H. Green (1965, pp. 186–7).

33 The function of loosening bonds or ropes of terror is a function mythologically sanctioned by Tiu, the legislator sovereign in the Germanic pantheon, according to Georges Dumézil (1973, pp. 39–48).

34 I see Hunferth as a fierce competitor, not as a fool, thus agreeing with John C. Pope (1986, pp. 180–1) and Stanley B. Greenfield that Hunferth speaks out of envy.

35 For a brief account of the range of feeling Hunferth may embody for the Danes, see Irving (1989, p. 47). During Beowulf's progress towards Hrothgar's permission, we can think of Hunferth's and Hrothgar's words at this point as a dual welcome, reflecting hope, warning, aggression, and anxiety. Hrothgar embraces Beowulf as a God-send, but no great hope and potential love could appear without provoking ambiguous feelings or hostile anxiety. Hrothgar has just given Beowulf a grim scenerio of brave but slaughtered Danes in Heorot. Hunferth expresses the overtly hostile

side of Hrothgar's feelings and, presumably, those of the Danes in general. His role for Hrothgar, psychologically, is to vent destructive emotions towards the would-be saviour-hero, emotions that then can give way to glad hope and, eventually, to love after the hero passes his challenges. George Clark (1990, pp. 60–1) convincingly defends Hunferth's role and responds to the ambivalences of the scene regarding relative prestige and honour but I think he overstates the Danish fear of being shamed should Beowulf defeat Grendel. Grendel literally and bitterly shames the Danes; Beowulf offers to lift the shame, if it is ever to be lifted. For martial honour lost, the Danes, and Hrothgar especially, can compensate through unstinting generosity should a foreign warrior do what they could not. Through such generosity they win fame.

36 See Mary Douglas (1986, pp. 40–1) for a perceptive account of how latent groups survive. Often the sense of group is enhanced by activities – such as taking up and believing conspiracy theories – that are not causally linked to the effect (the enhancement of the group). This would be the case with Hunferth's activities also, if we see them as on the group's behalf. For much discussion of that role see Morton Bloomfield (1951), Norman Eliason (1963), Fred Robinson (1974), Lewis Nicholson (1975), and Michel Vaughan (1976). R.D. Fulk (1987) has, I think, in etymology and naming customs found the grounds for refuting views of Hunferth's name as allegorical (e.g. 'Un-Peace,' 'Mar-Peace,' and so on). Hunferth is simply the warrior's name. Moreover, readers who see Hunferth as a fool underestimate his social role: Beowulf will later call Hunferth a 'widely known' man – an honourable, if not heroic appellation – and the poet adds that Hunferth spoke in his drink (thus formally and perhaps outside his proper person?) and does not, in facing the Grendel-kin's mere, dare risk his life, for which he loses fame (l. 1470b). One cannot lose what one never had.

37 See Bosworth and Toller, p. 384, for citations that include the phrases 'gedefne dom' and 'Ealra demena ðam gedefestan' 'fitting judgment' and 'the most proper of all judges.'

38 Mary Douglas (1987) has edited a collection of essays on drinking in different cultures, the key point of which is that drinking behaviour has different sanctions and functions in different cultures. We tend to deplore drinking, linking it to excesses, alcoholism, and even unmanliness (a real man can hold his drink and knows when to quit). We have overread Beowulf's remark about beer-drinking. See Helen Damico (1984, especially pp. 54–7 and 166–7) for enlightening accounts of the ritual functions involved in bearing and receiving the 'ful' – functions, of course, that can be turned sardonically, as in *Atlakviða* when Gudrun

comes out to meet Atli 'med gyltom kalki' (Dronke, 1969, v. 34, l. 3). On a socially enlightened view of drinking in *Beowulf*, see Hugh Magennis (1985) and Fred C. Robinson (1987, pp. 75–9).

39 D.H. Green (1965, pp. 518–27).

40 Jan de Vries (1935, vol. 1. p. 173).

41 Nolan and Bloomfield (1980, pp. 500, 511) show that boasting speeches are traditional forms of public speech that define the hero's purposes and establish his social identity.

42 However, uncompounded, or as the initial element of the compound, 'wuldor' refers to the deity in *Beowulf*.

43 See D.H. Green (1965, pp. 251–3) for the sacral and legal meanings of 'getruwian.' Michael Swanton (1982, p. 33) comments on the legal implications of 'treow,' while seeming to imply that it hardened into legal usage, away from an earlier sense of reciprocity, whereas its legal usage may well reflect a late and less reciprocal stage of its legal history. Also, for discussion of the sacral aspects of warrior life and kingship, see William A. Chaney (1970, pp. 121–56) and J.M. Wallace-Hadrill (1971, pp. 1–20); see also Gwyn Jones (1984, p. 156).

44 See S. Viswanathan (1979) for an account of the melting sword and the rope image within a suggestion of the providential: the Augustinian God releases us from the bondage of 'wyrd.' This suggestion is interesting but not in harmony with the immediate context. It does, however, reinforce the analogy between a True Measurer who 'unbinds' the terrible and the juridical warrior-hero whose actions accomplish the same, in effect.

45 This divine function may once have belonged to Tiu and is enacted through marriage as well as combat. The bride as peace-kin is an attempt to settle the terror of ongoing feud; the subliming of Đryth – who once 'settled' ('scyran') terror on warriors who so much as looked at her by having them bound and then slain with a damascened sword – occurs through her marriage in 'high love' to Offa.

46 D.H. Green (1965, pp. 248–51) discusses the vertical character of 'est' and its association with kinship ties. This kind of 'favour' is something an inferior kinsman renders up to a superior kinsman (as Beowulf does to Hygelac, l. 2149a) or something Wealhtheow shows to Beowulf, presumably out of a kindred-like friendliness. Beowulf in addressing Hrothgar, then, may be responding subtly to Hrothgar's 'adoption' speech. The term has reciprocal possibilities, especially when drawn into proximity with *comitatus*-like service (thus reflecting a point of intersection between kinship ties and the *comitatus*).

Chapter 4 The Economy of Honour in *Beowulf*

1 John Niles (1983, pp. 224–6. For Kaske (1958), Niles agrees that there is a case for some sense of wisdom, physical strength, and wise speech as virtues that become a theme, but not the controlling theme of the poem (p. 302n3).

2 Kathryn Hume (1975), especially p. 5.

3 See M.I. Finley (1967) for comments on gifts and counter-gifts and on the word 'gift' in Homeric Greek as 'a cover-all for a great variety of actions and transactions which later became differentiated' – transactions we would separate as rewards, payments, tribute, amends, loans, and so on (pp. 410–11). The range of functions is similar in *Beowulf* although *Beowulf* has a richly varied vocabulary of giving.

4 For comparisons in subsequent discussions I will rely on overviews of the Yanomami by Jacques Lizot (1985), of numerous American and Pacific peoples by Marshall Sahlins (1972), and on a global view that includes comments on the Germanic past by Marcel Mauss (1967). So far what has been said is not particularly new to *Beowulf* scholars, especially not to such readers as T.A. Shippey (1978, especially pp. 18–21). But scholars have focused either on the contractual bond of gifts and services or on the aspect of status and worth involved in possessing and giving rings, war gear, horses, and jewellery. This diminishes the social complexity of gift giving, reducing it merely to payment, in effect, no matter what the payment confers.

5 Marshall Sahlins (1972) sees these reciprocal functions as a kind of feedback system: in the first case, prevailing rank structure influences the system of exchange (Heremod is a king but not generous, hence not noble – becoming infamous, not famous); in the second, exchange initiates a rise in status (p. 207), as when the coastguard sets a watch for Beowulf's ship, the actual boatguard eventually receiving in turn a 'worth'-conferring sword, raising his status in the mead-hall. An in-between event occurs when Hunferth essentially acknowledges greater honour in the better man and thus accepts some loss of glory for himself, in lending his sword, Hrunting, for Beowulf's use against the mother. Beowulf accepts the loan, uttering and thereby honouring the sword's name and the sword in his great boast before descending into the mere. That Hrunting in the event fails to dent the 'sea-wolf' does not detract from its stature when Beowulf returns it to Hunferth, thus evening their exchange, with no debt on either side and Beowulf twice over the more glorious man.

6 George Clark (1990), rightly seeing no irony in the series of superlatives

through which the Geats praise their dead king, convincingly puts to rest readings of 'mildust' that would see it as intrusively Christian and potentially critical, especially when read in the context of 'lofgeornost,' which some readers read negatively at Beowulf's expense. Clark points out that Old Norse cognates for 'milde' regularly mean 'generous' and, when applied to princes, suggest the virtue of liberality (p. 140). He gives secular, heroic contexts in *Beowulf* for both 'milde' and 'liðe' (gracious). These points support the insightful but little read work by D.H. Green on the ethical vocabulary of the *comitatus* (which includes 'milde' but not 'liðe' or 'monðwærust,' terms of horizontal, kinship-like amity in *Beowulf*, terms special to the conception of generous kingship embodied in Beowulf as perceived by his people). Thus the Geats praise Beowulf in a mixed vocabulary of military and social ethics – he is, in their eyes, superlative in both spheres, which no doubt overlap.

7 Informed by a Hobbesian eloquence, Marshall Sahlins (1972) comments on Marcel Mauss's *The Gift*: '*The Gift* transposes the classic alternatives of war and trade from the periphery to the very center of social life, and from the occasional episode to the continuous presence. This is the supreme importance of Mauss's return to nature, from which it follows that primitive society is at war with Warre, and that all their dealings are treaties of peace. All the exchanges, that is to say, must bear in their material design some political burden of reconciliation ...' No exchange can be understood 'in its material terms apart from its social terms' (pp. 182–3). This burden always involves an awareness of instability and is, as such, an untranscended part of *Beowulf* as it probably is of the poet's world long ago. The tenth-century facts, say, of trade, markets, coinage, and even rents paid in part in coin do not necessarily affect the ethos of gift giving, especially in an aristocratic context. Trade is with others, not friends; honour and loyalty are not centrally involved; coins may supplement services in kind but on the whole their use is quite limited. Alfred's and Athelstan's mints were established to raise wealth for the maintenance of armies, to centralize internal trade and block foreign coins, and to pay tribute when necessary. For a comprehensive account of money and some of its uses in early and late medieval Europe, see Spufford (1989).

8 Jacques Lizot (1985, p. 183).

9 Helen Codere (1950) reviews work on this society by Boas, Benedict, and Mead in the course of an admirably concise account of potlatch as an incredibly competitive prestige game, one that seeks the humiliation of social competitors and avoidance of even the smallest loss in status or honour. Such a game can only sustain itself within a clan-like or self-

renewing group context – albeit Kwakiutl kinship has bilateral features – where the number of status positions is restricted and their relationships to one another are subject to change. C.A. Gregory (1980) shows the continuing expression of similar potlatch giving among contemporary Papuans (in a money economy) and argues convincingly that the principle of such giving is to give away more than one's competitors can, not to accumulate capital.

10 See Levin Schücking (1933, especially p. 41).

11 See Helen Damico (1984, pp. 84–6).

12 Ross Samson (1991, p. 90) uses the phrase quoted here and goes on to quote Elisabeth Vestergaard's note that, for Marcel Mauss, exchange 'is social communication and the important matter is that an exchange is going on rather than what is exchanged' (Vestergaard, 1991, p. 98).

13 That this is not a passing on of the succession is well stated by Edward B. Irving, Jr (1989, p. 115). But to see Beowulf's act as exclusively 'something intimate and affectionate within the bounds of a small warm family' is to miss the point about Wiglaf's undeniable deserts. By his actions he has become leader-worthy among the Geats; Beowulf's free gifts, expecting no personal return (an impossibility given his imminent death), necessarily honour Wiglaf even as they express close kinship. Thus through his actions and the honours bestowed, Wiglaf becomes king-worthy as he carries out Beowulf's directives and speaks his own mind as well. The plural verbs Beowulf uses ('fremmað' 'perform' and 'hatað' 'command') when he speaks in Wiglaf's presence about continued attention to the needs of the people cannot be addressed to Wiglaf directly, Irving thinks, but rather must be directed to the people at large (the collective nation should care for the people's needs?). Yet I think they are addressed to Wiglaf as the embodiment of the group (he reconstituted a miniature *comitatus* in the face of the dragon). This seems clear especially when we consider that Wiglaf immediately begins to assert leadership by exiling the cowards and later by organizing a recovery party to go into the barrow from among Geats not involved in the original expedition.

14 See D.H. Green (1965) for a discussion of 'milde' in *Beowulf*. David Turton (1979) carefully distinguishes between periodic, territorially competitive hostilities (between groups who may for periods of time also exchange with each other) and permanent hostilities. We do not know enough about Geats and Frisians to say what their relationship is. We know more about periodic war and peaceful exchange between Swedes and Geats. That the messenger does not expect generosity from the Merowingians may be ironic overstatement: he does not see them as opening up reciprocal exchanges, an impulse they simply have not had *since*

Hygelac's raid. He expects a period of warfare – and may be urging the Geats to prepare maturely for battle, as Irving (1989, pp. 125–6) nicely observes. However, the time indicators do not suggest permanent hostilities, either in the distant past or in the future.

15 Aside from exchange as a continuing affair, once begun, and the near-imperative of continuing reciprocity or else war (thus making the achieving of mutual exchange and friendship the poet's political ideal for relationships between groups), the outline of this is familiar to *Beowulf* scholars. Arthur Brodeur (1959) thinks of gifts given in Heorot as 'appropriate rewards' ... and the material pledge of Beowulf's adoption' (pp. 118–19). Edward B. Irving, Jr (1968) emphasizes the necessity that gift giving be entirely public (p. 131), whereas Margaret Goldsmith (1968) emphasizes Hrothgar's splendid gifts as symbols of social relationships that 'signal the munificence of the royal giver' as well as the worth of the receiver (p. 90). Charles Donohue (1975) thinks of Hrothgar's rewards for Beowulf's service as a counter gift, a potlatch (p. 26). Although interesting, none of these views is entirely accurate. Hrothgar's gifts are not pledge gifts; gift giving does not need to be public (see Beowulf's gifts of weapons to Wiglaf); Hrothgar's splendid gifts imply an invitation rather than only assert his munificence; and the idea of potlatch – a system of obligatory giving and receiving – does not apply because Hrothgar would both reward Beowulf and invite a new relationship, rather than exchange within an established, highly competitive relationship.

16 Compare Marshall Sahlins's discussion of group-to-group exchange (1972, p. 222).

17 Michael Swanton (1982, pp. 130–1) is one of many who make this mistake; most recently we could note it even in inspired departures from traditional criticism. Nicholas Howe's ground-breaking study of Bede's account of the Anglo-Saxon migration myth reifies geography to the status of theme and, almost, of character in *Beowulf*. Howe would reduce the poet's vision of political geography to a 'single axiom: Life in the north changes because individuals or tribes cross the seas to attack other tribes ... In this pagan world violence exists unrestrained by any sense of ethical or political good. Only the hero can hold feuds in abeyance, and he is constrained by his own mortality' (pp. 167, 172).

18 James Bellman (1985) notices that this alliance is 'not treated ambivalently or openly criticized by the poet' (p. 89).

19 Robert Kindrick (1981) has astutely surveyed the theme of wisdom in *Beowulf* and noted its decidedly political nature, referring approvingly to Schücking's (1929) discussion of Augustinian and stoic Christian backgrounds for the poem's political themes. But Kindrick also empha-

sizes Germanic notions of wisdom, especially of self-control, judiciousness, keeping one's own counsel when dealing with enemies, and so on (largely drawing upon Tacitus' accounts of Germanic peoples and the '*Hávamál* and old Norse gnomic poems). What is missing here is an illuminating account of contextual import and thus the specific content of references to (political) wisdom in the poem. When we look closely at the social drama of Beowulf's interactions with Hrothgar and the Danes, the possible influence of Augustinian ideas of judicious and prosperous kingship recedes quickly, whereas the wisdom of the *Hávamál* opens out into considerable complexity when transposed into an aristocratic world.

20 Ideas of affirmed relationship are discussed in Marcel Mauss (1967). Discussion of Germanic practice mainly occurs on pp. 59–62. See also Vilhelm Grønbech (1931). For Grønbech gifts possess a kind of magic that identifies the parties to and with each other (although the gift is probably not the giver's soul); gifts carry something that rightly should come back to the giver, which Grønbech (1931) thinks of as the giver's identity (see vol. 2, chap. 4). Mauss makes a similar assumption but Marshall Sahlins challenges this idea in analysing the vocabulary of gifts among the Maori (Mauss's source for the 'spirit' of the gift).

21 *Hávamál*, stanza 42 is notable: 'Vin sinom scal maðr vinr vera / oc gialda giof við giof; / hlatr við hlatri scyli holðar taca, / enn lausung við lygi' 'To his friend shall a man be a friend / and gift with gift repay; / laughter with laughter shall a man receive, / moreover, falseness with falsehood meet' (stanza 42 in Kuhn [1962]). Stanza 41 emphasizes the good of friends gladdening each other with gifts, for the friendship of gift givers lasts the longest, fate willing.

22 In *Maxims I* both the king and queen shall 'ærest / geofum god wesan' 'first be good with gifts' and the woman 'rumheort beon / mearum ond maþmum, meodorædenne / for gesiðmægen symle æghwær / eodor æþelinga ærest gegretan / forman fulle to frean hond / ricene geræcan, ond him ræd witan / boldagendum bæm ætsomne' 'shall be noble minded / with horses and treasures generously advised / at all times greet first at the banquet the protector of nobles / bring the cup first to the lord's hand / present to the ruler, and advice know for them both, hall-possessors together' (ll. 86b–92). The liberality, decorum, and (legal) counsel ('ræd') here all mark the juridical sovereign (especially the queen in this case). *Maxims II* tells us that 'cyning sceal on healle / beagas dælan' 'a king shall distribute treasure in the hall' (ll. 28b–29a).

23 Bede, *Ecclesiastical History*, ed. Colgrave and Mynors (1969, pp. 256–8). The king in question is Oswine, bounteous to nobles and commoners.

Noblemen come from every kingdom to serve him. Widsith's exchange is a gold ring given to his lord, for his lord's gift of lands. But Widsith refers to his giving as 'on æht sealde, / minum hleodryhtne' (ll. 93b–94a): he gave, but the ring came into the lord's possession as something due him. Ordinarily 'sellan' is reserved for the superior in a gift giving relationship.

24 Mauss (1967), p. 59: 'The nature and intention of the contracting parties and the nature of the thing given are indivisible.'

25 John Niles (1983) joins with many (e.g., Peters [1970]) in seeing Hrothgar as impotent for not defeating Grendel, for not preventing Danes from making heathen prayers, and for not reproaching Unferth. 'Hrothgar thus appears as only the shell of a good king. His piety, generosity, wisdom, and good intentions can be taken for granted ... [but his actions] never prove him to be a king of the stature of the aged Beowulf or the legendary Scyld Sceafing. The ferocity of these two kings wins them reigns of peace and prosperity' (p. 110). Recently Irving (1989) has endorsed and expanded this view; he acknowledges Hrothgar's lyrical strength, warmth, and royal munificence but he also sees Hrothgar virtually as someone who does nothing heroic, who speaks to very few, and who seems isolated and even querulous (when not simply aged, feeble, and pathetic) (pp. 54–7). By not rising above his post-Grendelian measure, Hrothgar does indeed lack heroic vigour but he is hardly isolated at the centre of Heorot's familial, social, and ritual life, and he remains noble, indeed, fame-worthy throughout. He certainly seizes the occasion to try and recruit Beowulf and, failing that, to seize Beowulf's offer of a lasting alliance. To think of him as feeble, isolated, and pathetic is certainly to overstate an ambivalence toward him – one that may reflect both an Anglo-Saxon and a modern sense of 'pollution' or 'contagion.' Once polluted by Grendel's terror, the Danes remain so until a purgative (shamanic?) warrior cleanses the hall. For comments on 'the laws' of sympathetic magic and contagion see Rozin and Nemeroff (1990).

26 The vocabulary of gift giving suggests this as well. In *Beowulf* it is richly varied, reporting that gifts are given ('sellan,' 'gifan') or indicating the nature of particular acts: 'feohgift,' 'gedælan,' 'beodan,' 'teohhian,' 'geteon,' 'forgyldan,' 'forgifan,' 'geywan,' 'leanian' and 'gemæne.' 'Gedælan' means 'to share' or 'distribute,' which distinguishes it from 'feohgift,' an act within a martial or heightened *comitatus* context (reward usually or a gift for expected services). 'Forgyldan' ('to repay') suggests a definitive (usually deadly) paying back; it is not mere reward or compensation, which is 'leanian.' The common word for 'give,' 'gifan,' appears repeatedly as something a superior does – in *Beowulf* and elsewhere in Old Eng-

lish poetry. In distinctly Christian poetry a noun form becomes God's gift or Grace. Some especially interesting items in *Beowulf* concern the inferior's giving of gifts to a superior or a giving of gifts outside of a lord to retainer relationship. The key items are 'geteon' ('to confer,' 'grant,' 'bestow') and 'geywan' ('to show,' 'bestow'). Bosworth and Toller give a definition for 'geteon' as 'to bring as an offering or gift, contribute, bestow, give.' In this sense Beowulf has the sword-hilt given to Hrothgar as though it were tribute already due him. 'Geywan' usually means 'to show, manifest, reveal' in Old English poetry and prose. In *Beowulf* it accompanies a phrase indicating that kindness is shown, such as when Wealhtheow gives gifts to Beowulf and Beowulf gives gifts to Hygelac. It shares a sense of 'bestow' with 'geteon.'

27 As far as I know, Wealhtheow's strength of mind and her imperative mood have been rarely noticed. Helen Damico (1984) offers an exceptional reading of Wealhtheow's counter argument or advice to Hrothgar's offer – a reading that includes seeing Hrothulf as Wealhtheow's 'nephew-son' and thus as someone on whose behalf she quite appropriately speaks (pp. 126–30). There is nothing pathetic or desperate in Wealhtheow's consciousness here. Cramer (1977) noticed Wealhtheow's imperative mood and her orientation towards 'the active present,' whereas Kliman (1977) sees her speeches as disjointed, 'unconnected to any request or demand of her' (p. 34). This latter response underlies Overing's (1990) unsuccessful effort to set Wealhtheow's speeches apart from everyone else's by referring to Wealhtheow's (presumed) 'double subjugation' – to the rule of language she seeks to assert and to the 'language of the masculine economy' (pp. 90–1).

28 For comments on kin-right and succession, see Fritz Kern (1970, especially pp. 12–13n3). On the etymology of Old High German 'kuning,' D.H. Green offers the following summary: 'Whichever of the rival etymological explanations we accept (derived from **kunjam* in the sense of *stirps regia* or in the sense of the people as a whole, or derived from **kunjaz*), it is clear that the basic element is nowhere that of the kinship as an institution, but instead the extended idea of "people" or the idea of "stock, lineage"' (1965, p. 317n4). Fritz Kern is in essential agreement only with the idea of lineage, focusing on kin-right as belonging to *any* member of the royal family – a position accepted by Tryggvi J. Oleson (1955) for one. Clearly the issue is not precise, tending toward extension and ambiguity. However, close blood ties within the royal family are not necessary nor is natural membership within a particular kinship. Hrothgar offers something that falls between legal adoption and mere fraternal spirit, although if Beowulf is involved through his Wægmunding kin-

dred with Onela's Swedes, then perhaps there is already an in-law, nephew-like relationship here, made official now by Hrothgar's statement and command.

29 The business of choosing a successor, which it seems a king can do, and the subsequent election remain largely mysterious. Peter Hunter Blair (1956, p. 198) thinks that Bede implies that a king can choose his successor, but nowhere does Bede clearly say so. D.A. Binchy finds that an agreeable suggestion and points to designation of a successor in Welsh law from the tenth century (1970, pp. 29–30). The Irish also chose a successor while the reigning king lived. Spenser, Binchy notes, says it is done at the inauguration of the king. But it is not known when or how this was done for the ancient Irish, for the Welsh (who in the tenth century borrow 'æðeling' to indicate the heir designate – Binchy, p. 29), or for the Anglo-Saxons. Tacitus mentions that among the Germans a successor might be carried about on a shield. Gregory of Tours tells of this for Sigibert of Cologne's successor, Clovis, for Sigibert, the son of Chlothar, and also for Gundobald Ballomer. The shield probably betokens the successor's crucial function as war-band leader and defender of the folk. In these named cases the successor is not in the direct line of descent. Janet L. Nelson (1977, pp. 54–7) tells us that we know nothing about the rites of election or much, anyway, about the cultural resonance of early ordinations. Tantalizing detail emerges, however, about the use of helmets in the earliest English ordinations (Nelson, 1975, pp. 44–5) and in the 'ordination' of the long-haired Clovis, who apparently put on a helmet of 'holy anointing.'

30 'Freond' is often associated with one's lord; see *The Wanderer*, in *Anglo-Saxon Poetic Records*, vol 3, p. 134, l. 28, and *The Dream of the Rood*, ll. 132, 144, in *Anglo-Saxon Poetic Records*, vol 2, p. 65. Toller and Campbell's *Supplement* lists a domain for 'freond' as 'one who wishes well to another, favours, supports, helps.' Under that, in the laws, a 'freond' is 'one who undertakes responsibility on behalf of another.'

31 For commentary on royal cult objects, particularly banners and helmets, see William A.Chaney (1970, pp. 121–56).

32 Notably Wealhtheow does not use it. We might understand 'wel' in this phrase as meaning 'rightly,' according to conferred or bestowed or recognized right.

33 Edward Irving (1968) sees Wealhtheow as worried about the adoption, which would make Beowulf a rival to her sons (p. 140). But Irving mainly thinks of Wealhtheow as casting 'brave fragile hopes' out over 'the uncontrollable future' (p. 141). For Irving on incantation, see *Reading*, pp. 141–4. Editors often assume a missing line somewhere around l. 1174.

But awkward syntax aside, Wealhtheow makes good sense and seems quite in command; she does not seem at all pathetic. Many twentieth-century readers of *Beowulf* are fond of female pathos, of dramas of intrigue and treachery. The *Beowulf* poet does suggest that something bad will eventually happen in or to Heorot, but does this mean that Hrothulf will prove treacherous to Hrothgar or to his sons by Wealhtheow? Helen Damico (1984) has doubts about whether Wealhtheow can be read as worrying about Hrothulf's loyalty and Kenneth Sisam (1965) has cautioned us all about Hrothulf generally.

34 The Mercian Offa apparently spilled much blood – perhaps even that of close kinsmen – in 'choosing' his son to succeed him, having Egfrith crowned as king.

35 The great necklace, which signifies Wealhtheow's sense of retainer solidarity, kindred amity, and group loyalty to Hrothgar goes from Beowulf to Hygd, Hygelac's young, new, but noble queen. Thus he confirms his loyalty and friendship to her. She gives the necklace to Hygelac, apparently, before his fateful raid into the land of the Frisians; this removes the necklace from the exchange world of the Geats, and perhaps leaves Hygd with a special debt to Beowulf – one she more than amply repays in her offer of the kingship, preferring Beowulf over her own sons. He, however, chooses to remain loyal to Hygelac through his sons, remaining their kinsman and powerful protector, not becoming their king. The poet's comparison of the necklace to that of the Brosing's (its possessor fled treachery and chose long-lasting counsel) is somewhat opaque; perhaps the comparison only suggests that such necklaces include the question of choosing well. Wealhtheow would have Beowulf take up her version of kinship, not Hrothgar's.

36 D.H. Green (1965, p. 166). He suggests an early date for *Beowulf* because of the ways in which this ethical vocabulary is used.

37 As noted above, drinking in the hall has sometimes been mistaken for loose drunkenness. Geoffrey Russom nicely disagrees with such readings; he sees the queen bearing a cup and urging men to drink as someone noble proffering a hospitality that has consequences (1988, p. 182). This essentially supports Helen Damico's insight into the strong role Wealhtheow has as bearer of the 'ful' (or vow eliciting cup cited in chapter 3, n38). For a comprehensive account of 'druncen' in *Beowulf*, see Fred Robinson (1987, pp. 75–9). He notes analogues for the ritual of the oath cup; suggests that Wealhtheow's words mean that the warriors 'have been confirmed [in] their devotion to the rulers by drinking the royal mead'; and adds that the Anglo-Saxon audience of *Beowulf*, if they felt contempt for the characters' drinking, would have realized that in the world

and age of the poem 'drinking the king's mead had a different social function.' Drinking thus becomes a motif that distances the poem's audience from the world of the poem. Robinson's observations about drinking behaviour are astute, but I do not agree with his final point, for reasons discussed in chapter 2.

38 Edward B. Irving, Jr (1981) responds to the general impression many readers take of anti-climax in Beowulf's return home and in his accounts to Hygelac. That response is sensitive to rhetorical nuance, especially to Beowulf's concern to clear himself of the suspicion that he may now serve two lords, but it unfortunately emphasizes Hygelac's questions as part of a challenge-speech and therefore Beowulf's replies as an heroic clearing of his reputation. Hygelac's doubts about Beowulf's mission, expressed after the fact upon Beowulf's return, no doubt reflect avuncular concern for his great retainer's safety as well as suggesting second thoughts about Beowulf's connections in the world, if not about his loyalties (after all Beowulf's father did become Hrothgar's thane). To think of Hygelac's questions as challenges is too aggressive, although the possible implications of continuing service over several nights may well trouble Hygelac (see also George Clark, 1990, p. 56, on this point).

Chapter 5 The Psychological World in *Beowulf*

1 A complex approach, more easily stated than practised and tenuously posed against comparative psychologies that seek either a mechanistic core or a transcendental guarantee. See Richard A. Shweder (Stigler, Shweder, Herdt, 1990, pp. 1–43) for this approach to and articulation of 'cultural psychology.'

2 That tradition goes back to Geza Roheim and has lately been taken up by Alan Dundes (1987). It has influenced the person in society psychology of such anthropologists as Mead, Kardiner, the Whitings, and LeVine.

3 Patricia A. Belanoff (1990) notes that in Old English lyrics (elegies especially) the language of emotion is curiously indirect, impersonal, and passive in that something comes into or acts on the speaker: the speaker does not 'long' for but 'is longed.' The large subject of emotion words in Old English poetry has not been examined, mainly because scholars are almost exclusively interested in intellectual themes and ideas.

4 Caroline Brady (1983).

5 Throughout this book I have assumed a poet-narrator, someone who responds to the material, usually in either moralizing or gnomic ways. Practically considered, this is the *Beowulf* poet. The poem includes his voice and might be seen (especially when regarding psychological mat-

ters) as everywhere and in every literary respect a reflection of his conflicts: the conflicts thus analysed are a kind of cloud-chamber of processes leading us back to the poet's primitive wishes and offering some sense of his idiosyncratic defences and accommodations within his culture. Such an analysis, however, would exceed the authority of present scholarship on the poem's provenance, language, and tone, not to mention the problems we face in reconstructions everywhere, but especially in the last third of the poem.

6 Max Gluckman (1963) offers an illuminating account of the 'peace in the feud': 'The Anglo-Saxon vengeance group, called the 'sib,' which was entitled to claim blood-money for a dead man, was composed of all his kindred, through males and females, up to sixth cousins. But the group which resided and worked together seems to have been some form of patriarchal joint family: again we find that the vengeance group did not coincide with the local group. And if you trace each man's kin up to his sixth cousins, they form a widely scattered grouping which could not mobilize.' That grouping probably never received wergeld, the Icelandic laws for distribution being clerical and legalistic more than reflections of established customs – see P.H. Sawyer (1982, pp. 44–5) on Scandinavian evidence, and Bertha Phillpott (1913, pp. 205–44) for English evidence making the same point. 'Each man, with only his full-brothers and full-sisters, was the centre of his own sib; ... in a long-settled district, where there had been much intermarrying, almost everyone would have been a member of everyone else's sib. Hence where vengeance had to be taken, or redress enforced, some people would have been members of both plaintiff and defendent sibs. They would surely have exerted pressure for just settlement. This is the position among the Kalingas of the Philippine Islands who have a similar kinship system' (p. 22). Gluckman is probably wrong about the Anglo-Saxon vengeance group, but not, I think, about the idea of 'peace' within the feud; the prominence of wergeld statements in the laws no doubt reflects usual and long-established custom rather than a desperate attempt to institute something other than violence. We have, I think, generally been misled by latter day feuds (sometimes fictionalized, as in the Hatfields and the McCoys) that are pernicious precisely *because* they are lawless, being carried on outside of well-established, juridical procedures. We have also been misled by a handful of heroic tales in which vengeance is disastrously urged (the context for which we usually mistake).

7 Assent, of course, is the most difficult response here. Critics dismayed by psychoanalytical studies even include once prominent practitioners (Frederick Crews comes to mind). I do not think that readers who reject

psychoanalytical studies are necessarily uninformed or defensive in some neurotic way: they may simply dislike what seems strange to them; they may dislike a regrettable reductionism that appears in many Freudian studies (as it does in other schools of criticism); they may be sympathetic to, yet confused by, the formidable and often surprising analyses of Freudian readers; or they may simply become incredulous when presented with the dark comedy of intrapsychic struggle. This latter point, no doubt tainted by my own ambivalence, seems the significant one, the kernel of justification. Too many studies, even non-reductionist ones, treat the literary work as a grim, psychic circus – an idiosyncratic one, to be sure – but analysable in ways that seem their own network of determinants. That a poet may actually perceive something, or have profound thoughts about something other than the clinical dynamic posited in the work (with 'insight' limited to the poet's working out of a textbook problem), or achieve moments of incredible, self-sufficient beauty – these judgments are usually pushed aside or undervalued. That is a pity even Freudians can admit. Perhaps psychological studies should remain as open as possible to the thinking and making that goes on in literature – processes that can qualify every awareness we bring to literary studies. Freudian awareness helps us understand what poets have done and where they can lead us, but we need to remain open to the poet's intuitions – intuitions that may undermine *any* body of certainties we bring to the literature studied.

8 See Freud (1960, pp. 24–5, 42, 44). The early debates in anthropological literature about the universality of the Oedipus complex hinged on Malinowski's discovery of an avuncular rather than a paternal dynamics among the Trobriand islanders. The dispute between him and Ernst Jones (with Jones emphasizing infantile sexuality and a generalized psychodynamics) was more a talking past each other, however, than a valid engagement. Anne Parsons (1967, p. 380) has reviewed that ricochet of minds and, on the basis of her field work and an analytical overview, has concluded the following: 'We began, with reference to the Jones-Malinowski debate, by considering the possibility that each culture is characterized by a distinctive nuclear complex whose roots lie in its family structure. Our subsequent task has been to pull together various orders of data concerning Southern Italy in such a way as to portray such a nuclear complex which differs both from the brother-sister-sister's son triangle characteristic of the Trobriand Islands and from the patriarchal complex isolated by Freud. In the South Italian data we have found that two cultural complexes, the sacred one centered on respect for the feminine Madonna figure and the secular joking pattern surrounding court-

ship and embodied in popular drama, also have their reflections in the actual patterning of family life and childhood experience and in the intrapsychic life of the individual as seen in projective tests. It is this continuity which has led us to the conclusion that it is possible to define a single global complex which can be perceived simultaneously either as intrapsychic or as collective, the representations of which are passed on from generation to generation on the social level coming to be internalized in the individual in the form of representations of the self in relation to objects.' My sketch for the psychology of the heroic world, as projected in *Beowulf*, focuses on just such a 'global complex,' which is both collective and reflected in and through the behaviour and commitment of particular characters, both individually and in their confrontations. For insightful work in cross-cultural or cross-civilizational areas, see Alan Roland (1988), Vincent Crapanzano (1980), and especially Gananath Obeyesekere (1990), the latter proposing that in relation to the world's cultures the western Oedipus 'complex' needs to be thought of as more like an undifferentiated cluster of intrafamilial and intrapsychic possibilities, strands of which different cultures actualize, project, and then make either numinous or almost plain in different ways; the results are psychologically healthy or not in terms of those cultures' Oedipal demands. Individuation in the Western sense need not occur and one can have social shame rather than individualistic guilt (see Levy, 1973, pp. 347–56).

9 Marilyn Strathern (1988, p. 134) subtly analyses gift exchange in various Melanesian societies as, in broadest terms, investing things with the social form of persons (rather than making persons into things). One gives in ceremonial contexts; what one gives and how much – these evidence one's capacity to make relationships, define in what capacity one makes the relationships, and thus alternately eclipse some possible relationships and reveal or else proffer and then institute others (pp. 166–7). Hrothgar does all of these things silently, as it were, in his giving to Beowulf (as discussed earlier).

10 Freud (1960, pp. 24–5, 44). In the same face-to-face society, a leader's super-ego identification with the father can be more or less coherent and reality-oriented or more or less fragmented and fantasized (see Kracke, 1978, especially pp. 229–34). Beowulf seems to have a coherent view of Ecgtheow as justifiably famous because of his war-prowess and his wise counsel. But fathers and kings in *Beowulf* are largely idealized figures; this suggests fantasy and some degree of destabilizing paranoia in this split world of good fathers and terrible monsters. Lately James W. Earl (1991, especially pp. 83–4) has raised the Freudian issue of ambivalent identification with the heroic lord in *Beowulf*. See also, in an Indian context, a

very interesting, culturally transformed 'oedipal pattern' in Sudhir Kakar's account (1990, pp. 442–3) of the father's envy directed at sons and thus of the son's persecution anxiety – an anxiety charged 'with the dread of filicide and with the son's castration, by self or the father, as a solution to the father-son competition.'

11 See Melanie Klein (vol. 1, 1984) and Hanna Segal (1955). Klein is a pioneer in pushing psychological conflicts back into early infancy and getting beyond some of the opaqueness of the famous oral, anal, and genital stages – for all of which such practitioners as John Bowlby and D.W. Winnicott applaud her. Klein posits very early dynamics, first a 'paranoid-schizoid' phase that gives way to (or evolves into, through reparative response) a 'depressive' position. She sees this staging as inherited and as fundamentally based on the death instinct. This gloomy view of early dynamics has been criticized appropriately for its small attention to environmental factors in infant development and for its primitive sense of how such mental dynamics as ego and super-ego development can split off from this beginning. See Harry Guntrip (1969, pp. 410–11); John Bowlby (1973, pp. 173, 387); D.W. Winnicott (1965, pp. 176–7). Winnicott especially admires Klein's achievements but would reform her vocabulary. He thinks of the 'depressive' stage as a stage of caring and anxiety for the object, while questioning how it is possible for an infant first to dread and then split its nurturing object before it can be said to have observable object relations, ego development, and projective capacities.

12 Daniel Miller (1987, pp. 90–3) summarizes the complex, interactive strategies of splitting, projection, introjection, partial integration, and so on in Melanie Klein's theory of evolving personality in the very young child. He notes, as other recent critics of Klein's work have not, that her view of these matters is basically developmental (but not markedly teleological) moving towards healthy integrations of affects within an eventually approximated, moral norm. As a projection, Grendel of course reflects a largely preintegrated state of psychic life, embodying bad impulses (frustration, pain, devouring anger); Hrothgar, Beowulf, and other noble characters largely embody the good (truth, law, generosity, right honour). Hence they cannot understand Grendel and, in Hrothgar's case anyway, simply feel persecuted. This is an aspect of his situation that justifies the impression of him as passive and somehow almost deplorable; see Niles (1983, p. 110) and Irving (1984, pp. 14–15). Another way of looking at this, in more integrative terms and at later levels of maturity, is to see that such oppositions may well underlie functional dissociations in strongly communal, gift-giving cultures. Robert Levy (1973, pp. 492–4) speculates that latent aspects of people's personalities in Tahiti

seem to have some organization and autonomy in being 'dissociated' rather than repressed. Strong social norms emphasize a limited repertoire of acceptable, adult emotions and behaviour, while emotions and behaviours disapproved of are allowed 'expression and interpretation in special, bounded contexts.' Certainly folk-tales, legends, and libidinous but public dances could be or could contain such contexts.

13 Stephen O. Glosecki (1989, especially pp. 181–210) sees the slow youth motif as residue from a shamanic past informing the kinds of bear and wolf-warrior tales out of which parts of *Beowulf* probably come. That shamanic past, or reflexes of it, appears uncannily in the poem's animal images, special weapons and armour, dangerous, initiation-like descent adventures, and the 'obsession' with bone, flesh and dismemberment. In these latter issues, shamanistic, dissociative submersion and travelling look decidedly like temporary regressions into the pre-Oedipal psyche. As for a more pedestrian view of the slow or slothful youth motif, we might liken it to ideas in many cultures of children as given to emotionalism, anger, and aggressiveness; as not having yet fully perceived and internalized communal values of active cooperation, mutuality, and social control. Perhaps as a youth Beowulf was slow to take up an adult mindfulness – in warrior terms perhaps he was slow to be bold or brave. See Briggs (1970, pp. 328–37) for an account of an Inuit group's negative emotion words in relation to children.

14 Stephen Glosecki (1989, p. 190) notes both positive and negative sides to the wolf image, associated with either outlawry or noble guardianship and power.

15 The perspective back to Cain is part of the poet's overview of God and cosmic feud, shared with his audience; see Irving (1984) and Osborn (1978). For our purposes here those wastelands come alive in their inhabitants – Cain originally, now monster mother and Grendel, but also giants, orcs, and elves long ago. Although Grendel is one of the many who awoke in successive occupations (given Cain's paternity), seeking specific sources and allegorical values for Grendel's link to Cain is not fruitful. But for intriguing connections between Cain and Ham, see John Block Friedman (1981) and Oliver F. Emerson (1906). For erudite renderings, see Niilo Peltola (1972), Stephen C. Bandy (1972), Ruth Mellinkoff (1979, 1981), and M. Andrew (1981). John Niles (1983, pp. 12–13) pragmatically suggests that the links to Cain give Grendel and creatures like him an actual existence in this here-and-now world, making them temporal and concrete (like any other people with its kin-line, I might add) rather than providing them with a devotional demonology. James Earl (1987), noting Grendel's association with Cain, sees him more as a prin-

ciple, 'an aspect of creation, than as a character ... Grendel is Heorot's shadow' (pp. 181–2). Somehow Grendel is a *necessary* punishment, perhaps because the heroic and the Grendelian define each other.

16 See S.L. Dragland (1977) for work on underlying commonalities between Beowulf, humans, and the monsters. It is true that Beowulf shares what we might think of as primal energies and ferocity with the monsters. He is capable of a terrible, Odinesque strength. But always he uses that strength in the service of what is lawful, right, and good.

17 John C. Pope (1981, pp. 350–2) makes a similar point: 'The poet's view of worldly existence and worldly values is much more complicated than that of the Wanderer ... [implicitly, through Beowulf] Mutability has not shaken his faith in the value of earthly existence, which he [Beowulf] counts in terms of achievement, the performance of *ellen* ... [which in several places can form into] admiration and awe at something time has not conquered'. Working within a sense of dual perspectives (the poet's and that of the poem's characters) Marijane Osborn comes to a similar conclusion: 'Whereas some movement from the secular level toward the spiritual occurs within the Wanderer's experience, no such progression occurs within Beowulf's world, where the two levels ... [give] us a framework within which to set particular feuds ... and to estimate men's valor ... [in effect supporting] the native grandeur of the human soul as it is understood by the noblest pagans in *Beowulf*' (1978, pp. 979–80).

18 Edward B. Irving, Jr. (1989) cannot think that Beowulf has 'a truly practical use for the treasure, such as building up the war-chest of national defense against future invasions' (p. 116). But Beowulf explicitly says that he is gratified to be allowed to acquire such treasure for his people ('minum leodum') before his death-day. They may of course do with it what they will, if they do not build up a warchest (whatever that could mean). In this world of reciprocity, Beowulf is thankful that his people will have the treasure for their exchanges. He could hardly mean anything else. That his people choose to make a free gift of it to the immolated Beowulf, in his great honour, and as an expression of their love – well, that is hardly something he anticipates.

19 I prefer to think of 'myth' here rather than theology, say, which might lead to seeing Grendel as a devil or as a Satan figure, although psychologically both Grendel and Satan share similar darknesses and, perhaps, such motives as devouring or destroying greed. Indeed, I think it is the poet's intuitions about monstrous impulses and the communal joys of conscientious life that indirectly encourage the cerebrations of neo-patristic readings of *Beowulf*, even for such vigorously intelligent readers as Betty S. Cox (1971, pp. 79–95), who strikes some fine, resonant

phrases in the service of theological explanations. Connecting Grendel to Christian accounts of worldly evil, Cox suggests how in Grendel the poet would 'make a cosmos out of chaos, Satanic though it was' (p. 79); the essentially Satanic is that desire deep in Satan 'to usurp the place of the Creator, followed by assault upon creation in a frenzy of hate which irrevocably dedicates itself to a continuous destruction of life' (p. 95), a quote she borrows from Roland M. Frye on Milton's Satan. I do not think it is wrong to note that Grendel in fact loves (his) life, lives happily in the created world once he undertakes his rapacious picnics in Heorot, and is primarily a hating hall-thane. In many ways, however, Cox's readings of the poem suffer from the ailment that afflicts top-heavy readings of any kind (perhaps especially devotedly distorted Freudian ones): a highly selective symbolizing of textual material, which moves quickly away from the clarities, complexities, and complications of the poem. However seductively articulated, such readings simply do not honestly engage the terms of the poem and live there.

20 George Clark (1990) suggests that Grendel may also charm the retainers to sleep (pp. 74–5) and that Beowulf's great wakefulness is a sign of his gigantic will. Glosecki (1989) notes saga parallels in which men become strangely sleepy just before being attacked. From a shamanic perspective they are bewitched by the 'hugr' or 'fylgja' (the spirit companion) of their enemies (pp. 184–5).

21 Melanie Klein (Segal, ed., 1955, p. 18) summarizes her findings on infant oral-sadism. She illustrates these findings expansively through case-studies, in Klein vol. 2 (1984).

22 Cast against various analogues, *Beowulf* seems as sublime at the narrative level as at the lexical and prosodic levels. Much of the poet's original folk- and hero-tale material, if we look to analogues, must have been simultaneously crude and ego-centred. Characteristically, the analogue material deals with murders between brothers, uncles and nephews, cousins, brothers-in-law, step-fathers and step-sons (although each tale needs to be read with traditional kinship structures and tensions in mind). The Oedipal pattern is deflected, but only just in such tales as *Hrolf saga Kraki*: one Athels slays Hrolf's father and marries Yrsa, Hrolf's mother and sister. Hrolf slays Athels with Yrsa's help – a slaying that involves slicing off Athels buttocks. Perhaps the *Beowulf* poet's lack of interest in sex and violence reflects his interest in the subliminal, his exploring of the pre-Oedipal, rather than a transcending of crude libido.

23 See R. Bruce-Mitford (1974, especially plates 14, 15, 57, 58, 59).

24 Beowulf's account of slaying sea-monsters by night and enduring severe distress in doing so looks like a literary account of the psychic combat a

Germanic warrior-initiate might have undergone: 'No ic on niht gefrægn / under heofones hwealf heardran feohtan, / ne on egstreamum earmran mannon; / hwæþere ic fara feng feore gedigde / siþes werig' (ll. 575b–579a). The severe distress must have been deeply somatic, as evident even today in trances undergone by shamans (see M. Eliade, 1972) and in manhood initiations by such warlike people as the Nuer of the Southern Sudan. As a youth Beowulf has a sorry reputation, but when he comes to the Danes he is already the strongest in might of mankind in those days. As an initiate he probably underwent battle with psychic beasts, perhaps as represented by the beast-clothed shamans depicted in Bruce-Mitford and remembered by him as the fierce binding of a giant family and the bloody, night-time slaying of water-monsters (the latter suggested by Glosecki, 1989, p. 158). If the Sigmundr story tells us anything, perhaps the initiate might even become his worst self – an outlaw, a marauder, a devouring slayer possessed of a bear's strength and a wolf's cunning – which he overcomes when emerging with super-ego mastery, a mastery imbued with the positive strengths of bear and wolf. We might compare this outlaw status with aspects of manhood initiation rituals among Australian aborigines (Geza Roheim, 1945, pp. 74–7): the pubescent boy is beaten (sometimes badly) by the tribe's women and then exiled to the bush for several weeks before being allowed back into the community for the somewhat painful subincision ceremony, in the healing of which the boy's mother participates vicariously, while the men of the tribe may in fact reopen their own subincision wounds, creating a bond with the initiate and helping the boy in his recovery. One of the justifications for the ritual is that without it the young men would become demons, fly up into the sky, and then return to devour all of the old men. Geza Roheim was a pioneer in psychoanalytic anthropology at a time when primal horde ideas and Oedipal patterns were still fixed in formulaic ways, emphasizing such matters as separation and castration anxiety for boys and the implacable demands of id-desire mobilized against the frustrating object or against the super-ego. But his analyses are still valuable, albeit tending towards the formulaic and (understandably enough given circumcision and subincision ceremonies) the genital. For the suggestion that Beowulfian-hero-against-monster-tales reflect a now lost, aristocratic ritual, see Nora K. Chadwick (1959).

25 M. Gerstein (1974) comments seminally on the outlaw as werwolf and on the warrior's functions, while Glosecki (1989) complements her research by noting that wer-bear and wer-wolf spirits could be positive as well as negative, depending upon how the energy is dedicated. As 'warg' (l. 1267a) Grendel is savage; as 'brimwylf' (l. 1599) the mother is terrible

and can only be killed by a giant-forged sword. Her imperviousness to man-made swords further indicates her spirit world, her demiurgic ancestry, according to Glosecki (1989, p. 168). Only dream-time weapons can kill dream-time foes, against whom one needs dream-time protection (much as Beowulf's corselet, given to him by Hrethel and probably made by the magic smith, Weland, protects him).

26 Alexandra Hennessey Olsen (1982) suggests than an 'aglæca' is one who violates a natural or a moral law (p. 67).

27 Edward B. Irving, Jr. (1989, p. 144) notes how Grendel brutally forces his way into Heorot's doorway – the hall's mouth – wrenching it apart and thus performing 'a gross violation of the hall's body as well as an act of sacrilege against the temple-like building.' Here and elsewhere, without recourse to anthropological help, Irving registers the many functions of the great house or hall: dynastic, family centre, centre of communal ritual, public place for hospitality, and a place for the sacred. His comment also suggests the hall's psychological aura as a body image. In purging the hall Beowulf evicts dark impulses from the social body.

28 Fred C. Robinson (1979, pp. 132–4) elegantly notes a motif of battle flame and of flame that seizes, bites, and devours, making hostile fire something of a 'living entity' in the poem.

29 This is an important development for views of the poem's three-part structure (see Kathryn Hume, 1975), although when seen from the perspective of gift giving and feud, *Beowulf* takes on a two-part look, with the first part in two segments.

30 See James Rosier (1963) for comprehensive attention to aggressive 'feasts' in *Beowulf*.

31 In registering the violent, almost sexualized language of the underwater fight, Irving (1989, p. 98) moves paradoxically a step or so in this direction. The difficulty of the fight when for a time Beowulf is 'blocked' may have as its deep basis a common, infant experience, 'the struggle of all infants against their monster parents, especially their mothers.' In fierce enactment of the father's law, Beowulf of course would overcome the monster mother; but the deeper motif here would be regressive – the monster-son desire for absolute possession of each other. In confronting that gallows-mindedness, Beowulf must dive deeper and struggle more fiercely than any other man could.

32 Recently several approaches to *Beowulf* have attempted to recover the 'mother' suppressed or erased and to read the poem even from these margins 'against itself.' These efforts are interesting and sporadically insightful, in many ways complementing my use of Freud and Melanie Klein, but too often they leave the poem's language and its confirming

associations and details behind in reader responses that create their own, quite eloquent poetry. Janet Thormann's 1990 MLA paper, 'The Body of the Mother in *Beowulf*,' discusses the instability of a world of rivalries and the structuring function of genealogies while offering a Lacanian language for the son's renunciation of the mother and an acceptance of the father's law. She notes that the '*Beowulf* narration denies, displaces, and distorts the imago of the phallic mother, the representation of the maternal body as primordial, in the monstrous itself.' From a Kleinian standpoint this is part of pre-Oedipal body-destruction anxiety (and aggression). Also, see Gillian R. Overing (1990) virtually *passim* but especially on Modthryth, pp. 104–5, where we are asked to suppose that Modthryth 'will not consent to be a feminine spectacle in a masculine arena, refusing to join the ranks of the gold-adorned queens who circulate among the warriors as visible treasure.' Modthryth's violence partly expresses her rejection of the masculine 'gaze' and partly reflects 'the poem's insistent connection between violence and signification.' The latter phrase, although apt concerning this study's emphasis on the retainer's readiness to take on the violent needs of his war-lord, does not redeem Overing's interesting fiction concerning Modthryth's undisclosed mind, let alone her purposeful underestimations of the power of hall-queens.

33 Hugh Magennis (1986) offers an overview of the ways in which Old English poets feel an expressive, elegiac, even psychological quality (passivity and dejection) in the image of sitting in sorrow.

34 James Earl (1991) argues for sober observation, in the main, given that the ideal hero is beyond criticism, that the retainer's role is to accept, not criticize, his lord, and that in epic the hero is simply as he is, free to do as he will (p. 82). Yet an impulse to criticize also shadows Wiglaf's comments and our reactions, given that both his and our relationship to the idealized hero is inevitably ambivalent – an ambivalence he and we live with.

35 Michael Swanton (1982, p. 140) differs, along with many readers, from those who would see no basic fault in Beowulf on this, Beowulf's last day alive. Swanton argues that Beowulf finally falls into 'the ultimate kingly sin, that of *oferhygd*' (although the poet only says that he scorns to take an army). Beowulf would not rely 'on his own natural, material strength alone, without any reference whatever to God.' That Beowulf initially thinks he may have offended God certainly requires attention here; Beowulf's uncustomary gloom is not a plausible source of overweening pride (of greed and arrogance in Hrothgar's 'sermon'); rather, we need to keep in mind the function of Beowulf's boasts throughout

the poem and consider everything he says, beginning with the stories of bitter, unavengeable deaths. Beowulf, in going alone, follows his hero's calling (which has always rightly rejected cautionary advice, such as Hygelac's, in the past) and summons up his utmost courage from out of a gloom that would have crippled lesser kings. Finally, he now does exactly what he did before the fight with Grendel's mother. God blessed him then with victory; He may do so now, despite Beowulf's forebodings of death.

36 Alan K. Brown (1980) offers an intriguing network, almost a music of tonal associations, for the consuming, terrible fire of the dragon as well as for the presumed theological resonances of the dragon fight. He poses the fight in relationship to various passages concerning battle against sin, the devil, leviathan, and consuming, inextinguishable fire, while backing away from an overt, allegorical, or spiritual reading. But is Beowulf a righteous heathen fighting leviathan out of vaunting pride? The affair just does not read in that way: Beowulf's sword is not 'false'; it just breaks; Beowulf's shield is not false pride; it is iron and it avails enough; Beowulf's corselet protects his body, as it is meant to, but not his exposed neck. If the dragon is 'sin and death and fiery devil' he is so in terms of crime and niggardliness, not hell, and he dies (unexplicated). Of course the dragon's energies remain in the world, as would the devil's work, in spite of the demise of a particular, seized-upon creature to do it.

37 Probably the lines surrounding this phrase will never come satisfactorily clear for us. Good discussions are in Wrenn (1973) and Swanton (1978). I prefer to think of the two 'swa' constructions in the passage (ll. 3066, 3069) as establishing a parallelism that separates the lines about Beowulf from the lines about disturbing the hoard.

38 See Howell D. Chickering (1977, p. 373) for a sense of how the dragon is echoed in language applied to Ongentheow.

Conclusion

1 See D.H. Green (1965) for a thorough review of the vertical force as well as reciprocal connotations of 'milde,' 'milts,' and 'milti' (Old High German). Most citations in Bosworth and Toller, *An Anglo-Saxon Dictionary*, give the Old English words a range of meaning from mildness to mercy, including empathetic qualities, and apply them often to God and to Christ. But Green insists that the Germanic form 'milti' in the earliest Germanic Christian literature often denotes the lord's or king's benevolent and especially generous disposition towards his inferiors (pp. 164–5). The usage in *Beowulf* may well reflect that meaning when we consider the range we

find in the poem. Wealhtheow would have Hrothgar speak 'mildum wordum' to the Geats, as a man should do, but he should leave the kingdom to his own kinsmen (implicitly, do not be too generous); the word appears next in her insistence that each warrior in the hall is true to each other and 'milde' in mind, while 'hold' toward Hrothgar, thus especially emphasizing its horizontal connotations, not its usual application to the superior in a relationship. Such is the case in the next appearance, when Wiglaf's messenger recites Hygelac's ill-fated raid and concludes that since that time the Merovingian king has withheld his favour from the Geats.

2 Gernot Wieland (1988) suggests that Beowulf takes on Christ-like attributes in terms of the half-line, 'manna mildost.'

3 I owe this distinction between social and cultural dimensions to Kirsten Hastrup (1990, p. 6), who in turn quotes Anne Knudsen (1989). But of course the social and the cultural interpenetrate: what we draw out as implications concerning the mentalities and the rich projections of people has much to do with the ways in which people in fact form their social relationships, not just their attitudes about those relationships. Regarding legends and stories as myth, Hastrup suggests (p. 193) that in an Icelandic context myths of the past, as encapsulated in sagas, provided a permanent image of who and what the Icelanders were, but an image at wrong angles to history. Rather than adjust their myths to new circumstances, the Icelanders just repeated them, producing then a serious disjunction between their cultural models and their contemporary experience (beginning in the twelfth century). Not knowing when *Beowulf* was composed or where, we cannot deeply entertain a similar line of consideration, but John Niles (1993), working with a highly plausible tenth-century, West Saxon context, suggests that the social and cultural work that *Beowulf* does is to legitimate national ambitions in mythic terms 'through invocation of a common, pseudo-Christian, Anglo-Danish past' (106). Furthermore, this reinvention of the ancestral past 'in the light of Christian doctrine and Danish presence, as well as ... [the articulation of] a system of values appropriate to this task [makes the poem] a site where cultural issues of great magnitude and complexity are contested' (p. 107). Along with this there are issues that transcend historical and social tensions, such as the oppositions of the poem between hero and monsters – issues that perhaps 'underlie civilization itself and its inevitable discontents.'

Works Cited

Allen, Judson B. 'God's Society and Grendel's Shoulder Joint: Gregory and the Poet of *Beowulf*.' *Neuphilologische Mitteilungen*, 78 (1977): 239–40.

Anderson, Earl R. 'Treasure Trove in *Beowulf*: A Legal View of the Dragon's Hoard.' *Mediaevalia*, 3 (1977): 141–64.

Andrew, M. 'Grendel in Hell.' *English Studies*, 62 (1981): 401–10.

Applebaum, Herbert, ed. *Perspectives in Cultural Anthropology*. Albany: State University of New York Press, 1987.

Arnold, C.J. *An Archaeology of the Early Anglo-Saxon Kingdoms*. London: Routledge, 1988.

Bandy, Stephen C. '*Beowulf*: The Defense of Heorot.' *Neophilologus*, 56 (1972): 86–92.

Belanoff, Patricia A. 'Women's Songs, Women's Language: "Wulf and Eadwacer" and "The Wife's Lament".' In *New Readings on Women in Old English Literature*, ed. Olsen, Damico 193–203. Bloomington: Indiana University Press, 1990.

Bellman, James Fredrick, Jr. 'The Institutional Environment of *Beowulf*.' PhD diss., University of Nebraska, 1985.

Benson, Larry D. 'The Pagan Coloring of *Beowulf*.' In *Old English Poetry: Fifteen Essays*, ed. Robert P. Creed, 193–213. Providence: Brown University Press, 1967.

Biebuyck, Daniel. 'The Epic as a Genre in Congo Oral Literature.' In *African Folklore*, ed. Richard M. Dorson, 257–74. New York: Doubleday & Co., 1972.

Binchy, D.A. *Celtic and Anglo-Saxon Kingship*. The O'Donnell Lectures for 1967–8. Oxford: Oxford University Press, 1970.

Black-Michaud, Jacob. *Cohesive Force: Feud in the Mediterranean and the Middle East*. New York: St. Martin's Press, 1975.

Blair, Peter Hunter. *An Introduction to Anglo-Saxon England*. Cambridge: Cambridge University Press, 1956; repr. 1959.

Bloomfield, Morton W. '*Beowulf* and Christian Allegory: An Interpretation of Unferth.' *Traditio*, 7 (1951): 410–15.

– 'Beowulf, Byrhtnoth, and the Judgment of God: Trial by Combat in Anglo-Saxon England.' *Speculum*, 44 (1959): 545–59.

– 'Patristics and Old English Literature: Notes on Some Poems.' *Comparative Literature*, 14 (1962): 36–43

Bloomfield, Morton W., and Barbara Nolan. 'Beotword, Gilpcwidas, and the Gilphlæden Scop of *Beowulf*.' *Journal of English and Germanic Philology*, 79 (1980): 499–516.

Boehm, Christopher. 'Ambivalence and Compromise in Human Nature.' *American Anthropologist*, 91 (1989): 921–39.

– *Blood Revenge: The Enactment and Management of Conflict in Montenegro and Other Tribal Societies*. 2nd ed. Philadelphia: University of Pennsylvania Press, 1987.

Bohannan, Paul. 'Concepts of Time among the Tiv of Nigeria.' In *Myth and Cosmos: Readings in Mythology and Symbolism*, ed. John Middleton, 313–29. Garden City: The Natural History Press, 1967.

– *Social Anthropology*. New York: Holt, Rinehart and Winston, 1963.

Bonjour, Adrien. *The Digressions in* Beowulf. Medium Aevum Monographs, 5. Oxford: Basil Blackwell & Mott, 1950.

Bosworth, Joseph, and T. Northcote Toller. *An Anglo-Saxon Dictionary*. London: Oxford University Press, 1898; repr. 1972.

Bowlby, John. *Attachment and Loss*. Vol. 2, *Separation Anxiety and Loss*. London: The Hogarth Press, 1973.

Brady, Caroline. '"Warriors" in *Beowulf*: An Analysis of the Nominal Compounds and an Evaluation of the Poet's Use of Them.' *Anglo-Saxon England*, 11 (1983): 199–246.

Branston, Brian. *The Lost Gods of England*. New York: Thames and Hudson, 1957; repr. 1974.

Bremmer, Rolf H., Jr. 'The Importance of Kinship: Uncle and Nephew in *Beowulf*.' *Amsterdamer Beitrage zur Alteren Germanistik*, 15 (1980): 21–38.

Brennan, Malcolm M. 'Hrothgar's Government.' *Journal of English and Germanic Philology*, 84 (1985): 3–15.

Briggs, Jean L. *Never in Anger: Portrait of an Eskimo Family*. Cambridge: Harvard University Press, 1970.

Brodeur, Arthur G. *The Art of* Beowulf. Berkeley: University of California Press, 1959.

– *The Climax of the Finn Episode*. University of California Publications in English, 3, no. 8. Berkeley: University of California Press, 1943.

Brown, Alan K. 'The Firedrake in *Beowulf*.' *Neophilologus*, 64 (1980): 439–60.

Bruce-Mitford, R. *Aspects of Anglo-Saxon Archeology: Sutton Hoo and Other Discoveries*. New York: Harper's Magazine Press, 1974.

Brundage, James A. *Law, Sex, and Christian Society in Medieval Europe*. Chicago: University of Chicago Press, 1987.

Brunner, H. *Deutsche Rechtsgeschichte*. 2 vols. Leipzig: Dunker und Humblot, 1887–92.

Burlin, Robert B. 'Gnomic Indirection in *Beowulf*.' In *Anglo-Saxon Poetry: Essays in Appreciation for John C. McGalliard*, ed. Lewis E. Nicholson and Dolores Warwick Frese, 41–9. Notre Dame: University of Notre Dame Press, 1975.

Byock, Jesse. *Feud in the Icelandic Sagas*. Berkeley: University of California Press, 1982.

Calder, Daniel G., ed. *Old English Poetry: Essays in Style*. Berkeley: University of California Press, 1979.

Calder, Daniel G., and T. Craig Christy, eds., *Germania: Comparative Studies in the Old Germanic Languages and Literatures*. Wolfeboro, NH: D.S. Brewer, 1988.

Camargo, Martin. 'The Finn Episode and the Tragedy of Revenge in *Beowulf*.' *Studies in Philology*, 78 (1981): 120–34.

Carsley, Catherine A. 'Reassessing Cultural Memory in Beowulf.' *Assays*, 7 (1992): 31–41.

Cassidy, F.G. 'A Symbolic Word-Group in *Beowulf*.' In *Medieval Literature and Folklore Studies: Essays in Honor of Frances Lee Utley*, ed. Jerome Mandel and Bruce A. Rosenberg, 35–8. New Brunswick, NJ: Rutgers University Press, 1970.

Chadwick, H. Munro. *The Heroic Age*. Cambridge: Cambridge University Press, 1926.

– *Studies on Anglo-Saxon Institutions*. Cambridge: Cambridge University Press, 1905.

Chadwick, Nora K. 'The Monsters and Beowulf.' In *The Anglo-Saxons: Studies in Some Aspects of Their History and Culture*, ed. Peter Clemoes, 171–203. London: Bowes & Bowes, 1959.

Chambers, R.W. *Beowulf: An Introduction to the Study of the Poem*. 3rd ed., with a supplement by C.L. Wrenn. Cambridge: Cambridge University Press, 1959.

Chagnon, Napoleon. *Yanomamo: The Fierce People*. New York: Holt, Rinehart and Winston, 1977.

Chaney, William A. *The Cult of Kingship in Anglo-Saxon England*. Berkeley: University of California Press, 1970.

Cheyette, Fred L. 'The Invention of the State.' In *Essays on Medieval Civilization: The Walter Prescott Webb Memorial Lectures*, ed. Bede Karl Lackner and Kenneth Roy Philip, 143–78. Austin: University of Texas Press, 1978.

Chickering, Howell D. *Beowulf: A Dual Language Edition*. Garden City, NY: Anchor, 1977.

Clark, George. *Beowulf*. Boston: G.K. Hall & Co., 1990.
– 'Beowulf's Armor.' *English Literary History*, 32 (1965): 409–41.
Codere, Helen. *Fighting with Property: A Study of Kwakiutl Potlatching and Warfare 1792–1930*. Seattle: University of Washington Press, 1950; repr. 1966.
Colgrave, Bertram, and R.A.B. Mynors, eds. *Bede's Ecclesiastical History of the English People*. Oxford: Oxford University Press, 1969.
Comaroff, John L., and Simon Roberts. *Rules and Processes: The Cultural Logic of Dispute in an African Context*. Chicago: University of Chicago Press, 1981; repr. 1986.
Cox, Betty S. *Cruces of* Beowulf. The Hague: Mouton, 1971.
Cramer, Carmen. 'The Voice of Beowulf.' *Germanic Notes*, 8 (1977): 40–4.
Crapanzano, Vincent. *Tuhami: Portrait of a Moroccan*. Chicago: University of Chicago Press, 1980; repr. 1985.
Dalton, George, ed. *See* Finley.
Damico, Helen. Beowulf's *Wealhtheow and the Valkyrie Tradition*. Madison: University of Wisconsin Press, 1984.
Davidson, Hilda Ellis. *The Battle God of the Vikings*: The First G.N. Garmonsway Memorial Lecture. York: University of York Medieval Monograph Series 1, 1972.
Devereux, George. *Ethnopsychoanalysis: Psychoanalysis and Anthropology as Complementary Frames of Reference*. Berkeley: University of California Press, 1978.
Diamond, A.S. *Primitive Law Past and Present*. London: Methuen & Co., 1971.
Donohue, Charles. 'Potlatch and Charity: Notes on the Heroic in *Beowulf*. In *Anglo-Saxon Poetry: Essays in Appreciation for John C. McGalliard*, ed. Lewis E. Nicholson and Dolores Warwick Frese, 23–40. Notre Dame: Notre Dame University Press, 1975.
Douglas, Mary, ed. *Constructive Drinking: Perspectives on Drink from Anthropology*. Cambridge: Cambridge University Press, 1987.
– *How Institutions Think*. Syracuse: Syracuse University Press, 1986.
– *Implicit Meanings: Essays in Anthropology*. London: Routledge and Kegan Paul, 1975; repr. 1984.
Dragland, S.L. 'Monster-Man in *Beowulf*.' *Neophilologus*, 61 (1977): 606–18.
Dronke, Ursula, ed. *The Poetic Edda* I. Oxford: Clarendon Press, 1969.
Duby, G. *The Early Growth of the European Economy: Warriors and Peasants from the Seventh to the Twelfth Century*. Trans. H.B. Clarke. Ithaca: Cornell University Press, 1974.
Dumézil, Georges. *Gods of the Ancient Northmen*. Trans. Einar Haugen. Berkeley: University of California Press, 1973.
– *Mitra-Varuna: An Essay on Two Indo-European Representatives of Sovereignty*. New York: Zone Books, 1988.

Dumville, David N. 'Kingship, Genealogies and Regnal Lists.' In *Early Medieval Kingship*, ed. P.H. Sawyer and I.N. Wood, 72–104. Leeds, 1977.

Dundes, Alan. *Parsing through Customs: Essays by a Freudian Folklorist*. Madison: University of Wisconsin Press, 1987.

Earl, James W. '*Beowulf* and the Origins of Civilization.' In *Speaking Two Languages: Traditional Disciplines and Contemporary Theory in Medieval Studies*, ed. Allen J. Frantzen, 65–89. Albany: State University of New York Press, 1991.

– 'Transformation of Chaos: Immanence and Transcendence in *Beowulf* and Other Old English Poetry.' *Ultimate Reality and Meaning*, 10 (1987): 164–85.

Eliade, M. *Shamanism: Archaic Techniques of Ecstasy*. Trans. Willard R. Trask. Princeton: Princeton University Press, 1964; repr. 1972.

Eliason, Norman E. 'The Arrival at Heorot.' In *Studies in Language, Literature, and Culture of the Middle Ages and Later*, ed. E. Bagby Atwood and Archibald A. Hill, 235–42. Austin: The University of Texas Press, 1969.

– 'The Pyle and Scop in *Beowulf*.' *Speculum*, 38 (1963): 276–84.

Emerson, Oliver F. 'Legends of Cain, Especially in Old and Middle English.' *Publications of the Modern Language Association*, 21 (1906): 831–926.

Enright, Michael J. 'Lady with a Mead-Cup: Ritual, Group Cohesion and Hierarchy in the Germanic Warband.' *Frühmittelalterliche Studien*, 22 (1988) 170–203.

Evans-Pritchard, E.E. *The Nuer: A Description of the Modes of Livelihood and Political Institutions of a Nilotic People*. Oxford: Clarendon Press, 1940.

Farrell, Robert T. 'Beowulf and the Northern Heroic Age.' In *The Vikings*, ed. Robert T. Farrell, 180–216. London: Phillimore & Co.: 1982.

– *Beowulf, Swedes and Geats*. Viking Society for Northern Research. London: University College, 1972.

Feld, Steven. 'Wept Thoughts: The Voicing of Kaluli Memories.' *Oral Tradition*, 5 (1990): 241–66.

Finley, M.I. 'Wealth and Labor [Archaic Greece].' In *Tribal and Peasant Economies*, ed. George Dalton, 397–17. New York: The Natural History Press, 1967.

Finnegan, Ruth. *Oral Poetry: Its Nature, Significance and Social Context*. Cambridge: Cambridge University Press, 1977.

Firth, Raymond. *Tikopia Ritual and Belief*. Boston: Beacon Press, 1967.

Flint, Valerie I.J. *The Rise of Magic in Early Medieval Europe*. Princeton: Princeton University Press, 1991.

Foley, John Miles. '*Beowulf* and the Psychohistory of Anglo-Saxon Culture.' *American Imago*, 34 (1977): 133–53.

Fortes, Meyer. *The Dynamics of Clanship among the Tallensi*. London: Oxford University Press, 1945.

– *Kinship and the Social Order: The Legacy of Lewis Henry Morgan*. Chicago: Aldine, 1969.

Fortes, M., and E.E. Evans-Pritchard, eds. *African Political Systems*. London: Oxford University Press, 1940; repr. 1962.

Frank, Roberta. 'The *Beowulf* Poet's Sense of History.' In *The Wisdom of Poetry: Essays in Honor of Morton W. Bloomfield*, ed. Larry D. Benson and Siegfried Wenzel, 53–66. Kalamazoo: Medieval Institute Publications, 1982.

Freeman, J.D. 'On the Concept of the Kindred.' *The Journal of the Royal Anthropological Institute of Great Britain*, 91 (1961): 192–220.

Freud, Sigmund. *The Ego and the Id*. Trans. Joan Riviere. New York: W.W. Norton & Co., 1960.

Friedman, John Block. *The Monstrous Races in Medieval Art and Thought*. Cambridge, Mass.: Harvard University Press, 1981.

Fulk, R.D. 'Unferth and His Name.' *Modern Philology*, 85 (1987): 113–27.

Galloway, Andrew. '*Beowulf* and the Varieties of Choice.' *Publications of the Modern Language Association*. 105 (1990): 197–208.

Gatch, Milton McC. *Loyalties and Traditions: Man and His World in Old English Literature*. New York: Pegasus, 1971.

Gerstein, M.R. 'Germanic *Warg*: The Outlaw as Werwolf.' In *Myth in Indo-European Antiquity*, ed. Gerald J. Larson, 131–56. Berkeley: University of California Press, 1974.

Gies, Frances and Joseph Gies. *Marriage and the Family in the Middle Ages*. New York: Harper & Row, 1987; repr. 1989.

Glosecki, Stephen O. *Shamanism and Old English Poetry*. New York and London: Garland Publishing, 1989.

Gluckman, Max. *Custom and Conflict in Africa*. Oxford: Basil Blackwell, 1963.

– *The Judicial Process among the Barotse of North Rhodesia (Zambia)*. Manchester: The University Press, 1955.

– *Politics, Law and Ritual in Tribal Society*. Chicago: Aldine, 1965.

Goodenough, W.H. 'Kindred and Hamlet in Lakalal, New Britain.' *Ethnology*, 1 (1962): 5–12.

Goody, Jack. *The Development of the Family and Marriage in Europe*. Cambridge: Cambridge University Press, 1983; repr. 1988.

– 'The Time of Telling and the Telling of Time in Written and Oral Cultures.' In *Chronotypes: The Construction of Time*, ed. John Bender and David E. Wellberry, 77–96. Stanford: Stanford University Press, 1991.

Goldsmith,Margaret. *The Mode and Meaning of* Beowulf. London: Athlone, 1968.

Green, D.H. *The Carolingian Lord: Semantic Studies on Four Old High German Words: Balder, Fro, Truhtin, Herro*. Cambridge: Cambridge University Press, 1965.

Greenfield, Stanley B. 'The Authenticating Voice in *Beowulf*.' *Anglo-Saxon England*, 5 (1976): 51–62.
– 'Of Words and Deeds: The Coastguard's Maxim Once More.' In *The Wisdom of Poetry*, ed. Larry D. Benson and Siegfried Wenzel, 45–51.
– '"Gifstol" and Goldhoard in *Beowulf*.' In *Old English Studies in Honour of John C. Pope*, ed. Robert B. Burlin and Edward B. Irving, Jr., 107–17. Toronto: University of Toronto Press, 1974.
Gregory, C.A. 'Gifts to Men and Gifts to God: Gift Exchange and Capital Accumulation in Contemporary Papua.' *Man*, n.s. 15 (1980): 626–52.
Grønbech, Vilhelm. *Vor Folkeoet i Oldtiden* (1909, 1929). Trans. William Worster. *Culture of the Teutons*. 3 vols. Oxford: Oxford University Press, 1931.
Guntrip, Harry. *Schizoid Phenomena, Object Relations and the Self*. New York: International Universities Press, 1969.
Hamilton, Marie P. 'The Religious Principle in *Beowulf*.' *Publications of the Modern Language Association*, 61 (1946): 309–31.
Hanning, Robert W. '*Beowulf* as Heroic History.' *Medievalia et Humanistica*, n.s. 5 (1974): 77–102.
Hastrup, Kirsten. *Nature and Policy in Iceland 1400–1800: An Anthropological Analysis of History and Mentality*. Oxford: Oxford University Press, 1990.
Hayoshi, Hiroshi. 'Felix Liebermann and Recent Studies of Anglo-Saxon Laws (I).' *Kenkyu Nenpou* [Gakushuin Review of Law and Politics], 16 (1981): 165–84.
Henderson, Alastair C.L. 'Live Connections: Reading Chaucer in the Presence of an Oral Culture.' Paper delivered at session on Implications of Orality. Modern Language Association Convention, Chicago, 1990.
Hill, John M. 'Beowulf and the Danish Succession: Gift Giving as an Occasion for Complex Gesture.' *Medievalia et Humanistica*, n.s. 11 (1982): 177–97.
– '*Beowulf*, Value, and the Frame of Time.' *Modern Language Quarterly*, 40 (1979): 3–16.
– 'Hrothgar's Noble Rule: Love and the Great Legislator.' In *Social Approaches to Viking Studies*, ed. Ross Samson, 169–78. Glasgow: Cruithne Press, 1991.
– 'Revenge and Super-ego Mastery in *Beowulf*.' *Assays*, 5 (1989): 3–38.
– 'The Good Fields of Grief: Remnants of Conversion in Three Anglo-Saxon Poems.' *Psychocultural Review*, 2 (1978): 5–26.
Hill, Thomas D. 'The Confessions of Beowulf and the Structure of Volsunga Saga.' In *The Vikings*, ed. Robert T. Farrell, 165–79. London: Phillimore & Co, 1982.
– '"hwyrftum sciþað": *Beowulf*, Line 163.' *Medieval Studies*, 33 (1971): 379–81.
– 'The Measure of Hell: *Christ and Satan* 695–722.' *Philological Quarterly*, 60 (1981): 409–14.
– 'Woden as "Ninth Father": Numerical Patterning in Some Old English

Royal Genealogies.' In *Germania: Comparative Studies in the Old Germanic Languages and Literatures*, ed. Daniel G. Calder and T. Craig Christy, 161–74. Wolfeboro: D.S. Brewer, 1988.

Holdsworth, William. *A History of English Law.* Vol. 2. 4th ed. London: Methuen & Co. & Sweet and Maxwell, 1936; repr. 1976.

Hollander, Lee M. *The Skalds: A Selection of Their Poems*. Ann Arbor: University of Michigan Press, 1968.

Howe, Nicholas. *Migration and Mythmaking in Anglo-Saxon England*. New Haven: Yale University Press, 1989.

Hume, Kathryn. 'The Theme and Structure of *Beowulf*.' *Studies in Philology*, 72 (1975): 1–27.

Hunt, Robert, ed. *Personalities and Cultures: Readings in Psychological Anthropology.* New York: The Natural History Press, 1967.

Irvine, Judith T. 'When Is Genealogy History? Wolof Genealogies in Comparative Perspective.' *American Ethnologist*, 5 (1978): 651–74.

Irving, Edward B., Jr. 'Beowulf Comes Home: Close Reading in Epic Context.' In *Acts of Interpretation: The Text in Its Contexts, 700–1600: Essays on Medieval and Renaissance Literature in Honor of E. Talbot Donaldson*, ed. Mary J. Carruthers and Elizabeth D. Kirk, 129–43.

– 'The Nature of Christianity in *Beowulf*.' *Anglo-Saxon England*, 13 (1984): 7–21.

– *A Reading of* Beowulf. New Haven: Yale University Press, 1968.

– *Rereading* Beowulf. Philadelphia: University of Pennsylvania Press, 1989.

Jackson, Michael. *Paths toward a Clearing: Radical Empiricism and Ethnographic Inquiry.* Bloomington: Indiana University Press, 1989.

Jones, Gwyn. *A History of the Vikings*. 2nd ed. Oxford: Oxford University Press, 1984.

Kakar, Sudhir. 'Stories from Indian Psychoanalysis: Context and Text.' In *Cultural Psychology: Essays on Comparative Human Development*, ed. James W. Stigler, Richard A. Shweder, and Gilbert Herdt, 427–45. Cambridge: Cambridge University Press, 1990.

Kardiner, Abram. 'The Technique of Psychodynamic Analysis.' In *Perspectives in Cultural Anthropology*, ed. Herbert Applebaum, 147–59. Albany: State University Press of New York, 1987.

Kaske, Robert E. '*Sapientia et Fortitudo* as the Controlling Theme of *Beowulf*.' *Studies in Philology*, 55 (1958): 423–57.

Keesing, Roger M. 'Nonunilineal Descent and Contextual Definition of Status: The Kwaio Evidence.' *American Anthropologist*, 70 (1968): 82–4.

– 'Shrines, Ancestors, and Cognatic Descent: The Kwaio and Tallensi.' *American Anthropologist*, 72 (1970): 755–75.

Ker, William Paton. *Epic and Romance.*2nd ed. London: Macmillan, 1908.

Kern, Fritz. *Kingship and Law in the Middle Ages*. Trans. S.B. Chrimes. New York: 1970.

Kiefer, Thomas M. *The Tausug: Violence and Law in a Philippine Moslem Society.* New York: Holt, Rinehart and Winston, 1972.

Kindrick, Robert L. 'Germanic *Sapientia* and the Heroic Ethos of *Beowulf*.' *Medievalia et Humanistica*, n.s. 10 (1981): 1–17.

Klaeber, Frederick, ed. *Beowulf*. 3rd ed. Boston: D.C. Heath, 1950.

Klein, Melanie. *Love, Guilt and Reparation*. Vol 1. New York: The Free Press, 1984.

– *The Psychoanalysis of Children*. Vol. 2. New York: The Free Press, 1984.

Kliman, Bernice W. 'Women in Early English Literature: *Beowulf* to the *Ancrene Wisse*.' *Nottingham Medieval Studies*, 21 (1977): 32–49.

Knudsen, Anne. *En O i Hostorien. Korsika. Historisk Antropologi 1730–1914* (An Island in History, Corsica. Historical Anthropology 1730–1914). Copenhagen: Basilisk, 1989.

Koch, Klaus-Friedrich. *War and Peace in Jalemo: The Management of Conflict in Highland New Guinea*. Cambridge, Mass.: Harvard University Press, 1974.

Kracke, Waud H. *Force and Persuasion: Leadership in Amazonian Society.* Chicago: University of Chicago Press, 1978.

Krapp, George Philip, and Van Kirk Dobbie Elliot, eds. *The Anglo-Saxon Poetic Records*. 6 vols. New York: Columbia University Press, 1931, 1932, 1936, 1942.

Kuhn, Hans, ed. *Edda*. Heidelberg: Carl Winter, 1962.

Kuper, Adam. *The Invention of Primitive Society: Transformations of an Illusion*. London: Routledge, 1988.

Lancaster, Lorraine. 'Kinship in Anglo-Saxon Society.' *The British Journal of Sociology*, 9 (1958): 230–50; 359–77.

Lawrence, W.W. *Beowulf and Epic Tradition*. Cambridge, Mass., Harvard University Press, 1928; repr. 1930.

Lea, Henry Charles. *Superstition and Force: Essays on The Wager of Battle – the Ordeal – Torture*. Philadelphia: Lea Brothers and Co., 1892.

Lee, Alvin A. *The Guest-hall of Eden*. New Haven: Yale University Press, 1972.

Levi-Strauss, Claude. *Structural Anthropology.* Trans. Claire Jacobson and Brooke Grundfest Schoepf. New York: Basic Books (Doubleday, Anchor), 1963; repr. 1967.

– *The Way of the Masks*. Trans. Sylvia Modelski. Seattle: University of Washington Press, 1988.

LeVine, Robert A. 'Infant Environments in Psychoanalysis: A Cross-cultural View.' In *Cultural Psychology: Essays on Comparative Human Development*, ed.

James W. Stigler, Richard A. Shweder, and Gilbert Herdt, 454–75. Cambridge: Cambridge University Press, 1990.

Levy, Robert I. *Tahitians: Mind and Experience in the Society Islands*. Chicago: Chicago University Press, 1973.

Liebermann, Felix, ed. *Die Gesetze der Angelsachsen*. 3 vols. Halle: S.M. Niemeyer, 1903–16.

Liggins, Elizabeth, M. 'Revenge and Reward as Recurrent Motives in *Beowulf*.' *Neuphilologische Mitteilungen*, 74 (1973): 193–213.

Little, Lester K. *Religious Poverty and the Profit Economy in Medieval Europe*. Ithaca: Cornell University Press, 1978; repr. 1983.

Lizot, Jacques. *Tales of the Yanomami: Daily Life in the Venezualan Forest*. Trans. Ernest Simon. Cambridge: Cambridge University Press, 1985.

Loyn, H.R. *Anglo-Saxon England and the Norman Conquest*. New York: St. Martin's Press, 1962.

– *The Governance of Anglo-Saxon England, 500–1087*. Stanford: Stanford University Press, 1984.

– 'Kinship in Anglo-Saxon England.' *Anglo-Saxon England*, 3 (1974): 197–209.

Lutz, Catherine A. *Unnatural Emotions: Everyday Sentiments on a Micronesian Atol & Their Challenge to Western Theory*. Chicago: University of Chicago Press, 1988.

Magennis, Hugh. 'The *Beowulf* Poet and His "Druncne Dryhtguman".' *Neophilologische Milleilungen*, 86 (1985): 159–64.

– '"Monig Oft Gesæt": Some Images of Sitting In Old English Poetry.' *Neophilologus*, 70 (1986): 442–52.

Malinowski, Bronislaw. *Argonauts of the Western Pacific*. New York: E.P. Dutton & Co., 1961.

– *Myth in Primitive Psychology*. New York: W.W. Norton & Co., 1926.

Malone, Kemp. *Studies in Heroic Legend and in Current Speech*. Ed. Stefan Einarsson and Norman E. Eliason. Copenhagen: Rosenkilde and Bagger, 1959.

Marcus, George E., and Michael M.J. Fischer. *Anthropology as Cultural Critique: An Experimental Moment in the Human Sciences*. Chicago: University of Chicago Press, 1986.

Marquardt, Hertha. *Die Altenglischen Kenningar: ein Beitrag zur Stilkund altgermanischer Dichtung* (The Old English Kenning: A Contribution to the Style of Old German Poetry). Schriften der Konigsberger Gelehrten Gesellschaft, Geisteswissen-schaftliche Kl. 14, Halle: M. Niemeyer, 1938.

Mattingly, H. trans. *The Agricola and the Germania* by Tacitus. Harmondsworth: Penguin, 1948; rev. trans. S.A. Handford, 1970.

Mauss, Marcel. *The Gift: Forms and Functions of Exchange in Archaic Societies*. Trans. Ian Cunnison. New York: W.W. Norton & Co., 1967.

McNamara, John. 'Beowulf and Hygelac: Problems of Fiction in History.' *Rice University Studies*, 62 (1976): 57–63.

Meany, Audrey L. 'Scyld Scefing and the Dating of *Beowulf* – Again.' *Bulletin of the John Rylands University Library of Manchester*, 75 (1989): 7–40.

Melinkoff, Ruth. 'Cain's Monstrous Progeny in *Beowulf*: Part 1, Noachic Tradition.' *Anglo-Saxon England*, 8 (1979): 143–62, and Part 2, 'Post-Diluvian Survival.' *Anglo-Saxon England*, 9 (1981): 183–97.

Miller, Daniel. *Material Culture and Mass Consumption*. Oxford: Basil Blackwell, 1987; repr. 1991.

Miller, William Ian. *Bloodtaking and Peacemaking: Feud, Law, and Society in Saga Iceland*. Chicago: University of Chicago Press, 1990.

Moisl, Hermann. 'Anglo-Saxon Genealogies and Germanic Oral Tradition.' *Journal of Medieval History*, 7 (1981): 215–48.

Murray, Alexander C. *Germanic Kinship Structure: Studies in Law and Society in Antiquity and the Early Middle Ages*. Toronto: Pontifical Institute of Medieval Studies, 1983.

Needham, Rodney, ed. *Rethinking Kinship and Marriage*. London: Tavistock Publications, 1971.

– Introduction and 'Remarks on the Analysis of Kinship and Marriage.' In *Rethinking Kinship and Marriage*. London: Tavistock Publications, 1971, pp. xiii–cxvii; 1–34.

Nelson, Janet L. 'The Earliest Surviving Royal *Ordo*: Some Liturgical and Historical Aspects. In *Authority and Power: Studies on Medieval Law and Government Presented to Walter Ullman*, ed. Brian Tierney and Peter Linehan, 29–48. Cambridge: Cambridge University Press, 1975.

– 'Inauguration Rituals.' In *Early Medieval Kingship*, ed. P.H. Sawyer and I.N. Wood, 50–71. Leeds: School of History, University of Leeds Press, 1977; repr. 1979.

Nicholson, Lewis E. 'Hunlafing and the Point of the Sword.' In *Anglo-Saxon Poetry: Essays in Appreciation for John C. McGalliard*, ed. Lewis E. Nicholson and Dolores Warwick Frese, 50–61. Notre Dame: Notre Dame University Press, 1975.

Niles, John D. Beowulf: *The Poem and Its Tradition*. Cambridge, Mass.: Harvard University Press, 1983.

– 'Locating Beowulf in Literary History.' *Exemplaria*, 5 (1993): 79–109.

Obeyesekere, Gananath. *The Work of Culture: Symbolic Transformation in Psychoanalysis and Anthropology*. Chicago: University of Chicago Press, 1990.

Oleson, Tryggvi J. *The Witanagemot in the Reign of Edward the Confessor*. London: Oxford University Press, 1955.

Olsen, Alexandra Hennessey. 'The Aglæca and the Law.' *American Notes and Queries*, 20 (1982): 66–8.

Opland, Jeff. *Anglo-Saxon Oral Poetry: A Study of the Traditions*. New Haven: Yale University Press, 1980.

Osborn, Marijane. 'The Great Feud: Scriptural History and Strife in *Beowulf*.' *Publications of the Modern Language Association*, 93 (1978); 973–81.

Overing, Gillian R. *Language, Sign, and Gender in* Beowulf. Carbondale: Southern Illinois University Press, 1990.

Owen, Gale R. *Rites and Religions of the Anglo-Saxons*. London: David and Charles, 1981.

Parsons, Anne. 'Is the Oedipus Complex Universal? – A South Italian "Nuclear Complex".' In *Personalities and Cultures: Readings in Psychological Anthropology*, ed. Robert Hunt, 352–99. Garden City, NY: The Natural History Press, 1967.

Peltola, Niilo. 'Grendel's Descent from Cain Reconsidered.' *Neuphilologische Mitteilungen*, 73 (1972): 284–91.

Pepperdine, Margaret W. 'Beowulf and the Coastguard.' *English Studies*, 47 (1966): 409–19.

Peters, Edward. *The Shadow King:* 'Rex Inutilis' *in Medieval Law and Literature, 751–1327*. New Haven: Yale University Press, 1970.

Phillpotts, Bertha Surtees. *Kindred and Clan in the Middle Ages and After: A Study in the Sociology of the Teutonic Races*. Cambridge: Cambridge University Press, 1913; repr. New York, Octagon, 1974.

Plummer, Charles, ed. *Two of the Saxon Chronicles Parallel*. Oxford: Clarendon Press, 1965.

Poole, Fitz John Porter. 'Transforming "Natural" Woman: Female Ritual Leaders and Gender Ideology among Bimin-Kuskusmin.' In *Sexual Meanings: The Cultural Construction of Gender and Sexuality*, ed. Sherry B. Ortner, and Harriet Whitehead, 116–65. Cambridge: Cambridge University Press, 1981.

Pope, John C. 'Beowulf's Old Age.' In *Philological Essays: Studies in Old and Middle English Language and Literature in Honor of Herbert Dean Meritt*, ed. James L. Rosier, 55–64. The Hague: Mouton, 1970.

– '*Beowulf*, 505, "gehedde," and the Pretensions of Unferth.' In *Modes of Interpretation in Old English Literature: Essays in Honour of Stanley B. Greenfield*, ed. Phyllis Rugg Brown, Georgia Ronan Crampton, and Fred C. Robinson, 173–87. Toronto: University of Toronto Press, 1986.

– 'The Existential Mysteries as Treated in Certain Passages of Our Older Poets.' In *Acts of Interpretation: The Text in its Contexts, 700–1600: Essays on Medieval and Renaissance Literature in Honor of E. Talbot Donaldson*, ed. Mary C. Carruthers and Elizabeth D. Kirk, 345–62. Norman: Pilgrim Books, 1981.

Pospisil, L. *Anthropology of Law: A Comparative Theory*. New York: Harper & Row, 1971.

Richards, Audrey I. 'The Political System of The Bemba Tribe – North-Eastern Rhodesia.' In *African Political Systems*, ed. M. Fortes and E.E. Evans-Pritchard, 83–120. Oxford: Oxford University Press, 1940.

Robinson, Fred C. 'Two Aspects of Variation in Old English Poetry.' In *Old English Poetry: Essays on Style*, ed. Daniel G. Calder, 127–45. Berkeley: University of California Press, 1979.

– Beowulf *and the Appositive Style*. Knoxville: University of Tennessee Press, 1987.

– 'Elements of the Marvellous in the Characterization of Beowulf: A Reconsideration of Textual Evidence.' In *Old English Studies in Honour of John C. Pope*, ed. Robert B. Burlin and Edward B. Irving, Jr., 119–38. Toronto: University of Toronto Press, 1974.

Rogers, H.L. 'Beowulf's Three Great Fights.' *Review of English Studies*, 5 (1955): 339–55.

Roheim, Geza. *The Eternal Ones of the Dream*. New York: International Universities Press, 1945; repr. 1971.

– *The Gates of the Dream*. New York: International Universities Press, 1952; repr. 1970.

Roland, Alan. *In Search of Self in India and Japan: Toward a Cross-Cultural Psychology*. Princeton: Princeton University Press, 1988.

Rosaldo, Michelle Z. *Knowledge and Passion: Ilongot Notions of Self and Social Life*. Cambridge: Cambridge University Press, 1980.

– 'Toward an Anthropology of Self and Feeling.' In *Culture Theory: Essays on Mind, Self, and Emotion*, ed. Richard A. Shweder and Robert A. LeVine, 137–57. Cambridge: Cambridge University Press, 1984; repr. 1988.

Rosier, James L. 'The Uses of Association: Hands and Feasts in *Beowulf*.' *Publication of the Modern Language Association*, 78 (1963): 8–14.

– ed. *Philological Essays: Studies in Old and Middle English Literature in Honor of Herbert Dean Meritt*. The Hague: Mouton, 1970.

Rozin, Paul, and Carol Nemeroff. 'The Laws of Sympathetic Magic: A Psychological Analysis of Similarity and Contagion.' In *Cultural Psychology: Essays on Comparative Human Development*, ed. James W. Stigler, Richard A. Shweder, and Gilbert Herdt, 205–32. Cambridge: Cambridge University Press, 1990.

Russom, Geoffrey R. 'The Drink of Death in Old English and Germanic Literature.' In *Germania: Comparative Studies in the Old Germanic Languages and Literatures*, ed. Daniel G. Calder and Craig T. Christy, 175–89. Wolfeboro: D.S. Brewer, 1988.

– 'A Germanic Concept of Nobility in *The Gifts of Men* and *Beowulf*.' *Speculum*, 53 (1978), 1–15.

Sahlins, Marshall. *Islands of History*. Chicago: University of Chicago Press, 1985; repr. 1987.

– *Stone Age Economics*. New York: Aldine de Gruyter, 1972.

Samson, Ross. 'Economic Anthropology and Vikings.' In *Social Approaches to Viking Studies*, ed. Ross Samson, 87–96. Glasgow: Cruithne Press, 1991.

Sawyer, P.H. 'Kings and Merchants.' In *Early Medieval Kingship*, ed. P.H. Sawyer and I.N. Wood, 139–58. Leeds: The School of History, University of Leeds Press, 1977.

– *Kings and Vikings: Scandinavia and Europe, AD 700–1100*. London and New York: Methuen, 1982.

Schlegel, Stuart A. *Tiruray Justice: Traditional Tiruray Law and Morality*. Berkeley: University of California Press, 1970.

Schücking, Levin L. 'Heldenstolz und Wurde im Angelsachsischen, mit einem Anhang: Zur charakterisierungstechnik im Beowulfepos.' *Abhandlungen der Philologische-historischen Klasse der sachsischen Akademie der Wissenschaften*, 42, no. 5 (Leipzig), 1933.

Searle, Eleanor. *Predatory Kinship and the Creation of Norman Power 840–1066*. Berkeley: University of California Press, 1988.

Seebohm, Frederic. *Tribal Custom in Anglo-Saxon Law*. New York: Longmans, Green and Co., 1911.

Segal, Hanna, ed. *New Directions in Psycho-Analysis*. London: Tavistock Publications, 1955.

Shippey, T.A. *Beowulf*. London: Edward Arnold Ltd., 1978.

Sisam, Kenneth. 'Anglo-Saxon Royal Genealogies.' *Proceedings of the British Academy*, 39 (1953): 287–348.

– *The Structure of* Beowulf. Oxford: Clarendon Press, 1965; repr. 1971.

Smithers, G.V. 'Destiny and the Heroic Warrior in *Beowulf*.' In *Philological Essays*, ed. James L. Rosier, 65–81. The Hague: Mouton, 1970.

Spolsky, Ellen. 'Old English Kinship Terms and *Beowulf*.' *Neuphilologische Mitteilungen*, 78 (1977): 233–38.

Spufford, Peter. *Money and Its Use in Medieval Europe*. Cambridge: Cambridge University Press, 1988; repr. 1989.

Stanley, E.G. *The Search for Anglo-Saxon Paganism*. Cambridge: D.S. Brewer, 1975.

– 'Two Old English Poetic Phrases Insufficiently Understood for Literary Criticism: *Þing Gehegan* and *Seonoþ Gehegan*.' In *Old-English Poetry: Essays on Style*, ed. Daniel G. Calder, 76–82. Berkeley: University of California Press, 1979.

Stenton, Frank E. *Preparatory to Anglo-Saxon England*. London: Oxford University Press, 1970.

Stigler, James W., Richard W. Shweder, and Gilbert Herdt, eds. *Cultural Psychology: Essays on Comparative Human Development*. Cambridge: Cambridge University Press, 1990.

Strathern, Marilyn. *The Gender of the Gift*. Berkeley: University of California Press, 1988; repr. 1990.

Swanton, Michael. *Beowulf*. Manchester: Manchester University Press, 1978.

– *Crisis and Development in Germanic Society 799–800: Beowulf and the Burden of Kingship*. Goppinger Arbeiten zur Germanistic, nr. 333. Goppingen: Kummerle Verlag, 1982.

Tarzie, Wade. 'The Hoarding Ritual in Germanic Epic.' *Journal of Folklore Research*, 26 (1989): 97–121.

Tennenhouse, Leonard. '*Beowulf* and the Sense of History.' *Bucknell Review*, 19 (1971): 137–46.

Thormann, Janet. 'The Body of the Mother in *Beowulf*.' Paper presented in the Old English Language and Literature Division, The Modern Language Association Convention, Chicago, Dec. 1990.

Tietjen, Mary C. Wilson. 'God, Fate, and the Hero in *Beowulf*.' *Journal of English and German Philology*, 74 (1975): 159–71.

Tolkien, J.R.R. '*Beowulf*: The Monsters and the Critics.' *Publications of the British Academy*, 22 (1936): 245–95.

– *Finn and Hengest: The Fragment and the Episode*. Ed. Alan Bliss. Boston: Houghton Mifflin Co., 1983.

Tripp, Raymond P. 'Lifting the Curse on Beowulf.' *English Language Notes*, 23, no.2 (1985): 1–8.

Turton, David. 'War, Peace, and Mursi Identity.' In *Warfare among East African Herders*, ed. Katsuyoshi Fukui and David Turton, 179–211. Osaka: National Museum of Ethnology, 1979.

Turville-Petre, G. *Myth and Religion of the North: The Religion of Ancient Scandinavia*. London: Weidenfeld and Nicolson, 1964.

Vaughan, Micel F. 'A Reconsideration of "Unferð".' *Neuphilologische Mitteilungen*, 77 (1976): 32–42.

Vestergaard, Elisabeth. 'Gift-Giving, Hoarding, and Outdoings.' In *Social Approaches to Viking Studies*, ed. Ross Samson, 97–104. Glasgow: Cruithne Press, 1991.

Viswanathan, S. 'On the Melting of the Sword.' *Philological Quarterly*, 58 (1979): 360–3.

Vries, Jan De. *Altgermanische Religionsgeschichte* 1. 2 vols. Berlin: Walter de Gruyter & Co., 1935, 1937.

Wallace-Hadrill, J.M. *Early Germanic Kingship in England and on the Continent*. Oxford: Clarendon Press, 1971.

Waterson, Roxana. *The Living House: An Anthropology of Architecture in South-East Asia*. Singapore and Oxford: Oxford University Press, 1990.

Wentersdorf, Karl P. '*Beowulf*: The Paganism of Hrothgar's Danes.' *Studies in Philology*, 78 (1981): 91–119.

Whallon, William. 'The Idea of God in *Beowulf*.' *Publications of the Modern Language Association*, 80 (1965): 19–23.

Whitelock, Dorothy. *The Audience of* Beowulf. Oxford: Clarendon Press, 1951; repr. 1967.

– *English Historical Documents, c. 500–1042*. London: Oxford University Press, 1955.

– *History, Law and Literature in 10th and 11th Century England*. London: Variorum Reprint, 1981.

Whiting, John, and Beatrice Whiting. 'A Strategy for Psychocultural Research.' In *Perspectives in Cultural Anthropology*, ed. Herbert Applebaum, 181–98. Albany: State University of New York Press, 1987.

Wieland, Gernot. '*Manna Mildost*: Moses and Beowulf.' *Pacific Coast Philology*, 23 (1988): 86–93.

Winnicott, D.W. *The Maturational Processes and the Facilitating Environment: Studies in the Theory of Emotional Development*. New York: International Universities Press, 1965; repr. 1974.

Wormald, Jenny. 'An Early Modern Postscript: The Sandlaw Dispute, 1546.' In *The Settlement of Disputes in Early Medieval Europe*, ed. Wendy Davis and Paul Fouracre, 191–205. Cambridge: Cambridge University Press, 1986; repr. 1992.

Wormald, Patrick. 'Bede, *Beowulf* and the Conversion of the Anglo-Saxon Aristocracy.' In *Bede and Anglo-Saxon England*, ed. Robert T. Farrell, 32–95. Oxford: British Archaeological Reports, 46, 1978.

– '*Lex Scripta* and *Verbum Regis*: Legislation and Germanic Kingship, from Euric to Cnut.' In *Early Medieval Kingship*, ed. P.H. Sawyer and I.N. Wood, 105–138. Leeds: The School of History, Leeds University Press, 1977.

Wormald, Patrick, James Campbell and Eric John. *The Anglo-Saxons*. Oxford: Phaidon Press, 1982.

Wrenn, C.L., ed. *Beowulf*. Revised by W.F. Bolton. New York: St. Martin's Press, 1973.

Yorke, Barbara. *Kings and Kingdoms of Early Anglo-Saxon England*. London: B.A. Seaby, 1990.

Index